ROME IN LATE ANTIQUITY

Everyday Life and Urban Change, AD 312–609

BERTRAND LANÇON
TRANSLATED BY ANTONIA NEVILL

EDINBURGH UNIVERSITY PRESS

For Isabelle

English edition, revised and expanded by the author, first published 2000 by
Edinburgh University Press Ltd
22 George Square
Edinburgh
Scotland

Translation © Edinburgh University Press 2000
Introduction and Guide to Further Reading © Mark Humphries 2000

First published 1995 by Hachette Littératures
74 rue Bonaparte
75006 Paris
France
© Hachette Littératures 1995

English edition published with the aid of a translation
subvention kindly given by the French Ministry of Culture

Typeset in 11 on 13 pt Goudy Old Style
by Hewer Text Ltd, Edinburgh, and
printed and bound in Great Britain by
The University Press, Cambridge

A CIP Record for this book is available from the British Library

ISBN 0 7486 1239 4 (hard cover)
ISBN 0 7486 1240 8 (paperback)

Contents

CONTENTS

List of maps

List of illustrations

1. Western end of the Roman Forum. Left foreground, platform of the Rostra, extended northwards *c.* 470; behind, the arch of Septimius Severus (203). Right, the Senate house (*curia*) as rebuilt in the late third century after the fire of 283. Photo B. L.
2. Roman Forum. Base of the column for the *decennalia* of Galerius and Constantius Chlorus (303). Bas-relief showing the procession of senators. Photo B. L.
3. Roman Forum. Surviving part (north wing) of the building known as the 'Basilica of Maxentius' begun by him but completed by Constantine. Photo B. L.
4. Colossal head of Constantine (height 2.60m; Capitol, courtyard of the Palazzo dei Conservatori). It was part of the colossal statue situated in the Basilica of Maxentius. Photo B. L.
5. Foreground: the arch dedicated to Constantine in 315. Background: the Flavian amphitheatre. Photo B. L.
6. Bust of Constantius II as a young man (Capitol, courtyard of the Palazzo dei Conservatori). Photo B. L.
7. Roman Forum. Base of a statue. Inscription in honour of Constantius II, dedicated by Vitrasius Orfitus during his second urban prefecture (357–9). (*CIL*, VI, 31395.) Photo B. L. Inscription reads: 'To the propagator of Roman power. Our Lord Flavius Julius Constantius, the greatest, victorious and triumphant over the whole earth, forever Augustus, Memmius Vitrasius Orfitus, *vir clarissimus*, prefect of the city for the second time, judge of the sacred hearings for the third time, devoted to his emperor's divinity and majesty, set this up.'
8. Roman Forum. Base of a statue transferred by Petronius Maximus during his second urban prefecture (before 433). (*CIL*, VI, 36956.) Photo: B. L. Inscription reads: 'Petronius Maximus, *vir clarissimus*, urban prefect for the second time, restored this.'

9. Colosseum. Inscription of Decius Marius Venantius, *clarissimus* and *illustris*, prefect of the city, *patricius* and ordinary consul (484), who at his own expense restored the arena and balcony which had been destroyed by an earthquake. (CIL, VI, 32094.) Photo: B. L. Inscription reads: 'Decius Marius Venantius Basilius, *vir clarissimus* and *illustris*, prefect of the city, patrician and ordinary consul, restored at his own expense the arena and the balcony which the destruction of a terrible earthquake had destroyed.'

10. Fourth-century mosaic representing gladiatorial combats. The names of famous gladiators are mentioned. Rome, Galeria Borghese. © Fratelli Alinari/Giraudon.

11. Aurelianic walls. Porta Appia, after the modifications carried out at the beginning of the fifth century.

12. Aurelianic walls. Porta Ostiensis.

13. Ivory diptych presented to Honorius by Petronius Probus, ordinary consul in 406. The emperor is pictured as a soldier victorious in Christ's name. Treasury of the Cathedral of Aosta. © Alinari/Giraudon.

14. Mosaic in the nave of Sta Maria Maggiore (fifth century). This Old Testament scene depicts the appearance of the three men to Abraham at Mamre. The three angels are dressed in Roman style, in this instance the *toga praetexta*. © Fratelli Alinari/Giraudon.

15. Marriage chest of Secundus and Projecta. (Rome, late fourth century.) London, British Museum. © British Museum.

16. Allegorised as a seated woman, wearing a plumed helmet, Rome possesses the attributes of power (the spear), victory (orb, surmounted by a winged victory presenting the palm and the crown, the symbols of victory) and wealth collected and dispensed (the bag and amphora of coins). Seventeenth-century copy from a ninth-century manuscript, itself copied from a fourth-century original. Rome, MS Romanus 1, Barb. lat. 2154, fol. 2. © Vatican Library, Rome.

Abbreviations

BG   Procopius, *De bello Gothico*
CIL   *Corpus inscriptionum Latinarum*
CNRS   Centre National de la Recherche Scientifique
CSEL   Corpus Scriptorum Ecclesiasticorum Latinorum
ILS   H. Dessau, *Inscriptiones Latinae Selectae*, 5 vols (Berlin, 3rd edn, 1962)
ICUR   G. B. de Rossi, *Inscriptiones Christiane urbis Romae septimo saeculo antiquiores*, 2 vols (Rome, 1857–61 and 1886); supplement, vol. I, ed. Gatti, 1915)
ILCV   E. Diehl, *Inscriptiones latinae christianae veteres*, 3 vols (Berlin, 1924–31; rev. edn, J. Moreau and H. I. Marrou, 1967)
MAMA   Monumenta Asiae minoris antiqua
NS   New Series

Preface

It is the aim of the book to present a picture of the city of Rome between the early fourth and early seventh century, emphasising the material details of its inhabitants' daily life. Why this time frame? From 312 onwards (and, indeed, for much of the previous half century), Rome was a capital without emperors. They preferred to reside in other cities, such as Nicomedia, Antioch, Sirmium, Trier, Arles, Milan, Constantinople and Ravenna. Maxentius was the last ruler to live there, until his death in 312. Subsequently, they made only irregular and brief stays; certain emperors merely passed through, while others did not even set foot there and never glimpsed it.

Nevertheless, Rome remained the *Urbs, the* city *par excellence* and retained its immense prestige. Its monuments, ancient or more recent architectural remains, were its captivating adornment. In the fourth century, emperors continued to embellish it by erecting new buildings, at the same time restoring the old ones. Encircled by a new defence wall since the reigns of Aurelian (270–5) and Probus (276–82), the city preserved its topographical extent without increasing its population. Because of its monumental nature, the presence of the richest and most numerous aristocracy and its urban institutions, it remained a model for other cities; but this model was changing, losing its power yet continuing to develop. It was above all the place of conservatism and tradition, but also of novelty; hence its appearance of expansion rather than decline. Of course there was nostalgia for the past centuries, but Rome was not merely a relic of times gone by. On the contrary, the transformations it underwent between the fourth and sixth centuries bear witness to a remarkable vitality.

At the close of antiquity, Rome was a large and beautiful city which did not always have the means to maintain its architectural heritage. It was also a bruised and battered city, captured in 410 by the Goths, in 455 by the Vandals, and in 472 by the patrician Ricimer; it experienced its darkest hours in the middle of the sixth century, however, at the time of the Italian war, initiated by the emperor Justinian, between the forces of the eastern empire and the Ostrogoths. Before 536, Rome was still the most populated and monumental city in the west: in 555, when the eastern imperial forces finally vanquished the Goths, it was a mere shadow of its former self, and made a difficult recovery. In addition to its habitual problems with provisions, the city thus endured the ordeals of destruction, the impoverishment of its population and losses through exile. Even so, new buildings were continually being erected. The rising tide of Christianity had two important consequences for the city: on the one hand, the expansion of the episcopal see of Rome; on the other, the construction of many new religious buildings.

The pontificate of Gregory the Great (590–604) has often been considered by scholars to put the final full stop to Roman antiquity. That is due not only to the personality of this pope, who both inherited all that was Roman and yet was simultaneously an innovator (of so much that is deemed by us to be medieval), but also to a number of events which seem to close one epoch and begin another: the end of Roman magistracies, the erection of the last monument – the column of Phocas – in the Forum (608), the transformation of Agrippa's Pantheon into a church. Of course, *Roma christiana* had been a reality since the beginning of the fifth century but, with Gregory, it began to be for western Christendom what it had formerly been for the empire – a capital.

Foreword to the English translation

This book, aimed at the 'educated general reader', first appeared in France in 1995 as part of the wide-ranging series on 'La vie quotidienne' ('Daily Life') in history published by Hachette. The cornerstone of that series had been Jérôme Carcopino's *Rome à l'apogée de l'Empire*, a book which saw great success in English translation as *Daily Life in Ancient Rome*. My vision was to produce a sequel for the period of late antiquity – a presumptuous undertaking, no doubt, but a pinch of recklessness and immodesty is often necessary if we are to fulfil our ambitions.

Since the appearance of Carcopino's famous book, a great deal of water has passed under Rome's bridges. Much research has led to a reassessment of the later history of the Roman empire, and the abandonment of the idea of decline; for that very reason the word 'apogee' in Carcopino's title is obsolete today. After all, belief in the idea of apogees is implicitly a belief in that of declines. Carcopino belonged to a generation who still thought of history, whether it was past or present, in those grand terms, and a regrettable outcome of this belief was his participation in the Vichy government, in the role of Minister of Public Education. His generation also thought the Roman empire had reached its apogee under the Flavians and Antonines, and had then sunk into long decline. Moreover, it included anti-clerical historians who, in the wake of Gibbon, saw Christianity as a major cause of that decline. This book is written as a rebuttal of that view of things and, following in the wake of many illuminating studies, offers a portrait of late antique Rome stripped of this hierarchy of 'apogee' and 'decline', and of fallacious causalities. It was important to show that Rome never 'fell' from one world to another; rather, it remained profoundly itself, becoming very slowly transformed. The Christian Church fully took over the city's historical and cultural heritage, was nurtured and formed by it. The determination of its bishops preserved for Rome its nature and design as *caput mundi*; in other words, in spite of undeniable changes, the chief characteristic of the city, between the fourth and sixth century, seems to me to have been continuity.

I should like to express my deep gratitude to Dr Mark Humphries, of the National University of Ireland, Maynooth, who read my book with kindly and learned attention, and suggested particularly pertinent additions. It is thanks to his recommendation that it has been translated, and I am greatly in his debt. I should also like to express my warmest thanks to Mr John Davey, who brought it to the attention of Edinburgh University Press, and Mrs Antonia Nevill, who translated it.

Bertrand Lançon
Brest, 1999

Introduction: The city between antiquity and the Middle Ages
Mark Humphries

In this book, Bertrand Lançon provides a lively account of how, between the conversion to Christianity of the emperor Constantine in 312 and the pontificate of Pope Gregory the Great (590–604), Rome was transformed from the capital of the classical Roman empire to the centre of medieval Christendom. Perhaps the most striking manifestation of this change is offered by the city's topography, where churches came to dominate where once there had been pagan temples and imperial monuments. Such architectural developments have long fascinated scholars, to the extent that studies of Rome's development in late antiquity have often concentrated on this aspect to the exclusion of almost all other areas of life. In this respect, Bertrand Lançon presents us with a more wide-ranging analysis of Rome's metamorphosis. His focus is as much on the everyday lives of the city's ordinary inhabitants as on the achievements of emperors, popes and aristocrats, and he sets architectural changes side-by-side with those in society, institutions and the economy. The result is a nuanced picture of Rome's evolution between antiquity and the Middle Ages. Yet Rome's experience in these centuries, although it certainly boasted local peculiarities such as the rise of the papacy, was part of a wider process of transformation undergone by urban communities throughout what had once been the Roman empire. By way of setting the scene, therefore, it is worth considering these changes in broader perspective, since they do much to underline the importance of the subject of Bertrand Lançon's book.

In the middle of the second century AD, in a speech praising the achievements of Rome, the Greek orator Aelius Aristides remarked:

> When have there ever been so many cities, both inland and on the coast, or when have they ever been so beautifully equipped with everything? Was there ever a time when a man could travel through the country, as we do, counting the cities

by the days, and sometimes riding on the same day through two or even three cities, as if he was passing through only one?[1]

For Aristides, the achievements of Rome were inseparable from the great flourishing of urban life that occurred under the empire's aegis. Modern historians of the Roman world have readily agreed with him: from Britain to north Africa, from Spain to Syria, cities were the very engines of empire, through which Roman administration and culture permeated life in every region.[2] But if the urban form is emblematic of the success of Roman imperial civilisation, then any assessment of the transformation of the Roman world must pay particular attention to the fate of its cities. Many reflections on this subject – not least that by Edward Gibbon (1737–96), whose great history of the collapse of the Roman empire was inspired by the awful vista of Rome's ruins – have couched themselves in the emotive language of decline and fall. More recent analyses, however, have highlighted the need for a precise definition of what is meant by 'the end of the ancient city', even if notions of 'decline' are retained. In a penetrating survey of late antique urbanism, Wolfgang Liebescheutz has reminded us that:

> Many sites of ancient cities are occupied by flourishing cities today. Not a few of them have continuous histories since Antiquity. So the Ancient city can be said to have come to an end only in a special sense, the disappearance of those characteristics which distinguished the Graeco-Roman city from others.[3]

Indeed, when we turn to contemporary appraisals of urban change in late antiquity, we find a keen appreciation of precisely this sort of transformation. Writing in Gaul in the late sixth century, Gregory of Tours, in his account of the Seven Sleepers of Ephesus, eloquently describes the most basic changes in urban form in late antiquity. During the persecution of the emperor Decius (249–51), seven devout Christians, who had refused to recant their faith and offer sacrifice to the pagan gods, were punished by being bricked up and left to die in a cave outside the city of Ephesus in Asia Minor. Two hundred years later, during the reign of the Christian emperor Theodosius II (408–50), they were reawakened miraculously, and as one of them returned to Ephesus he was amazed by the metamorphosis of the city he had known so well:

> Approaching the city gate, he saw above it the sign of the cross and he marvelled [at it] . . . in astonishment. Entering the city he heard men swear oaths in Christ's name and he saw a church, a priest who was rushing around the city, and new walls. Being greatly astounded he said to himself: 'Do you think that you have entered another city?'[4]

In Gregory's lively account we are presented with two of the most striking changes undergone by the urban form in late antiquity: the construction of new defensive walls, the increased architectural and social prominence of the Christian Church.

In itself, this represented a radical redefinition of the image to the city. To observers in antiquity itself, there were various ways in which a city might be defined. First there was the physical presence of urban amenities. Hence the surprise of Pausanias, writing a description of Greece in the second century AD, that the community of Panopeus in Phocis could call itself a city 'when it has no state buildings, no training ground, no theatre, and no market square, when it has no running water at a water-head, and when they live on the edge of a torrent in hovels akin to mountain huts'.[5] In the late Roman period, the possession of grand buildings remained an index of city status. Thus the fourth-century historian Ammianus Marcellinus, remarking on the deplorable conditions of the southern Gallic city of Aventicum (modern Avenches), commented that it was 'formerly of no mean significance, as its half-ruined buildings still show in our own day'.[6] But buildings by themselves did not make a city: from the archaic age of Greece to the Roman imperial period, a city was defined not only by its physical amenities, but also by its population and institutions. Indeed, the possession of specific types of institution distinguished certain communities as cities rather than villages. For example, when, in the 320s AD, the people of Orcistus in the middle of Asia Minor appealed to the emperor Constantine for recognition as a city, it was precisely upon such factors that they called in support of their plea. The emperor reported to the local praetorian prefect that the Orcistans had 'claimed that in times past their village flourished with the splendour of a town, being adorned with the insignia of annual magistracies, possessing a large number of town councillors, and filled with a large population of citizens', and that it possessed, moreover, a favourable location and fine public amenities. In consideration of such factors, Constantine continued, it was inconceivable 'that so deserving a place should lose the appellation of a city'. Buildings, amenities and institutions together then, were the hallmarks of the city, but at Orcistus we can already see hints of a shift towards a new definition. The last piece of evidence cited by Constantine in favour of raising Orcistus from a village to a city was that 'all the inhabitants are said to be devotees of the most holy religion'. It seems that the canny Orcistans had appreciated the emperor's religious leanings in favour of the Church, and persuaded him that they were all Christians.[7]

Turning to the early Middle Ages we find that while buildings, amenities and institutions remained important in the definition of the city, their nature had changed. Like Ephesus in the legend of the Seven Sleepers, many cities had acquired new walls. In the western European provinces of the Roman empire particularly, there seems to have been a surge in the construction of such defensive circuits in the third century, with sporadic new building and renovation thereafter. While their construction was, for the most part, a response to increased insecurity and vulnerability to barbarian attack, the possession of walls soon came to be an important qualification for city status by the early Middle Ages. Hence in the seventh century, when the Lombard king Rothari (636–52) conquered parts of north-western Italy, he ordered the cities there to be stripped of their walls and demoted to the status of villages.[8] Yet walls by themselves were not enough to grant a city prestige. In the centuries that followed Constantine's conversion to Christianity, the calibre of a city's bishops, church buildings and saints' cults provided a new focus for competitive civic pride. Throughout the Mediterranean world, the rapid appearance of massive, sumptuously decorated churches provided a concrete manifestation of the rising social power of Christianity. The centrality of the Church to the urban self-image is eloquently attested in two verse eulogies written in eighth-century northern Italy, describing the cities of Milan and Verona. Both poems hark back to the classical past, describing the Roman buildings still visible in each city; but in addition, both poets celebrate their cities' Christian heritage, enumerating distinguished bishops, impressive church buildings and saints whose cults brought Milan and Verona prestige far and wide.[9]

These transformations of cities in late antiquity have attracted a great deal of attention in recent years.[10] Such research has shown that the process was by no means uniform or linear, as the pace and nature of change varied considerably in different parts of the Mediterranean world. For instance, the account of the change in urban society given above is itself a limited one, since it accounts only for Christian Europe. In the Middle East particularly, the rise of Islam had a profound impact on the transformation of cities. It brought the appearance not only of distinctive religious buildings but also of specific types of secular architecture associated with early Arab society. In many Near Eastern cities shops invaded the elegant colonnaded streets, so that the thoroughfares become blocked with walls, and movement was restricted to narrow alleys. Thus networks of passages typical of medieval souks here replaced the grand processional routes characteristic of ancient cities.[11] Contrast this, however, with the cities of northern Italy where to this day the ancient street grids are frequently well preserved, a circumstance that owes much to the conscientious maintenance of such public rights of way by early medieval rulers.[12]

Yet even in northern Italy the mixture of continuity and discontinuity is more haphazard than the preservation of street grids might lead us to believe. We have already seen that in the eighth century the city of Verona could still be praised by reference to its ancient buildings. Their impact on the appearance of the city can be seen in a ninth-century topographical drawing that shows clearly the Roman theatre, amphitheatre and bridge which can still be seen there today. Moreover, Verona is one of those cities where the ancient street grid is particularly well preserved. While this may seem to imply strong continuity between the Roman and medieval periods, other evidence shows that there was very real disruption between these periods. Excavations in the centre of Verona, on the site of its Roman forum and so the centre also of the ancient city, yielded a layer of dark earth which strongly suggested that this area had fallen into disuse for some time during late antiquity. Moreover, it is clear that the decay of parts of Verona's forum began as early as the fourth century. Ever since the city's foundation, its forum had been dominated by a temple of Jupiter. At some time between 379 and 383, however, an imperial official removed from the temple a statue that had lain toppled from its base for a considerable time. This is enough to suggest that already by the later fourth century, one of Verona's finest public buildings, and one that had sat at the Roman city's monumental heart, was falling into ruin.[13] When viewed together with evidence of the layer of dark earth in the middle of the forum, it shows that any history of Verona in the passage from antiquity to the Middle Ages must account, on the one hand, for the resilience of the city's ancient street grid and certain public buildings and, on the other, for the decay of its ancient civic centre.

None of these physical transformations occurred in a vacuum: they reflect broad social and ideological changes. Just as the dilapidation of temples reflects the eclipse of paganism by Christianity, so also society came to be dominated by a Christian élite. In some respects, this was achieved through members of the existing upper classes, who simply focused their patronage on Christian projects. Thus, from Constantine onwards, emperors acted as patrons of ecclesiastical building in the great imperial cities, as well as in a few centres of peculiarly Christian interest, such as Jerusalem and Bethlehem. At the level of local society, such acts of patronage were performed, as they had always been, by members of the civic aristocracy. Yet from the fourth century onwards, a major new power emerged in the empire's cities: the Christian bishop. Favoured by imperial exemptions from such onerous duties as serving on town councils, invested by emperors with judicial powers and acting as spiritual guides to an increasingly Christian population, bishops became important power brokers in urban society throughout the late Roman world. In many places – such as Gaul in the fifth century – this led to a merging of secular and ecclesiastical aristocracies, as grandees like Sidonius Apollinaris extended the range of their official titles to include the episcopate.[14] Even where such assimilation did not occur, bishops increasingly became the chief politicians of their cities, overseeing the minutiae of urban administration and providing leadership in times of trouble. The most striking examples of this change come from periods of crisis when, with no imperial administration to turn to for help, urban communities looked to their bishops for guidance. When the Lombards invaded north-eastern Italy in 568, for example, it was bishop Felix of Tarvisium (modern Treviso) who negotiated his city's surrender. Around the time, and even more drastically, bishop Paulinus of neighbouring Aquileia led the inhabitants of his city on an exodus, abandoning their old settlement for a more secure one on an island in the nearby coastal lagoons.[15] With such events we have clearly left behind the classical world with its town councils and magistrates far behind and moved into the social landscapes of medieval Christendom.

As Bertrand Lançon shows, the increased social and political prominence of bishops was a crucial factor also in the transformation of late antique Rome. Already during the Gothic and Hunnic invasions of Italy in the fifth century, the popes showed themselves to be energetic diplomats seeking to preserve the city from attack. It is above all the presence of the papacy that gives Rome's metamorphosis in this period its special significance. Of course, Rome represents a special case, since the magic of its ancient reputation continued to beguile the medieval imagination. Thus the seventh century saw the erection of the last imperial monument, a column in honour of the emperor Phocas (602–10), in the Roman Forum, and a final, disastrous attempt to re-establish Rome rather than Constantinople as the empire's capital by Constans II (641–68).[16] The barbarian conquerors of the Roman west too were bewitched by the city's former majesty and even sought to revive it. Such aspirations reached their climax on Christmas Day 800, when the Frankish king Charles the Great – Charlemagne – had himself crowned Augustus of a revived Christian Roman empire by Pope Leo III.[17] Yet Charlemagne's coronation, however much it sought to evoke the grandeur of Rome's imperial past, took place in a radically transformed city, where the age-old traditions of the Caesars could not simply be revived. Rome was home to a bishop whose spiritual jurisdiction stretched far beyond the territories that comprised Charlemagne's empire. Throughout the cermonies of Christmas 800, Pope Leo acted as impresario, lending the proceedings his sanctifying significance. In this respect, Charlemagne's installation as emperor at Rome possessed a different texture to those coronations of Roman emperors that continued to occur at Byzantine Constantinople. Whereas in the east the figure of the emperor retained its ancient supremacy, in the city of Rome that pre-eminence belonged firmly to the pope. The complex processes that yielded this difference provide the thread that unites Bertrand Lançon's narrative.

Department of Ancient Classics
National University of Ireland, Maynooth

I

Maiestas Quirini: *The majesty of the Quirinal*

CHAPTER 1

Looking at the city

— PAST AND PRESENT —

No other city than Rome can offer the modern tourist such an impression of the way in which the various ages of history have overlapped and been superimposed. Let us step into the shoes of a visitor going through the city, by Vespa like Nani Moretti in his *Intimate Diary* and Gregory Peck and Audrey Hepburn in *Roman Holiday*, or by motorcycle as in the nocturnal epilogue to Fellini's *Roma*, or even on foot, like a brave tourist. Let us suppose that this visitor has read and enjoyed Julien Gracq's *Around the Seven Hills*, and that he or she likes the Roman canvasses of Pierre de Valenciennes, Hubert Robert and Corot. As he paces through the streets, Respighi's music fills his soul: indeed, the pines and fountains are the least changed witnesses of what the ancient city must have been. Despite a sometimes remarkable state of preservation, the ancient vestiges of Rome are ruins which make us view it in the light of a grandeur that is past. Even if, by an effort of imagination, one tries to reconstruct a picture of what it could have looked like, it is difficult to escape the romantic view which writers and painters have bestowed upon it.

In the very same way that the ceiling of the Sistine Chapel, now that it is restored, is nearer to its original appearance in the time of Michelangelo, so our tourist will form a more accurate picture of what the city was like in the early fourth century by going to see the model of Rome in Constantine's day. This great model, created by I. Gismondi, can be found in the Museo della Civiltà Romana (Museum of Roman Civilisation), in the EUR (Esposizione Universale di Roma) district which was conceived and realised in the Fascist era.[1] One therefore has to overcome a reluctance that is both aesthetic and ideological. If we refer to the model and the knowledge we have of the architectural decorations of antiquity, we have to admit that the most disparaged monument in contemporary Rome is the one which best reflects its ancient reality: the Monument of Victor Emmanuel II, the white bulk of which has loomed at the foot of the Capitol since the achievement of Italian unity. Most people find it hideous, and consider that its bad taste detracts from its surroundings. Yet there is nothing more quintessentially Roman than this monument! There is no doubt at all that the fourth-century Romans would have adored it. What we today like in ruins, they liked brand new. Where we see bare bricks and stones, the domain of basking cats and rampant weeds, the Romans used to admire dazzling facings of travertine, marble or coloured stucco. They deplored the patina and signs of wear that we admire nowadays, while meditating on the destiny of empires.

It was partly for those reasons, I suspect, that Alma-Tadema's paintings were so disparaged in the twentieth century. Where people expected poetic ruins in the manner of Piranesi, he attempted to show the marbles unchanged, exactly as Romans in antiquity would have seen them. This agonising struggle between the ruined, on the one hand, and the new and the bold plan, on the other, is perfectly embodied in the character of Stourley Kracklite, the protagonist in Peter Greenaway's film *The Belly of the Architect*. Certainly he is preparing an exhibition on the plans of Étienne-Louis Boullée; but his studio is located in the Victor Emmanuel Monument. Distracted from his work, he paces the Roman ruins, sadly meditating on the fatal illness that tortures him. It is as if the ruins were the metaphor for his belly and, at the same time, the only womb in which he can curl up in peace. Rome has therefore not stopped being for us, as for the ancients, like a mother and the relationship one has with it reflects its ambiguities and paradoxes.

Although 1500 years separate us from the Rome of AD 500, the Romans living in 500 were separated by 1250 years from the town's foundations, which means that they themselves had more than a thousand years of architectural palimpsest before their eyes. They were witnesses to the disappearance of ancient buildings, their dilapidation and possible restoration, as well as the construction of new buildings. They also experienced nostalgia, sadness and wonderment at the sight of the changing landscape of their city.

Why did the choice of the EUR model fall on the Rome of Constantine rather than on Antonine Rome? The answer is simple. It was in fact in Constantine's reign (306–37) that the last great building works were finished, with the erection or completion of baths and a basilica. This era represents the last state of the 'pagan' city, before its gradual but radical transformation by the construction of Christian buildings. The other reason is documentary. Roman topography of the fourth century is in fact the best known to us, for from this era we have preserved the regionnary catalogues, which list the names of the Roman buildings, district by district.

– A FORTIFIED TOWN –

Passing through the gates of Rome, we can today admire the well-preserved stretches of a fine defence wall, but this must not make us forget that, until the last quarter of the third century, only the centre of the city was fortified by the so-called Servian Walls, erected in the fourth century BC. The new circuit, built on the initiative of Aurelian (270–5), with the consent of the Senate, and completed by Probus (276–82) around 279, is indisputably the greatest architectural enterprise of late antique Rome. However, it is not an isolated construction. Aware of the threat from the barbarians, Aurelian had had a number of western towns fortified, such as in Gaul, where the fine walls of Le Mans are apparently contemporary with those of Rome. The perimeter at Rome is 18.8 kilometres, and embraced the best part of the city's fourteen *regiones*, or slightly more than 100 square kilometres and, a little later, encircled the Trastevere region on the right bank of the Tiber.

The base of the edifice is stone rubble faced with brick, four metres thick, and the wall itself is twenty feet high, or slightly under six metres. Sixteen gateways were made in the whole length, three of which were on the right bank, and it was punctuated by 381 square towers, located every thirty metres, comprising a room with loopholes. Built in a mere ten years or so, this large-scale construction had a few weak points, such as the lack of ditches, the inadequate height of the walls and the absence of towers giving on to the Tiber, north of the Campus Martius.

Erected on a base of about 19 metres in width, its construction implied the compulsory acquisition of some 350,000 square metres of land, where there were houses, villas, gardens, cemeteries and public buildings (aqueducts, mausolea). In order to save time and money, it incorporated preexisting architectural elements such as houses or aqueducts. Excavations have brought to light one house wall in which the statues had not even been removed from their niches. The walls of another house, datable to the third century, and therefore recent, had been filled in; archaeologists found ornamental pavings, mosaics, frescoes and a marble staircase still in place.

Several planned campaigns were undertaken later in order to repair and strengthen the wall, at the same time trying to overcome its most obvious faults. The first took place under Maxentius, between 309 and 312; the second under Honorius, in 401–3, was undertaken by the city prefect Longinianus.[2] Towers were added and the curtain wall raised to sixty feet. Maxentius also initiated the digging of a ditch. Honorius raised the height of the walls to some fifteen metres, and had them crenelated. The gates and towers were restored and large amounts of rubble cleared away. Also during this period the wall was extended to the right bank, encircling part of Trastevere. When Honorius began his sixth consulship at Rome, early in 404, he was therefore welcomed within an enlarged fortifying wall, bristling with towers, with a fresh look that, according to the poet Claudian, imparted an air of renewed youth to the city. Subsequently, works were carried out regularly, especially after the Goths sacked the city in 410. Thus the fifth *novella* (decree) of Valentinian III (425–55) ordered the prefect of the city to repair the parts of the wall that had collapsed or were threatening to crumble, making use of Roman trades guilds for this purpose. Further restoration works were similarly carried out in the sixth century, during the war between Justinian and the Ostrogoths.

The construction of the defensive walls and later works resulted in raising the city's ground level. In Aurelian's time, rubble from the wall's foundations had been thrown to the inside, which created banks that reached three metres in height. The fresh debris due to the digging of the ditch was spread out in 403, thus raising the level of the ground outside the walls. Archaeologists found that the bases of several gates in the wall lay at a level three or four metres higher than the bases of first-century buildings.

– The *POMERIUM* and the *REGIONES* –

The wall of Aurelian and Probus and its successive restorations do not reflect only the town's fear of sieges; Rome in late antiquity, unlike Rome of the early empire, was a powerfully fortified town, not just for honorific purposes but also for defence. There is no doubt that this was a sign of the times, but the construction of the wall had a further consequence in terms of the *pomerium*, Rome's sacred boundary, which Aurelian had adjusted to fit in with his new circuit of walls. Until then the *pomerium* had been demarcated by *cippi* (boundary stones). Claudius, Vespasian and Hadrian had altered its boundaries, so that its circumference, before Aurelian's time, had been about 14.9 kilometres. With Aurelian, Rome experienced the last, but not the least, of its pomerial extensions. The 18.837 kilometres of the fortified circuit marked out an area of 1372 hectares, or three-quarters of the surface area of the city's fourteen *regiones* (administrative districts), which encompassed some 1800 hectares. The path of the wall did not meet military needs. It attempted, in fact, to follow as closely as possible to the outline of the *pomerium* in AD 175.

In his *Panegyric on the Consulship of Stilicho*, Claudian marvels at the sight of the incomparable expanse of the city, which could not be taken in at one glance. In his view, there was no greater city that the air encompassed on the earth.[3] It is true that, during late antiquity, Rome remained the largest city in the west, taking precedence over Carthage and Milan. Since the time of Augustus its 1800 hectares had been divided into fourteen *regiones* of unequal size and population. These were sub-divided into quarters, the *vici* placed under the charge of *vicomagistri*. In the middle of the third century, on the decision of Pope Fabian, seven ecclesiastical regions were super-imposed. These were at first purely of concern to the Church, with seven regional deacons organising aid to the poor. In the mid-fifth century, however, they received an administrative framework, with Pope Leo the Great appointing to each of them a sub-deacon, *defensores* (legal officials) and notaries. By the time of Gregory the Great, these ecclesiastical arrangements may be said to have supplanted the old division into fourteen districts. It must be pointed out that these districts, which remained seven in number until the twelfth century, had nothing in common, including topographically, with the *diaconiae*, food distribution centres, which are mentioned for the first time under the papacy of Benedict II, in the late seventh century.[4]

– Roads –

The road network leading to or departing from Rome was the same as in republican times. Together with the Tiber, it was the finest example of the city's permanence. To the south, the Via Appia led to Campania and thence towards Brindisi; to the north, the Via Cassia led to Milan by way of Etruria, and the Via Aurelia to Liguria; the Via Flaminia went by way of Umbria to the Adriatic; to the south-west, the Via Ostiensis and Via Portuensis, twice as wide as the others, established a land link with Rome's ports. Beyond the *pomerium*, the town's cemeteries followed the lines of these roads. They were the first places where buildings were put up in honour of the martyrs.

Within the city, the streets had no proper names. In texts, there is a consequent lack of precision in fixing locations, the points of reference mentioned usually being the nearest monuments. Only the largest streets were straight, and were paved and had pavements for pedestrians. The rest were narrow, and, although some were paved, many were not. Those which were made of beaten earth and crushed and compacted pieces of stone suffered more from running water and the passage of carts and chariots, and became full of potholes and ruts.

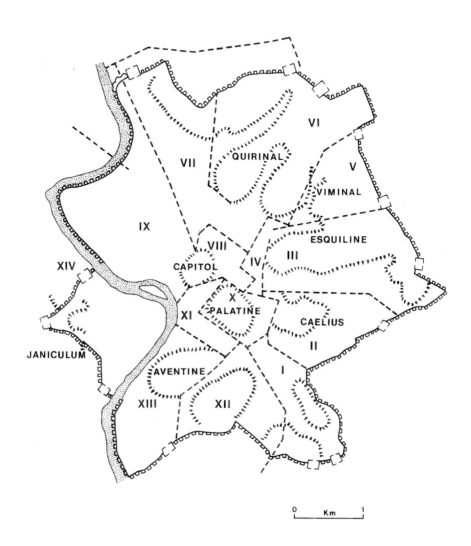

Map 1.1 Regions and hills

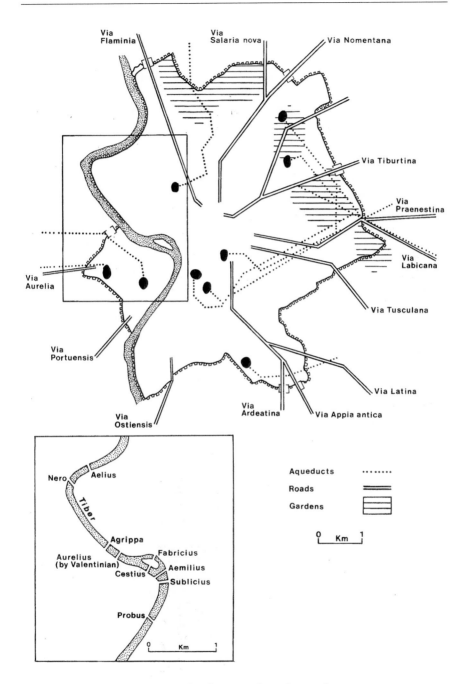

Map 1.2 Gardens, roads and aqueducts

– THE TIBER –

The Tiber is a modest river, but it is Rome's own, a fact which has conferred upon it a fame that is disproportionate to its unassuming course. Elevated to the status of a god, it had had a cult devoted to it in republican times. Not only was it indissociable from Rome but, like the seven hills, it was also a kind of metonym. According to the poet Claudian, when Honorius arrived at Rome in 404, his first act, before entering the city, was to hail the Tiber and make a libation with its water.[5]

Its length, of some 400 kilometres, and its width are those of a small river. It also presented some disadvantages for Rome: on the one hand, its somewhat capricious flow rendered it liable to high levels that caused flooding; on the other, the low-lying areas of the city and Latium were consequently marshy. But it also had immeasurable advantages: it was navigable, especially over the thirty-five kilometres of its course separating Rome from the Tyrrhenian Sea, and it provided the city with a sewer.

As the Tiber's source was in the Apennines, its flow had the character-istics of a mountain watercourse. In the spring, its waters were swelled by the melting snows, so it often overflowed its banks. Claudian refers to one of the floods which, from time to time, afflicted the city. This one probably took place during the famine brought about by the war against the African Gildo in 398–9. The Tiber flowed into houses, covering them to roof-level. At this point its level had risen so much that, in Claudian's somewhat exaggerated dramatisation, it threatened to reach the hilltops. The walls of Claudian's home were submerged, and he assures us that he saw boats sail over them. The low-lying areas were of course totally under water and the Forum was filled with the sound of oars.[6] At the beginning of the tenth book of his *Histories*, Gregory of Tours mentions a serious flooding of the Tiber in 589. Returning from Rome in November of that year, a deacon of the Church of Tours, Agiulf, told of a flood of such dimensions that it caused the collapse of ancient buildings and, submerging the cereal store-houses of the church, destroyed thousands of bushels of wheat. John the Deacon, Gregory the Great's biographer, notes the detail that snakes and livestock were floating adrift. In addition, defects in the drainage of the surrounding countryside made it a malarial zone.

The banks of the Tiber were an object of great concern to the Romans; not that they were well tended – quite the reverse. The only place where they had been well fitted out were the quays, landing-stages and ware-houses. On the Campus Martius, the structures of the *navalia* (dockyards) were preserved until the sixth century. It was there that Procopius saw an ancient galley moored, piously preserved by the Romans as Aeneas' boat.[7]

In this district also late imperial sources mention the prettily named 'Perched Swans' – *Ad ciconias nixas*: it was there that eagerly-awaited wine was unloaded, destined for the Romans' consumption. In addition, there were floating mills on the Tiber.

From the time of Augustus, there were magistrates whose duties were to supervise the Tiber and its banks, and they were answerable to the prefect of the city. This arrangement lasted until the fifth century, when the whole system was reconstructed. The magistrate's title, in Constantine's time, was *consularis alvei Tiberis et cloacarum sacrae urbis* (the ex-consul with responsibility for the bed of the Tiber and the sewers of the sacred city). In fact the town's drains emptied straight into the Tiber, a fact which no doubt helps to explain why the guild of fishermen experienced a decline. In the early fifth century, the *Notitia dignitatum* mentions a new magistrate with duties connected to the river: the Count of the river banks and Tiber bed and sewers. Justinian's *Pragmatic Sanction*, dated 554, still refers to the *cura alvei Tiberis*.

– BRIDGES –

In late antiquity there were eight bridges across the Tiber listed in the regionary catalogues. Among them, one was restored and two were built during the fourth century. These works show how the city continued to benefit from the concern of the emperors. In this way, although they resided in Rome only for brief stays, the emperors showed the perennial eminence of the city as the heart of the empire. They demonstrated this not only by such liberality but also by their desire to see their names associated with the monuments, by means of inscriptions, and thus to take their place among the names of the rulers who had preceded them. The Pons Aurelius, a bridge with three supports and four main arches which had been restored by Antoninus in the second century, underwent further renewal in the reign of Valentinian I (364–75). On this bridge, today known as the Ponte Sisto, a fragment of inscription was discovered at the end of the nineteenth century, bearing the eight letters 'NTINIANI' in capitals forty-five centimetres high. Restoration work commenced during the prefecture of Aurelius Avianus Symmachus (364–5), whose name appears in the dedication, and was completed a little later. Another bridge, attributed to Valentinian's son Gratian, dates from the same period: the dedicatory inscriptions lead us to believe that it was opened in 370. The masonry was not secured with mortar, but with iron tenons embedded in the stone and sealed with lead. Such fragility led to its subsidence, and it was destroyed at the end of the nineteenth century. The last bridge datable to this period is that of Theodosius, the building of which involved some corrupt practices. Symmachus, the son of the prefect of 364–5, was in his turn prefect of the city in 384–5, and in his *Relationes* – the official dispatches he sent to the emperor – and letters speaks of the many problems experienced in its construction.

According to Claudian, the Tiber's only island within the city's territory seemed to lie between two sister-towns – *geminae urbes*. Indeed, opposite it, the banks were lined with walls and towers, rising up like cliffs. Since the republican period, the island had been the site of the temple of Aesculapius, and many Romans went there to try by incubation (sleeping in a holy place) to find ways of curing illnesses.

– PORTUS AND THE DECLINE OF OSTIA –

Reading Diocletian's famous Edict on Maximum Prices of 301, we gather that Rome was at that time the principal maritime destination. The Tiber remained 'the centre of considerable maritime traffic' up to the sixth century.[8] There is an abundance of literary evidence on this point, much of it indicating a continuous influx of goods.

Written sources and excavations combine to show that from the late fourth century the port of Ostia was abandoned in favour of Portus, which was situated slightly more to the north. Indeed, excavations have revealed that there were no public buildings erected at Ostia during the late empire. The old defensive circuit, dating to Sulla's time (82–79 BC), was in a very bad state of repair and was not restored. Nevertheless, they also show that houses were built during the fourth century by adapting existing structures, but it seems that in the fifth century there was an abrupt halt, turning Ostia into 'a sort of fifth-century Pompeii',[9] as Federico Guidobaldi has called it.

Written sources stopped mentioning the use of this port; and Procopius, in the sixth century, makes the point in his account of the Gothic war that the Via Ostiensis was no longer maintained.[10] Ostia was used only in exceptional cases; for instance, Belisarius had his ships berthed at Ostia because Portus was occupied by the Goths.[11] It has been suggested that Ostia's decline was due to silting up, but, criticising this argument, others blame a fall in mercantile traffic. However, a study of the *annona* (Rome's grain supply) indicates that this fell only during the fifth century, at a time when Ostia's decline was well under way. Moreover it is hard to see why a drop in trading traffic should have caused a displacement of port activities from Ostia to Portus. Procopius states that the two branches of the Tiber were navigable in the sixth century, but specifies that people avoided using the left one – to the south – because of its sandbanks.[12]

In contrast, texts and archaeological remains indicate that Rome's port activity was concentrated in the three basins of Portus. It was the port invaded by the Goths at the start of the sieges of 408–10 and 537, in order to reduce Rome to starvation, since grain was in fact landed and stored in warehouses here before being conveyed up the Tiber. Portus' supremacy over Ostia already existed in the early fourth century, and Constantine had the town surrounded by a wall. As Ostia had been in earlier centuries, Portus was a place where cargoes were sorted. Landed from sea-going vessels, after checks on the quantities and quality of those cargoes concerned with the *annona*, the goods were transferred onto boats with less draught, and these were then towed some thirty kilometres to the city's quays.

– Aqueducts –

In the late period, the city had eleven aqueducts at its disposal for its water supply, with eight additional channels. Their construction was mostly of an earlier date for almost all of them had been built between 312 BC and AD 109. They represented a little over 500 kilometres of water conveyance and supplied the city with an estimated daily output of around one million cubic metres, or a volume of one cubic metre of drinking water daily per inhabitant: that was double the quantity available to the Romans in 1968.[13] Of course, that was an average, for a large part of the flow fed the baths and *naumachiae* (venues for mock sea-fights). The courses of these aqueducts finished, in the city, in large reservoirs. According to the *Curiosum*, in the fourth century, these supplied 11 large public bath complexes, 926 smaller public baths, 1212 fountains and 247 water tanks.

After the first thirty years of the third century no large aqueducts were built in Rome. The last large-scale construction was the Aqua Alexandrina, built by the emperor Severus Alexander in 226. The 22-kilometre (14-mile) aqueduct had been made to keep the baths of the Campus Martius supplied with water. A public heritage of the utmost usefulness, the aqueducts were vigilantly monitored and scrupulously maintained under the supervision of a magistrate of senatorial rank, the *curator aquarum*. They also underwent redevelopment. Thus the Aqua Marcia, which dated to 144 BC, had been restored by Titus, then by Septimius Severus and Caracalla. One section of 1500 metres was later added to it, under the name Marcia Iovia, which has led to the belief that it might have been built in the time of the Tetrarchy, when Diocletian and his Caesar Galerius bore the title of *Iovii* (men of Jupiter). The Marcia was restored by Honorius, using funds raised from confiscation of the rebel African Gildo's possessions, and again in the 460s by two 'counts of the aqueducts'. In 537 the Janiculum aqueduct was restored; it kept the grain mills supplied with water and for this reason played a fundamental role in feeding the city.

– POPULATION –

Assessing the size of the Roman population in the imperial period has always been a matter of controversy. In the absence of censuses, historians have fine-toothed-combed the evidence that might enable them to propose arguments supported by figures. The surface area of the city, the number of its *insulae* (apartment blocks), the number of those entitled to food distributions – all have been assembled and meticulously examined for that purpose. The estimates that have emerged are fairly variable. For the early empire they range from 750,000 to 2 million inhabitants, but an average of slightly over a million is generally accepted. The absence of aqueduct building in Rome after the first three decades of the third century may well indicate that the city's population ceased to increase after that period, but the water supply was so plentiful that one may also think this an insufficiently decisive criterion on which to base a judgement.

Though the population seems to have remained stable during the fourth century, the events of the fifth and sixth centuries caused its reduction, until the dramatic low-water mark in the mid-sixth century, at the time of the Gothic war. The main source enabling their numbers to be estimated is the figure given for those entitled to the public food distributions.

In the fourth century there were 200,000 *incisi* (inscribed names) in the official lists of those who were eligible. If we agree with Jean Durliat, who estimates that they formed about 30 per cent of the civic population, we may reckon that the citizens were between 550,000 and 700,000 in number, and that the Roman population consisted of from 700,000 to 900,000 individuals.[14] Let us keep to an average assessment of 800,000. In the fourth century, this population was very unevenly distributed among the city's districts. In contrast with densely populated zones were other, monumental, non-residential areas.

Highly populous, Rome was none the less a green town. Since the republican period, the city had been endowed with large and beautiful gardens, situated on the hills to the north, east and west. Some were private and lay within the grounds of the great houses of noble families; others, such as Caesar's gardens, had become public as a result of legacies.

An initial demographic fall took place in 408–19: the reform of the *annona* which occurred during 419 leads to the supposition that the population had declined by some 300,000 inhabitants. If the period is considered as a whole, Rome enjoyed a remarkable stability until the early fifth century. Then, between 408 and 530, the city lost nine-tenths of its population, with haemorrhages owing to the circumstances of sieges and devastation, and at the end of this period its population is estimated to have shrunk to 80,000.[15]

This dwindling of the population was accompanied by a migration to the city's interior. Archaeological evidence indicates that the higher zones were abandoned during the sixth century, as the populace became concentrated in the lower areas, especially in the loop of the Tiber.

In demographic terms, Rome's population was characterised by cosmopolitanism and youth. By cosmopolitanism must be understood that people came from every region of the empire to visit or to live in the city. Funerary inscriptions, which quite often mention the geographical origin of the deceased, are eloquent; moreover, a notable number were written in Greek. We know that as early as Juvenal's time there were many Greeks in Rome,[16] for he disparaged them with strongly xenophobic feelings. Similarly Jews, with their powerful sense of community, formed a large group, and had their own cemeteries, four of which have been identified.

As in the empire's provinces, the under-twenties represented slightly over half the population. Studying the ages at death mentioned on Rome's Latin epitaphs, Attilio Degrassi discovered an average life expectancy of 15.3 years.[17] This low figure, lower than those found in the provinces, must be treated with some caution, since the epitaphs of dead youths make more frequent mention of the age at which they died the better to emphasise the grief provoked by such premature death, a frequency that has led to an over-representation of infant and juvenile mortality in the statistical corpus.

− RESIDENTIAL AREAS −

Archaeology has not revealed the existence of specifically late antique quarters in Rome which would have been occupied for the first time in the fourth century, so it may be said without risk of error that the topography of Rome's residential areas was the same as in the early empire. If there were changes affecting the city, they were in the form of the construction of some large public buildings, in the fourth century, and numerous Christian edifices, between the fourth and sixth centuries. In addition, the decline in the Roman population from the early fifth century led in the sixth century to a redeployment of empty and occupied areas within the city. But in this respect, Rome was by no means unique; in this period, the layout of a good many western towns fluctuated inside their ancient *pomerium* as if in clothes that were too big for them.

One of the characteristic forms of Roman dwelling, between the end of the republic and the third century AD, had been the *insula*. *Insulae* were residential properties, of four storeys and more, divided into apartments intended for rent. One of the striking changes in Roman residential accommodation is that *insulae* were no longer built after the Severan era. At present, the last construction of which traces have been found is a large *insula* of Caracalla's time, on the Via Lata. But this had not been completed and had never been lived in. Why was this the case? Was the enterprise no longer profitable owing to a declining demand for such accommodation? This is the most likely explanation, yet the fourth-century regionnary catalogues mention a total of 46,602 *insulae* for the city of Rome. At first sight, this might appear to be an embarrassing contradiction of the archaeologist's evidence, so the question has been raised whether the term *insula*, as used in the catalogues, might have indicated a single apartment. In 1951, Léon Homo advanced the theory that in the fourth century the term *insulae* no longer designated residential blocks, but individual premises for rent.[18]

It certainly seems that henceforward the requirements of the Roman population tended towards a type of non-collective dwelling, the *domus*, and there was a notable boom in this sort of building during the fourth century. The term covers a variety of houses, ranging from – to use modern Italian expressions – a modest *casetta* to a sumptuous *palazzo*. Their owners were nearly all nobles, who lived there themselves or leased them. The *Liber Pontificalis* notes that renting could bring in an average income of a pound of gold, or seventy-two *solidi*. As Constantine had filled out the administration and increased the number of senators from 600 to 2000, one may well imagine that such bureaucrats and new members of the élite stepped up the demand for *domus*, both to buy and to rent. Merely by reading the biographical notes of the urban prefects we discover that a proportion of them came from elsewhere in the empire and therefore had to find accommodation in Rome. Thus the African Aradius Rufinus, prefect at the beginning of the fourth century, obtained a house near Caracalla's baths. The *domus*, which regionary catalogues number at 1790, needed more ground space than the *insulae*, or housed fewer people on an equivalent surface area. The development of this type of dwelling was therefore accompanied by the occupation of ground that had not been built on or had been left vacant by the destruction of ancient buildings. Of course, existing structures were also used. This restructuring revealed an attention to decoration: fountains, marble facings and apses indicate the spread of a luxury formerly reserved for imperial residences. Based on the results of excavations, it could be said that in the fourth century Rome went through a phase of embellishment, but this new town planning was not matched by urban expansion. After the first sack of Rome, in 410, many great *domus* were left abandoned.

CHAPTER 2

Transforming the city's image

— THE URBAN HERITAGE: THE CITY AS A MUSEUM —

When the emperor Constantius II visited Rome in 357, he processed through the city following a route which enabled him to admire its architectural riches. It was a chance for Ammianus Marcellinus, in his account of this visit, to paint a picture – biased, of course, but vibrant with admiration – of Rome in the mid-fourth century.[1] When he reached the Forum, Constantius was dazzled by the array of wonders accumulated over the centuries. During his brief stay, he toured the city, marvelling at its monuments, both old and new: the temple of Tarpeian Jupiter 'dominating everything as the sky dominates the earth'; thermal baths 'as big as provinces'; the Flavian amphitheatre, 'whose summit the eye can reach only with difficulty'; the Pantheon and its grandiose cupola; the columns bearing the statues of former emperors; and the temple of Venus and Roma and the Forum of Peace, the Odeon, Pompey's theatre and Domitian's stadium (now the Piazza Navona). He was amazed particularly at the sight of Trajan's Forum, 'a monument unique under all the heavens', which he visited in the company of the Persian prince Hormisdas. Wanting to leave his mark on Rome, he must have reflected a long time before deciding to erect a second obelisk in the Circus Maximus. But the tone of Ammianus' text clearly shows that Constantius, who for the most part had resided at Antioch, felt almost overwhelmed by the city's architectural and historic majesty.

Early in the fifth century, in the years preceding the Goths' first sack of the town, Rome had lost nothing of its ancient splendour, in the opinion of the poet Claudian: plated with bronze, the roofs of the buildings still rivalled the sun's rays in their brilliance. The triumphal arches and monuments of Roman victories were still standing, like the temples the forms of which soared skywards. Everywhere, he says, the eye was dazzled by the glitter of metals and quivered at the sight of so much gold.[2]

Architectural and epigraphic remains are not the only sources enabling us to picture Rome in late antiquity. In addition, there are the descriptive pieces to be found in literary texts and the regionary catalogues. The latter are little inventories, written in the fourth and fifth centuries and passed down by way of medieval manuscripts, setting out a list of the monuments each contained, district by district. Examples are the *Notitia regionum*, the *Laterculus* of Polemius Silvius and the *Libellus de regionibus urbis Romae*. The latter, known through two manuscript versions, includes the *Curiosum urbis Romae*. First, they tell us that in late antiquity Rome had retained the administrative division into fourteen districts imposed by Augustus. In addition, the *Curiosum* and *Notitia* give a detailed catalogue of the city's buildings and curiosities:

> 28 libraries, 6 obelisks, 8 bridges, 7 hills, 8 *campi* (level open areas), 11 forums, 10 basilicas, 11 public baths, 19 aqueducts, 29 avenues, 2 citadels, 2 circuses, 2 amphitheatres, 2 colossi, 2 columns decorated with spiral reliefs, 2 markets, 3 theatres, 4 gladiators' schools, 5 venues for sea-fight spectacles, 15 *nymphaea* (sanctuaries for the nymphs), 22 equestrian statues, 80 gold statues of gods, 74 in ivory, 36 marble arches, 37 gates, 423 neighbourhoods and the same number of temples, 46,602 *insulae* (residential blocks, rented premises), 1,790 *domus* (houses), 290 *horrea* (storehouses), 856 baths, 1,352 lakes, 254 bakeries, 46 brothels, 144 public latrines, 2,300 oil sellers.[3]

The only thing missing from this list is the Tiber's river rats![4]

− Imperial palaces −

At the time when Claudian was composing his panegyric of Stilicho, the imperial palaces still raised their lofty silhouettes above the Regia and the Rostra, the platform for public speaking. But they were becoming old and neglected, on the Palatine hill that had given them its name. Indeed, since Maxentius, ruler between 306 and 312, no emperor had chosen to make his ordinary residence there. Even before this the western Tetrarchs had installed themselves in Milan and Trier. In 330 Constantine had founded Constantinople, a new Rome on the Bosporus, where his successors lived in between their numerous journeys. During late antiquity, therefore, the immense imperial *domus* on the Palatine received only emperors or members of the imperial family who were making a short stay in the city. The most monumental, the Domus Augustana, had been built in Domitian's time; it was never replaced and was used as a temporary residence for emperors in transit until the end of the empire, a fact which Claudian regrets. On the Palatine, he said, power possesses more grandeur, and the masters of the

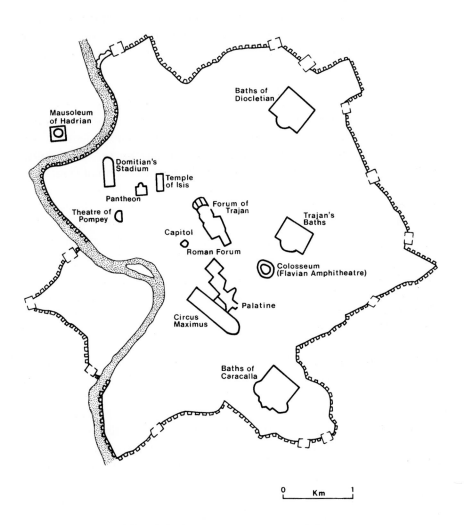

Map 2.1 Ancient monuments and forums

world could not imagine a more noble dwelling-place. For how long, he asks, invoking the image of the *paterfamilias* in his home, must the *potestas* (power) be thus exiled from its Lares (household gods), and, now appealing to military images, the *imperium* (authority) wander far from its head-quarters? He therefore implores the emperor Honorius, on a visit in 404 for his sixth consulship, to settle there. In his view the imperial presence would make the city's laurels grow green once more.[5]

– FORUMS –

Known to be the oldest of the city's forums and endowed with the most ancient remains, the Roman Forum is none the less rich in evidence of late antiquity. Between the reconstruction of the Senate house, shortly after 283, and the erection of the last great monument, the column of Phocas, in 608, it was enriched by many architectural adornments. The *curia*, the usual – but not exclusive – meeting place of the Roman Senate, was destroyed in the great fire that ravaged the western part of the forum in 283, in Carinus' reign. It was almost immediately reconstructed by Diocletian and Max-imian, its floor paved with marble tiling, and it is this edifice that can be seen today. The fire also raged in Caesar's Forum, destroying the Julian Basilica, the temple of Saturn and the slave market known as the Grae-costadium.

Maxentius had begun a basilica to be named after him on the site of the spice warehouse (*horrea piperataria*), but it was incomplete when he died in 312 at the battle of the Milvian Bridge, and was therefore finished by Constantine. Occupying a large part of the Velia (a northward extension of the Palatine Hill), it was indisputably one of the most imposing monuments of the entire imperial era, both for the area enclosed under its roof (100 x 65 metres) and its height (35 metres for the central aisle, nowadays in ruins). In 1487, the discovery was made in the western apse of pieces of the colossal statue of Constantine which are at present in the courtyard of the Palazzo dei Conservatori on the Capitol. It was most certainly an acrolith: the head (2.60 metres high), arms and legs were sculpted in marble, while the rest of the body was of bronze. Here we have one of the loftiest expressions of fourth-century imperial ideology. In the early empire, the Augustus was a *princeps*, an outstanding citizen endowed with great powers; by the time of Constantine, he had become a *dominus*, an almost inaccessible lord and master, of imposing majesty, who aroused somewhat apprehensive admiration.

Last but not least was Trajan's Forum, built between AD 107 and 113 on an area of 300 x 185 metres. Intact, it astounded Constantius II during his visit in 357. In the centre was an equestrian statue of Trajan, apparently wonderful since Constantius was seized with the desire to have a similar one made in his own likeness.

We must not forget the many public buildings that housed offices and surrounded the forums. Foremost amongst these offices were the prefecture of the city, located near the temple of Tellus, and that of the *annona*. The density of these public buildings in the heart of Rome imposed considerable restrictions on the availability of land for new construction, especially for the large churches of Constantinian and post-Constantinian periods, many of which had to be erected in peripheral sites.

– TEMPLES –

In 404, Claudian mentions the temple of Jupiter Tonans ('the Thunderer') and says that the statues standing on the rooftops of the temples seemed to be dancing amid the clouds. St Jerome, his contemporary, did not see them from the same viewpoint. After leaving Rome for good in 385, he wrote that the same rooftops were inhabited only by owls.[6] The adornments of the city, the temples were also the homes of Rome's traditional gods and, in the eyes of Christians, who were increasingly numerous in the city during the fourth century, were material evidence of idolatry. Where Claudian is happy to see the signs of Rome's continuity and grandeur still intact, Jerome scoffs at the tottering remains of superstition. Here, then, we have two versions that are biased, and we probably have to imagine a reality that lay somewhere in between. Rome's temples remained in use throughout the fourth century, and, although they were closed by Theodosius at the beginning of they 390s, they continued to be a respected ornament of the city. As public buildings, they were protected by the urban prefect from depredations, in accordance with imperial directives; but their stones and columns were a great temptation to people to remove and use them in the construction of new buildings. In the end the law permitted this practice for those which could no longer be restored, so that in the fifth century many of their columns were to be found in Christian basilicas.

– PUBLIC BATHS –

Each region possessed modest bathing establishments, but one could also go to the big public baths built by the emperors, such as those of Caracalla, in the south of the city, of Diocletian, in the north, and of Constantine, on the Quirinal hill. Shortly before 433, the prefect of the city saved the last from ruin thanks to a subsidy from the Senate.[7] They were dependent for their water supply on the aqueducts, which were still carefully supervised and maintained. They were cut off only in time of war in the sixth century, but were later restored.

Until that war the baths remained, as they had always been, centres of hygiene and sociability. It was possible to do gymnastics there, have a massage, relax in the warm room, sweat in the hot room and revive oneself in the cold room. In addition, there were the pleasures of conversation and reading, as the baths generally had a library. This style of living managed to survive only with extreme difficulty after the ravages of the sixth century. Moreover, the Roman population was now greatly diminished. Designed to meet the needs of several hundred thousand inhabitants, the imperial baths were no longer suitable when the number fell to a few tens of thousands.

– Circuses and amphitheatres –

The fires of 217 and 250 had not affected the majesty of the Flavian amphitheatre, better known as the Colosseum, the biggest in the Roman world. It was struck by lightning in 320, and seismic activity in 429, 443 and 486 caused some damage, but that was promptly repaired. An outstanding focal point for urban society, no monument in Rome was more cherished by the prefects of the city. In 438 Paulus had the *podium* (balcony), entrance and *cavea* (auditorium) restored. Most probably after the earthquake of 443, Lampadius had the arena, *podium* and gates renewed and the tiers of seating repaired. The arena was again restored in 470 by Severus, and in 484 by Venantius.[8]

Gladiatoral fights were held there until the early fifth century, but *venationes* (wild animal hunts) continued to be presented thereafter. Nets four metres high were firmly placed round the arena in order to protect the spectators from the animals – after all, were not the front rows occupied by the *clarissimi*, Rome's senatorial élite? The last show that we know of from the documentary sources – a letter from the Ostrogothic King Theodoric to the consul Maximus – was presented there in 523.

To the south of the Palatine, the Circus Maximus remained the public venue which, in Rome, allowed the largest number of the population to assemble: it could hold around 120,000 people, a capacity which few modern football stadia can equal. This building, which was regularly maintained, fulfilled a central function in the rituals of imperial ideology. Thus all cities that became imperial residences, such as Trier or Constantinople, received a vast circus. This was a fundamental element of the palatial complex; it was the conduit between the ruler and the citizens, the place where he could display himself to the people. In Rome the last circus was built by Maxentius, between 306 and 312, in the neighbourhood of his great villa on the Appian Way.

– ARCHES –

The Roman Forum had four triumphal arches, from one end of the Via Sacra to the other. That of Augustus has vanished, leaving those of Titus, Septimius Severus and Constantine. Titus' had been erected to commemorate his triumph in the war against the Jews (AD 66–70).

Constantine's arch was dedicated on 25 July 315, at the time of the emperor's tenth jubilee celebrations. Its height of twenty-five metres made it, as far as we know, the most imposing triumphal arch in the Roman world. It is possible, though not yet proved, that it was built by adding to an earlier arch that may have been on the site. There were probably no longer enough workshops in Rome able to cope with such a large order in three years, therefore the bas-reliefs adorning this arch are a real assortment of sculptures lifted from other monuments and new ones executed between 312 and 315. Indeed, there are reliefs from the times of Hadrian, Commodus and Constantine himself, which makes this arch, to use archaeologist Filippo Coarelli's words, a veritable 'museum of official Roman sculpture' of the imperial era.[9]

– COLUMNS AND STATUES –

In its *piazze* Rome had a number of statues in stone, metal or mixed media. Whereas those of deities were to be found in temples or their grounds, those of mere men were offered to the daily view of passers-by either in the open spaces or in the large public buildings. They certainly included statues of emperors. The one considered to be the finest stood in Trajan's Forum, and was an equestrian statue of its founder; but the emperors were not the only ones to have their statue erected. Prefects of the city were often presented with one by the emperor, the Senate or towns and guilds of which they were patrons. For instance, the prefect Orfitus was offered statues by the five guilds of which he was a patron, and these were placed in front of his house.[10] It appears to have been an honour much prized by *clarissimi*, rewarding the beneficent acts they had performed and, according to Ammianus in one of his caustic asides, sought after by those who had performed none. Many orators also received the honour of a statue; for the most part, these were grouped around the libraries in Trajan's Forum. Today, only the bases are preserved in their original locations, while surviving works of sculpture are housed in museums. So we have to imagine Rome, above all in its monumental centre, bristling with statues of various sizes, standing on the roofs of temples, on columns and pedestals carved with dedicatory inscriptions. The favourite place for these ornaments, the Forum, must have resembled a veritable museum of sculpture in the round, if not an incredible hotch-potch.

If we read the inscriptions on numerous statue pedestals, as well as texts such as the *Relationes* of Symmachus, we realise that the urban prefects erected and moved many statues. Such statues were manifestations of loyalty towards emperors and faithfulness to traditional Roman values: for men, just as much as monuments, were regarded as the ornaments of the city. The prefect of 334–5, Anicius Paulinus Iunior, had a statue of Constantine put up in the Forum.[11] Shortly before his death, the latter suggested to the Senate the erection of a statue of the current prefect, Aradius Valerius Proculus Populonius.[12] A few years later, the prefect Fabius Titianus had statues transferred to the Roman Forum.[13] In the middle of the fourth century, Orfitus installed statues in the Aventine thermal baths, and had those of Constantius and Julian placed in the Forum.

All these statues formed a remarkable historical and artistic heritage, and they were therefore placed under the supervision of prefectural dignitaries, the *centurio rerum nitentium* (centurion with responsibility for beautiful things) and, chiefly, the *curator statuarum* (curator of statues). Nevertheless, the city lost a number of its statues between the fourth and sixth centuries. In the first place, Constantine had many of them removed to adorn his new capital at Constantinople: then in 455 the Vandals had filled an entire ship with them; finally many of the gods' statues were destroyed by radical Christians who could not abide the sight of what in their view were idols.

– Obelisks –

Egyptian, or Egyptian-style, obelisks formed an original adornment to the city. Fifth-century Romans were able to see some half-dozen of these prismatic needles rising to the sky, and they still adorn some Roman *piazze*. Ammianus Marcellinus, the greatest Latin language historian of the fourth century, mentions several. The earliest had been installed in Rome by Augustus after the annexation of Egypt following his victory at Actium (31 BC). The only one remaining in place, and also one of the earliest erected in Rome, is the obelisk that today stands in St Peter's Square. It was put up by Caligula near the circus he had had built on the site of the Vatican. It was neither demolished nor transferred like its fellows. Two were to be found on the *euripus* (a low wall dividing the circus lengthways) of the Circus Maximus, at the foot of the Domus Augustana on the Palatine. If we are to believe Pliny the Elder, the first, dating from Pharaoh Seti I, was placed at the east of the track on Augustus' orders. Three centuries later, the circus was enlarged eastwards by Constantine, and his son Constantius II had the second placed there. The history of this obelisk, described by Ammianus Marcellinus after his account of Constantius II's visit to Rome in 357, is worth repeating.[14] It was one of the tallest obelisks in Rome in 357, standing 32.15 metres high. Erected at Aswan by Tuthmosis III (in the fifteenth century BC), it had later been moved to Egyptian Thebes (modern Luxor). Constantine wanted to have it erected in the circus of his new capital, Constantinople, but in 337 the emperor died while the obelisk still lay in the docks of Alexandria. Constantius II, visiting Rome from 28 April to 29 May 357, was dumbfounded by the city's architectural magnificence. He was anxious to add his own piece of stone to those of his predecessors, and therefore had the obelisk brought to Rome. It came up the Tiber on a boat, was placed in the Villa of Severus on the Aventine, and was then taken to Rome through the Ostian Gate over a land route of some 4.5 kilometres. Finally, it was set up on the *euripus* of the Circus Maximus, to match that of Augustus. On the four surfaces of its granite base six Latin lines were carved. It was surmounted by a bronze globe and a gold leaf, but these were struck by lightning and replaced by a bronze figure bearing a torch. Augustus' obelisk, still standing in the fifth century according to the *Notitia*, today graces the Piazza del Popolo. As for that of Constantius, it appears to have been knocked down early in the fifth century. Did it fall victim to vandalism by the Goths, who took the city in 410? But if so why did they leave Augustus' obelisk in place? Perhaps destruction by Christian fanatics is to blame. That is the theory of some historians, such as Rodolfo Lanciani, but it is debatable. In any case, the obelisk stands today in front of the Basilica di S Giovanni in Laterano.

Between the fourth and sixth centuries, two obelisks also adorned Augustus' mausoleum, near the Tiber, in the north of the city, and are mentioned by Cassiodorus. One now stands in Piazza del Quirinale, the other in the Piazza del' Esquilino, behind Sta Maria Maggiore. We may also note those on the Esquiline, put up in the second half of the first century, in imitation of Heliopolis, and mentioned by the *Curiosum*. The one in the gardens of Sallust on the Pincio is referred to for the first time by Ammianus in the fourth century; [15] today it stands in front of the church of the Trinità dei Monti, at the top of the Spanish Steps.

The obelisk now in the Piazza Navona is a special case: it does not, in fact, belong to the pharaonic era. Domitian had it sculpted and then transported from Egypt to adorn the temple of Isis in Rome. In 309, following the death of his son Romulus, Maxentius had a sanctuary and circus built at one of his villas and dedicated to his son's memory. On this occasion he had the obelisk from the temple of Isis transferred to the *spina* of the new circus situated on the Via Appia. An obelisk was still to be seen on the Campus Martius, another in the Varianus Circus and a further three whose date of import to Rome is unknown. The one on the Campus Martius, built on a base of red granite, had been used as the *gnomon*, or pointer, for the enormous sundial described by

Pliny the Elder. It could have functioned accurately for only some twenty years, but later it remained in position, and, indeed, is mentioned in the *Curiosum*. If we are to believe the manuscript of the itinerary of Einsiedeln, dated between 638 and 852, it was still standing, and would therefore have been the only one, with that of the Vatican, not to have been torn down during the fifth and sixth centuries.

It is thus evident that the majority of the obelisks adorned the *spina*[16] of circuses, amplifying their monumental nature. Their presence reveals the Egyptomania of the early empire, whereas only one was sent from Egypt to Rome during late antiquity. Rather than interpreting this as some sort of hypothetical decline in terms of financial means, or the fact that Egypt had gone out of fashion, I see the erection of this last obelisk as an effort to perpetuate an aesthetic tradition and an extravagant element, as eccentric as it was conspicuous, of imperial benefaction.

One last question remains: these obelisks' destruction. The sources make it certain that the obelisks were not all demolished at the same time. Must the Goths in 410 and the Vandals in 455 be incriminated? Did responsibility lie at the door of radical Christians, hostile to circus games? None of these hypotheses can be ruled out. At a time when historians believed that the Roman empire's collapse was an apocalyptic event, it was tempting to blame that for their destruction. Indeed, barbarian ravages and Christianity were at one time suggested as causes of the 'fall' of Rome. Such acts of deliberate destruction are not improbable, but it must be remembered that in late antiquity Rome also experienced earthquakes that might well have toppled these slender-based monuments, which the popes later re-erected in the *piazze* of Baroque Rome.

– CHRISTIAN INNOVATIONS –

Until the fourth century Christian communities in Rome had not had specific buildings, called churches or basilicas, available for their religious assemblies. They were regularly received in houses which ordinary citizens placed at their disposal. Their legal name, *tituli*, indicates that these were private properties, and therein lies the great difference from official religion which, subsidised by the state, was housed in public buildings. There were some twenty *tituli* in Rome at the beginning of the fourth century, the earliest being located within the ancient Servian walls. They were scattered throughout the districts, primarily on the fringes of densely populated and aristocratic quarters – hence there were none in the populous Velabrian and Suburan areas. This distribution shows that there was no specifically Christian quarter in Rome, and also means there was no ostentatious architectural sign of the existence of Christianity in Rome before Constantine's building campaigns.

– CONSTANTINE'S BUILDING PROJECTS –

In 311 Maxentius began handing back to the Christians the possessions that had been confiscated from them. Two years later, the so-called 'Edict of Milan' gave permission for Christian worship, inaugurating for the Church a period of peace that was to alter the city's ecclesiastical – and, indeed, religious – geography profoundly. In that year a council took place in Rome, under the presidency of Bishop Miltiades. It was held in the *domus Faustae*, at the Lateran, and a wish was expressed that the synodal court should possess its own meeting-place. Then, at his own expense, Constantine had a Basilica built for the Church of Rome. Started before 324, this, the Lateran basilica, was built in the south-east of the city, on an imperial domain, on the site of the barracks of the *equites singulares* and the *schola curatorum* which was destroyed. The great size of Constantine's Lateran Basilica broke away from the modesty of previous Christian edifices. Constructed on a basilican plan with five aisles, it measured 100 x 55 metres, thus equalling in size Maxentius' basilica in the forum. As its walls had been clad with yellow marble, it was given the name *basilica aurea* (the golden basilica). It was flanked by a baptistery, then a palace which later became the bishop's residence and seat of his administration. The first episcopal church, today it remains Rome's cathedral, under the name of S Giovanni in Laterano. The Roman cathedral's situation away from the centre is connected with its origins; as Constantine could not undertake large-scale monumental building in the city centre, he had to see his plans materialise on a readily available space, an imperial property where there was a barracks whose cavalry unit, which had supported Maxentius, had been disbanded after his defeat in 312. With the Lateran, the Roman church had at its disposal for the first time a place that enabled many of the faithful to assemble, which was not without liturgical consequences. Moreover, this first Christian complex received donations from the emperor, ensuring an annual revenue of 4390 *solidi* for the basilica and 10,234 for the baptistery. The latter was richly ornamented; if we are to believe the figures quoted in the *Liber Pontificalis*, three tons of silver and three and a half quintals (100 kilograms) of gold were used for this purpose.

The second of Constantine's great building projects was the basilica raised on the site of St Peter's tomb on the Vatican Hill. It was built near Caligula's circus, which was apparently abandoned, and cut into a pre-existing burial site. At the time, this extra-urban space was planted with trees and vines. Commenced between 319 and 322, it was fully completed in 329, though work continued on it after Contantine's death. Extensive

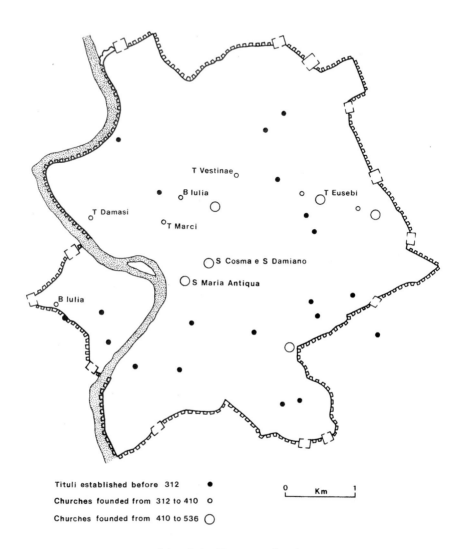

Map 2.2 Christian churches

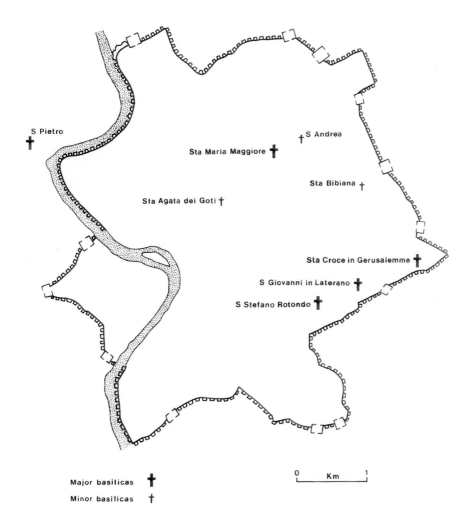

S Pietro ✝

S Andrea ✝

Sta Maria Maggiore ✝

Sta Bibiana ✝

Sta Agata dei Goti ✝

Sta Croce in Gerusalemme ✝

S Giovanni in Laterano ✝

S Stefano Rotondo ✝

Major basilicas ✝

Minor basilicas ✝

0   Km   1

Map 2.3 Christian basilicas

excavations on the site of St Peter's tomb revealed that already in the third century it had been the object of several successive reworkings. Peter's *memoria* (shrine), also called his 'trophy', was a small edifice of porphyry and precious materials capped, at the time when the basilica was built, by a little baldaquin of six wreathed columns in white marble, and its walls covered with a protective coating. Not far from this original structure stood the altar, with the gold cross presented to the basilica by Constantine and his mother, Helena. St Peter's basilica was larger than that of the Lateran (122 x 66 metres), but less well endowed, with 3708 *solidi* per annum. In addition, two or three suburban churches seem attributable to Constantine, including a shrine to St Paul and the basilica of St Laurence (S Lorenzo fuori le Mura). In the same period, Constantine's mother, Helena, had a wing of her Sessorian palace, situated in the south-east of the city, transformed into a Christian basilica named *Hierusalem* (Sta Croce in Gerusalemme). An apse was added, and colonnades divided the basilican lay-out into three aisles.

The basilicas of the Constantinian period have something in common: they were constructed according to the canons of imperial architecture then in force for civil basilicas and palatine *aulae* (audience chambers), with a few adaptations such as apses. The new amount of room available to Christians allowed the development of a more solemn liturgy, in more spacious and grandiose surroundings for the increased number of faithful. Rituals and processions certainly took their inspiration from palatine ceremonials.

THE FLOWERING OF THE CHURCHES: FROM JULIUS TO LEO THE GREAT (337–440)

Between 312 and 410 at least eight churches were founded in Rome, among them five titular churches, bringing the *tituli*, just before the sack of Rome, to their final number of twenty-five. Former *tituli* were reorganised. Popes Julius (337–52) and Liberius (352–66) were keen builders. Julius had five basilicas built, three outside Rome and two within the walls. On the Esquiline, Liberius had a large basilica constructed which became one of the great places for the city's Christians to assemble. With these new buildings, the Roman church now had at its disposal premises at the centre of the ancient city.

The pontificate of Damasus (366–84) was a high point in the organisation of the Roman church. He undertook numerous works of restoration and embellishment in existing buildings, and had the suburban tombs of the martyrs refurbished, with magnificently carved inscriptions in verse added. Thus he contributed to the development of the cult of martyrs in Rome, making the city an important centre for pilgrimages. His successors, Siricius and Anastasius, carried on his work, increasing the density of churches within Rome, in the middle of residential quarters. In 386, the emperors ordered the prefect of the city to divert a road in order to allow a more monumental construction of the basilica of S Paolo fuori le Mura,[17] begun at the end of Damasus' pontificate, and completed during that of Siricius (384–99). The new structure exalted the apostle of the gentiles to the point of placing him on an equal footing with Peter.

Bishops were not the only ones to order building work. Flavius Macrobius Longinianus, prefect from 401 to 402, who made a name for himself by restoring the city's walls, had a baptistery built near the church of Anastasius in the Velabrum.[18] After the Gothic sack in 410, few churches were founded. The bishops dedicated themselves chiefly to rebuilding and embellishment, adding marble, mosaics and enamels to the interiors. Celestine (422–32) had Pope Julius' basilica of Sta Maria in Trastevere restored. At his own expense, he endowed the brand-new church of Sta Sabina with carved wooden doors and mosaics, and had its walls clad with marble *opus sectile*. The *titulus* of the Apostles, on the Esquiline, was restored with the help of the imperial family; as it contained St Peter's chains, it received the name St Peter-in-Chains (S Pietro in Vincoli). Among other works, Sixtus III (432–40) rebuilt the Lateran baptistery, and the Liberian basilica, which he dedicated to the Virgin (known today as Sta Maria Maggiore). It was the first time that a bishop had financed out of his own pocket the building of a church of this size (72 x 32 metres). He did it in the old style, using Ionic columns and covering the vault of the apse with mosaic. From the second third of the fifth century, works of public benefaction declined and the construction of Christian edifices became the prerogative of the papacy.

It must be added that church architecture began also to diverge from the basilican lay-out. For instance, Sta Costanza, built in the mid-fourth century, and S Stefano Rotondo, copied from the Anastasis of the Church of the Holy Sepulchre in Jerusalem at the end of the fifth century, were both constructed on a circular plan.[19]

– FROM LEO TO GREGORY (440–604) –

The aspect of Christian Rome altered a little during the sixth century. The basilica of S Lorenzo fuori le Mura was enlarged, and churches were embellished with mosaics. Few new churches were built, but among them, on the Caelian hill, Sto Stefano Rotando, erected by Simplicius (468–83), was given an original circular lay-out. Hilarus flanked S Lorenzo fuori le Mura with a baptistery complete with baths, an open-air pool and two libraries, one Greek and the other Latin: we can see from this example that

Christianity had not swept away the Roman art of living. St Paul's (S Paolo fuori le Mura), St Laurence's (S Lorenzo fuori le Mura) and St Peter's were the three great extramural sanctuaries, around which grew residential quarters. In 480 a church dedicated to St Andrew, Peter's brother, was built in the former villa of the prefect Junius Bassus, which had become property of the Goth Valila, who had bequeathed it to the Church of Rome. Such plundering of existing structures was quite common. A number of churches constructed in Rome during the fourth and fifth centuries reused columns, capitals and entablatures taken from temples that had become unrestorable. Among the most spectacular examples are the forty-two columns of green marble in the Lateran basilica, the twenty-four Corinthian columns of Sta Sabina and the twenty Doric columns of S Pietro in Vincoli.

The great innovation of the sixth century was the installation of two churches in the Roman Forum: hitherto no church had been introduced into the old monumental centre of the city. Now, two centuries after the building of the Constantinian edifices on the city's periphery, its heart had been reached. Bishop Felix IV (526–30) created the churches of SS Cosmas e Damiano and Sta Maria Antiqua from two abandoned secular buildings. Situated on the Via Sacra, the first received a splendid mosaic on the *cul-de-four* vault of its apse, which can still be admired; Felix himself is represented (albeit heavily restored) on the left, offering a model of the building to the saints. Under Gregory the Great (590–604) alterations were made to the interior arrangement of St Peter's basilica. Four of the six baldaquin columns were moved and the floor raised to form a platform over the saint's tomb. Henceforward Mass would be celebrated over rather than in front of the tomb. An opening – *fenestella* – was fitted on the west side to give access to the relics.

The topography of Rome's Christian buildings was not the fruit of some carefully premeditated strategy. Originally it had been based on the *tituli* which were located in private houses. It was subsequently developed on private properties, belonging at first to the imperial family and wealthy donors, and later to the Church itself. However, we may see a design in certain creations: Damasus' plan was to build a circle of martyrs' tombs around the city. His successors intended to fill in the empty spaces, so that by the end of the fifth century every Roman, no matter where he lived, was sure of finding a church less than 500 metres from his home.[20] This density is certainly the most important transformation in the Roman landscape of late antiquity.

– The maintenance of public buildings –

The maintenance of Rome's public buildings in a suitable condition created severe problems in late antiquity, in the first place, of course, because their upkeep and restoration were expensive. Irregular, or even non-existent, maintenance could lead to their dilapidation. In addition, there was the damage caused by frequent fires, either accidental or, in the case of the sackings in the fifth and sixth centuries, deliberate. Earthquakes, some of which are attested by written sources, formed an additional factor in their deterioration. For all these reasons, on the initiative of the prefect of the city, regular maintenance work proved necessary. Thanks to the inscriptions, we know about several campaigns of restoration in the Colosseum, which, as we have seen, was the object of very special concern on the part of the prefects.

The fourth *novella* of the emperor Majorian is a major source for the condition of Rome's public buildings in the fifth century. It was addressed by Majorian, at the start of his reign, on 11 July 458, to the prefect Aemilianus. The document begins with a report: public buildings had been destroyed on the initiative of the urban prefecture itself, and stones had been taken to construct new buildings or rebuild old ones. Even worse, the public officials had authorised ordinary citizens to come and take stones away for their own private use. The *novella*'s tone is one of indignation and outraged majesty, with the emperor protesting that he will no longer put up with people altering the city's appearance, above all by destroying great edifices in order to restore small ones. This implies that Rome no longer had enough masonry workshops available to meet the volume of work being carried out. It also shows how useful deteriorated buildings could be as quarries for pre-cut stone. This practice was economical as well, suggesting that funds available were insufficient to have ready-cut stone brought from elsewhere. Yet by 458 the practice was far from new: the emperors Valens, Gratian and Valentinian II had already prohibited it in 376.

Majorian, however, would not allow this pillaging to continue. The aim of his *novella* was to preserve public buildings, temples and other structures. If temples were explicitly referred to, it was probably because they were the first victims of the removals. In theory, they had been closed since the end of the fourth century, and doubtless lack of maintenance had been responsible for some structural damage. In addition, when the city was sacked much destruction had been caused. According to Procopius, in 455 the Vandals had removed half the roofing, which was made of the finest bronze covered with gold, from the temple of Jupiter Capitolinus. To Romans who considered the temples useless Majorian put up the opposing argument of the traditional splendour of this the most sacred of cities. He therefore prohibited the removal of building materials, which became a crime carrying heavy penalties. If a public official was found guilty of having authorised any such removal, he would henceforward be liable to a fine of fifty pounds of gold. This sum, equal to 3600 *solidi*, was immense, being the equivalent of one-tenth of the annual property income of a senator! This leads one to think that the size of the fine may have been fixed according to the wealth of the magistrates, who must have been of senatorial rank. If subordinate staff, servants, or accountants, were convicted of involvement in a similar affair, they were likely to be beaten and to have their hands amputated.

Even so, Majorian did not decide on an absolute ban. Exceptions could be authorised, provided a strict procedure was followed. This stated that if architectural plans involved the need to demolish an ancient edifice, or if a building proved irreparable, a detailed request for permission to carry out the demolition had to be addressed to the Senate. After much deliberation, the latter would then make a report to the emperor, with whom the final decision rested. Quite apart from its explicit concerns over Rome's decaying fabric, there is no doubt that this law sought to restore a preferential link between Rome and the reigning emperor, a link that had slackened during the fourth and fifth centuries.

CHAPTER 3

The phoenix city: War and invasion in the fifth and sixth centuries

– ROME WITHOUT AN EMPEROR –

It is customary to say that Rome lost its status as capital of the empire when it lost its emperor, at the time of Constantine's creation of Constantinople in the 320s, but that is a schematic view. Because of its prestigious past, its personality, its name conferred upon the empire, Rome could not cease to be a capital. Furthermore, as Gilbert Dragon has shown so eloquently, the creation of Constantinople between 324 and 330 was not effected in opposition to Rome; it was conceived as a second Rome, likely to strengthen the image of the first.[1] In the literary texts of late antiquity, Rome continued to be venerated. Although its population, power and prosperity had indeed diminished, in the view of cultured people it remained *the* city. Certainly, in the late fourth century, Ammianus Marcellinus regarded it as the *Urbs venerabilis*, which had entered old age.[2] But whatever complaints he may have had against it, he described it as 'mistress and queen' – *domina et regina*. His contemporary Claudian, thought its 'Quirinal majesty' – *maiestas Quirini* – intact, and exalted it as 'mother of kings and leaders' – *mater regum ducumque*.[3] Of course, this enthusiasm may be tempered by ascribing it partly to patriotic fervour, but, in the minds of the educated, Rome never lost its individuality and pride of place in the power to arouse emotions. In 440, Valentinian III, who lived at Ravenna, addressed his fifth *novella* to 'the city of Rome, which we quite justifiably revere as the capital of our empire'. This means the imperial residence there did not make Ravenna a capital; that title remained the prerogative of Rome.

In fact, from the end of the third century Rome ceased to be the emperors' principal residence. The last to live there more or less continuously was, technically, a usurper, the *princeps* Maxentius, between 306 and 312. After that date the Augusti were there only in passing, for fairly short stays. In the west, they preferred to live in Milan and Trier, then, from early in the fifth

– 35 –

century, in Ravenna. Nevertheless, the Romans were familiar with the august countenances, for as soon as they were proclaimed the emperors sent their portrait, together with that of their empress, the Augusta, to the Senate. The latter then exhibited the portraits in the city. Besides, their visits demonstrated that Rome remained, *Senatus Populusque* (Senate and People), the umbilicus of the empire. It must also be pointed out that Rome continued to see members of the imperial families living within its walls. In 388, before engaging in hostilities against Maximus, Theodosius sent the empress Justina, together with her children Valentinian II and Galla, to Rome, thinking that they would be warmly received.[4] We also know that at the time of the Gothic siege of 408–10, the widow of emperor Gratian, Laeta, with her mother, Tisamena, were living there, and were provided for its relief at the state's expense.[5] Galla Placidia, Honorius' sister, was also present. When the Vandals seized the city in 455, they captured the empress Eudoxia and her two daughters, Eudocia and Placidia. So although Rome was without an emperor, the imperial residences were not unoccupied.

Several episodes and pieces of writing bear witness to the Romans' wish to have their emperor back. In the personification of Rome composed by Claudian in his panegyric for Honorius' sixth consulate, the city insistently asks the ruler to return and live there. Indeed, his power would possess more grandeur. How great would its emotion be to see the curule chair once more on the *Rostra*, and the lictors (his ceremonial guard of honour) again making their way through Trajan's Forum!

– 410: 'THE MOTHER OF THE WORLD IS MURDERED' –

In the wake of intrigues in Constantinople in 400–2, the Goths who were settled in the Balkans and Illyria made a move towards Italy. In late 401, they besieged Milan, where the emperor Honorius was, and unleashed a wind of fear that reached Rome. But this first incursion was repulsed by Stilicho, supreme military commander of the western empire, who defeated them in the spring of 402 at Pollentia and then Verona. During 406, a second Gothic raid took place, led by Radagasius. He avoided Ravenna and made a thrust towards central Italy. According to Orosius, the danger, now closer still to Rome, provoked a wave of panic, but Stilicho defeated the Goths at Fiesole. They then retreated to Pannonia, under the command of Alaric. Stilicho, faced with eastern aspirations to political supremacy over the west, claimed Illyricum for the western empire, and in 407 decided to appoint Alaric supreme military commander for this diocese. But this astute decision, which helped him in his struggle against the usurper Constantine III in Gaul, rebounded on Italy in the following year. Alaric asked the

Romans for a sum of 4000 gold *librae*, equal to 288,000 *solidi*, the equivalent of the annual property revenue of a senatorial family. Summoned to the imperial palace by Honorius, who was staying in Rome between November 407 and May 408, the senators rejected this possibility although Stilicho, on the contrary, advocated it. In Lampadius' view, it meant buying not peace but servitude. Afraid that he would be the victim of harassment, he took refuge in a nearby Christian church.[6]

However, as a result of intrigues led by the nobility, Stilicho was disgraced, arrested and executed in the summer of 408, leaving Italian troops lacking a great military leader. At the same time, Alaric, who was no longer receiving corn supplies for his troops, had moved from Epirus towards Noricum, still demanding the 4000 gold *librae* which Stilicho had hoped to pay him as the price of peace. In October 408 he crossed the Alps and invaded Venetia, then besieged Ravenna, where Honorius resided. The sources indicate, however, that the city was almost impregnable as it was surrounded by marshes, and because of this the Goths moved on to lay siege to Rome. The city had restored its defence wall in 402–3 but had no adequate garrison, so the people of Rome had taken up arms and been trained to handle them. Alaric set up a blockade; in November he seized Portus, helping himself to the recently unloaded African wheat. By applying this kind of pressure, he intended to obtain a treaty of alliance from Honorius, together with lands and positions of command, but Honorius refused and the siege of the city began in December. Alaric doubtless thought he could obtain from the Romans the money the emperor would not give him. Famine, then epidemics, began to sap the Romans' physical strength and morale. They had to make do with half, then a quarter, of their usual daily bread ration. Various kinds of indigestible food substances were tried, notably acorn flour. As the dead could no longer be buried outside the *pomerium*, 'the city became the tomb of the dead', writes Zosimus.[7] Gratian's widow and her mother, who lived in Rome, helped the population as best they could. A Roman embassy handed over 5000 gold and 3000 silver *librae* to the Goths, together with 4000 silk garments, 3000 scarlet hides and 3000 *librae* of pepper, entirely provided by the senators. This tribute was even supplemented by the jewels adorning the gods' statues, some of which were melted down.[8] When he had received these riches, Alaric allowed the Romans to come to Portus for three days to get fresh supplies. Purchases and bartering went well, but Goths attacked the Romans returning from Portus and seized their food supplies. Alaric had to put a stop to it to ensure that his word of honour was respected. Taking advantage of greater freedom of movement, slaves fled and joined the besiegers. Honorius despatched a body of 6000 Dalmatian solders to lift

Rome's blockade, but they were defeated. At that point the prefect of the city, accompanied by two senators, went to Ravenna to try to influence Honorius. But the emperor refused to accept the conditions laid down by Alaric for lifting the siege, especially the provision of hostages. The Goths then turned to demanding ransoms, restoring the Roman aristocrat Maximilianus to Marinianus, his father, for a payment of 30,000 *solidi*.[9]

In January-February 409 the Goths tightened their blockade. A second Roman embassy reached Ravenna, adorned this time by the assuredly persuasive presence of Pope Innocent I. This time Honorius agreed to negotiate. His praetorian prefect, Jovius, met Alaric at Rimini, but, when negotiations were broken off, Alaric returned to besiege Rome. At the end of the summer, the Romans again began talks with the Gothic king. A third embassy went to Ravenna, led by Attalus, prefect of the city, and Innocent I. They asked Honorius to grant the Goths land and supplies in the Alpine province of Noricum. As the Roman grain supply fleet had been kept at Carthage by the count Heraclian, the Goths were in fact also suffering from shortage of food. Faced with a new rejection, Alaric resumed the blockade and attempted a political manoeuvre. In December, he had Attalus proclaimed emperor, had him baptised according to the Arian rite, and had the title of *Magister Militum* (supreme military commander) bestowed upon himself.

In January 410, Alaric and his 'hostage emperor' marched towards Ravenna, and Jovius came over to their side. But Honorius received a reinforcement of eastern troops, as well as the *annona* and taxes coming from Africa. During the summer, Alaric, now under pressure, deposed Attalus, and Honorius then decided to lift the African embargo on Rome. But, attacked by the emperor's troops, Alaric returned yet again to besiege Rome, making the famine unendurable. The Romans tried to come to some arrangement with him, which resulted in the Goths entering the city. In fact, the capture and sack of Rome in the summer of 410 should not be regarded as some great feat of arms, but very probably the outcome of an agreement negotiated between Romans, in a state of utter physical and psychological exhaustion, and a very determined king. The Goths entered the city by way of the Porta Salaria and indulged in pillage for three whole days, from 24 to 27 August. There were fires, murders and kidnappings for ransom purposes. Some Romans were able to seek shelter in St Peter's basilica, which the Goths respected. On 27 August they left Rome for the south, with considerable booty and distinguished hostages: for example, Galla Placidia, Honorius' sister, and the former urban prefect Attalus. But they did not carry off everything. Orosius recounts how the vessels and sacred objects of St Peter's were saved from pillage by Alaric's religious fear.[10] He had permitted houses to be looted but had specified that St Peter's basilica should be a refuge for people and possessions. Lightning, which struck buildings shortly afterwards, added to the damage committed by the Goths.

When Gainas, another Gothic leader, had taken Constantinople in 400, the event had not caused much stir outside the eastern empire. In contrast, the sack of Rome in 410 had enormous repercussions throughout the empire. Learning of it in his Bethlehem retreat, Jerome wept hot tears: 'It is taken, the town that conquered the whole world!' For the Gallic poet Rutilius Namatianus, it was as if 'the mother of the world is murdered'.[11] The shock wave was spread by numerous refugees who had left Rome for Africa and the east, such as Pinianus and Melania. Their accounts diffused a feeling of desolation which only increased the emotion aroused by the knowledge that the capital of the Roman world, inviolate since the Gaulish raid of 390 BC, eight centuries earlier, had been taken. More lurid details were to follow: we are told in Jerome's 130th letter that the Count of Africa, Heraclian, who had withheld the grain supplies at Carthage during the siege, sold young refugees to oriental brothels.

The city's inhabitants had certainly been traumatised. For two years they had endured anxiety, hunger and illness. The losses of money and precious objects were immense and impoverished the city. There was also the shock to morale: if the city that had given its name to the empire was not invulnerable, could not the same apply to the empire itself? The event gave rise to reflection on the moral causes of this misfortune, and on the way to face up to it in the future. Augustine, bishop of Hippo, thus came to write his monumental *City of God* between 411 and 425. In his view Rome, like any earthly city, could be destined only to perish; the celestial city alone is eternal and unchangeable. But such clear-sightedness should not cause an attitude of resignation. However mortal it might be, the earthly city as built by the Romans deserved every effort to perpetuate it.

Rome tended its wounds and recovered rapidly. In the fifteen years following the sack restoration work increased. In 412–14, the *Secretarium Senatus* (Senate offices) and Aventine baths were rebuilt. In 414, Aginatius Albinus had the baths of Sura, on the Aventine, restored;[12] two years later, Rufius Probianus had the Julian basilica restored and adorned with new statues; at the end of Honorius' reign, it was the turn of the portico of the urban prefecture's offices. Within a few years, then, the sack had already been relegated to the back of Romans' memories, as various pieces of evidence reveal. Consider, for instance, the testimony of Rutilius Namatianus. After a few years' stay in Rome, during which he was urban prefect in 414, this Gaulish aristocrat left the city in October 417. He recounted his return in a long poem, of which only the first book and beginning of the second are preserved. Having arrived at Portus on the first evening after his departure, he perceived sounds coming from Rome and thought he was suffering from an illusion:

> Several times the echo of the circus resounded in my ears,
> The applause announcing that the theatres were full.[13]

In the same year, Orosius completed his *Histories against the Pagans*, which he had undertaken at Augustine's request. In it he says that the sack of Rome was of course a recent memory, but to listen to the Romans one would have believed nothing had happened. Only the last ruins left by the fires still bore witness to it. All the evidence suggests, however, that Alaric had no wish to subvert the Roman empire in the west, or even to settle in Rome. He wanted to obtain from Honorius a grant of land and revenues for the Gothic immigrants, as well as the dignity of a Roman title for himself. It was therefore a matter of desire for integration and, in the face of the Palace of Ravenna's refusal, he had no other solution than to take as his hostage the city that was still the symbol of the empire.

– 455: THE VANDAL SACK –

In 454, the patrician Aëtius was murdered by the emperor Valentinian III and his friends. This imposing figure had occupied an eminent position for thirty years, during which he had rendered the western empire notable political and military services. In his death the chronicler Marcellinus *Comes* sees the death of the empire. The following year, Aëtius' friends avenged him by assassinating Valentinian III, and, on 17 March 455, Petronius Maximus, one of the Roman aristocrats most in the public eye, was proclaimed Augustus by soldiers who had been bribed. Seeking to legitimise his accession by a link with the moribund Theodosian dynasty, he forced Eudoxia, the widow of Valentinian III, to marry him, at the same time wedding his son to Eudocia, the imperial couple's daughter. At this time, an atmosphere of upheaval pervaded Roman society. In Vandal Africa, King Gaiseric refused to recognise Petronius Maximus and demanded from him the Balearic Islands, Corsica, Sardinia and Sicily, as well as various smaller islands. The extravagance of these claims leads one to think they were intended to precipitate a refusal that would constitute a *casus belli*. Yet Gaiseric had an additional reason for rancour: Valentinian III, with whom he was bound by a treaty, had promised his daughter Eudocia to the Vandal king's son, Huneric, an understanding that Petronius Maximus had therefore clumsily violated. Gaiseric then made ready a naval expedition directed against Rome. Certain sources allege that Eudocia's mother, the dowager empress Eudoxia, herself appealed to Gaiseric for help, but it is impossible to test the reliability of such claims.

The Vandal expedition against Rome was a simple raid, and not the prelude to an invasion of Italy. At the end of May 455, the Vandal fleet, which at that time was the only one in the western Mediterranean worthy of the title, moored at Ostia and landed Vandal warriors supported on the flanks by Moorish auxiliaries. Petronius Maximus immediately took flight, and panic seized the Roman population. In the confusion, Petronius Maximus was recognised and lynched. The bishop of Rome, Pope Leo, came to meet Gaiseric outside the walls and begged him to spare the city, which was empty of defenders and had no intention of putting up any resistance, from massacres and fires. The Vandal king accepted the request, but insisted on the right to pillage the city for fourteen days. During June 455, therefore, Rome endured two weeks of an organised, systematic sack, very different from the hasty looting of 410. The Vandal vessels then set sail for Africa, their holds laden with vast booty, including furnishings seized from the imperial residences on the Palatine, as well as bullion. Among these was the treasure of the temple of Jerusalem, brought back to Rome by Titus in 70. The famous Menorah was thus unloaded at Carthage among the gold and precious objects amassed in Rome over several centuries. Procopius notes, however, that the ship carrying plundered statues was reported missing in the course of the crossing. Perhaps he interpreted it as some divine portent. There were also thousands of hostages, including the empress Eudoxia and her two daughters, as well as Gaudentius, the son of Aëtius. Eudocia was married to Gaiseric's son, Huneric, while Eudoxia herself and her other daughter, the wife of Olybrius, one of the more distinguished members in the Roman Senate, were sent to Constantinople.

Rome did not undergo destruction and massacres, but was weakened by the exodus of its wealth and its élite. The Roman Church had lost the liturgical furnishings of its *tituli*, which Pope Leo had to renew in their entirety. The Vandal sack, in this instance, had been a profitable act of piracy coupled with diplomatic victory: Gaiseric was now able to impose a treaty in his favour on the western empire.

– 472: CIVIL WAR –

In April 467, the emperor Leo I sent to the west troops and an Augustus appointed by himself, Anthemius, an experienced soldier and son-in-law of the late emperor Marcian. The strong man in the western empire at this time was the patrician Ricimer, who asked for and obtained the hand of Anthemius' daughter in marriage.

In 471, against Ricimer's advice, Anthemius decided to intervene against the Visigothic king, Euric, who was installed in Aquitaine. With the backing of Roman senators, he recruited barbarian mercenaries in Illyricum, sending them to Gaul with his own son, Anthemiolus, but they were defeated, and the disagreement between the emperor and the patrician soon degenerated into civil war. Ricimer rebelled early in 472, and came to besiege Rome, where Anthemius and his supporters were entrenched. During the siege, Ricimer embarked on a complex series of political intrigues and managed to persuade the emperor Leo to appoint the aristocrat Olybrius as emperor in place of Anthemius. In April, Olybrius landed with eastern troops and was proclaimed Augustus in front of the soldiers below the walls of Rome. Although he had been dropped by Leo I, Anthemius was by no means resigned to submitting. Ricimer summoned the Burgundians to his side, while Anthemius obtained the help of the Ostrogothic king, Vidimer, who arrived to harass the besiegers. However, Anthemius' hopes swiftly vanished, as Vidimer lost his life and his son negotiated with Ricimer. The siege had then lasted several months and, as in 410, the Romans were suffering from famine and epidemics. Early in the summer, the besieged city capitulated, and on 11 July 472 Ricimer's troops entered Rome, which they proceeded to sack. Anthemius tried to flee in disguise, but was discovered and killed.

– 535–52: THE DEVASTATION OF THE GOTHIC WAR –

After the deposition of the last Augustus of the west in 476, Rome was for a time under the rule of king Odoacer, and then came under the Ostrogoths of Theoderic. Like the emperors of the fifth century, he preferred to reside at Ravenna, and Rome preserved its institutions in their entirety. Games continued to be held there, and public buildings were still being restored. But there was some friction between the king and the Roman Senate, which culminated in the execution of Boethius in 525.

As soon as he had reconquered Vandal Africa in 533–4, the emperor Justinian turned towards Ostrogothic Italy. Advancing northwards through the peninsula from Sicily, the east Roman general Belisarius waged a campaign that enabled him to take Rome in 536. The conflict had serious repercussions for the survival of Rome's ancient fabric, as statues were used as makeshift missiles, catapulted at the Goths. This first campaign was completed in 540, with the capture of the Gothic king Witigis. But the latter's successor, Totila, put up a stubborn resistance which made the war in central Italy last until 552. Rome was one of the chief victims of these seventeen years of bitter fighting. It was besieged and captured may times, and went through its darkest hours in late antiquity.

In 537 Belisarius was at Rome. Witigis besieged it and the Romans suffered hunger and thirst. In fact, the besiegers captured Portus and helped themselves to the grain storehouses of the *annona*. In addition, Witigis had cut off the water supply to the city's fourteen aqueducts, and the Romans had to make do with scarce and very expensive water from springs situated within the walls. The next year, reinforcements asked for by Belisarius arrived. The eastern *Magister Militum*, John, landed at Portus with troops and at once loosened the stranglehold. Witigis negotiated with Belisarius, who was able to reprovision the city, and the theatre of war then shifted towards central Italy. In 540, Belisarius succeeded in taking Ravenna and brought Witigis to Constantinople with him, but two years later Totila resumed hostilities. In 543, he devastated Campania and besieged Tivoli, and, in 544, he laid siege to Rome, whose defences were commanded by John. The following year, Belisarius was again sent to Italy, where he replaced John with Bessas. At that time the situation for the Romans was very delicate, since Totila, who had just occupied Lucania and Bruttium, was now besieging Rome for the second time. Catastrophe struck on 17 December 547: by means of a ruse of the Isaurian troops, Totila managed to enter Rome, which he subjected to violent treatment: walls were demolished, houses set on fire and property and inhabitants, including senators, were handed over as booty. Kept in captivity, the Romans were deported to Campania. The continuator of the *Chronicle of Marcellinus Comes* reports that the city remained for at least forty days devoid of its population 'to the point where neither man nor beast lingered there'. Of course, there is some exaggeration here, but it seems as if Totila's aim was to annihilate the very substance of Rome, which he left wide-open and dead. This desolation lasted until the return of Belisarius, who immediately repaired part of the defensive circuit, while John pursued the war in Campania. In 553, Justinian sent Narses, a great dignitary, to Italy. With the backing of the Lombards, he succeeded where Belisarius had failed, defeating and killing Totila, and subsequently defeating his Frankish allies and the remainder of the Goths still in Italy. Like the whole of Italy Rome emerged dreadfully bruised from this war. It was the final blow after the misfortunes of the fifth century, from which it had recovered fairly well. Nevertheless, the Aurelianic walls were rebuilt; the aqueducts were renovated and were once more able to function; bridges and roads – such as the Nomentana in 552, the Salaria in 565 – were restored. The respite was short-lived, however, for in 568 a new threat loomed – the Lombards (*Longobardi*).

Rome was henceforward a diminished city, but preserved its claim to be a capital thanks to the presence of the pope.

From these events it will be seen that, if Rome was besieged so many times during the fifth and sixth centuries, it was because it remained a major prize. It would be hard to understand why a weakened, impoverished city, reduced to a second-class role, should have aroused such covetousness, were it not that it undoubtedly remained a vibrant symbol, to the extent of forming a major political objective for Romans and barbarians alike. To hold Rome was to possess an unchallengeable political ascendancy, to show clear evidence of supremacy. But we must not forget that the prospect of rich booty competed with strategic considerations. Rome attracted also by virtue of the rich stores of precious metals it possessed; to the treasure amassed in the course of its conquests must be added the imperial furnishings and, since the Constantinian era, liturgical treasures such as chalices, sacred urns, paterae and candelabra. Little wonder, then, that the Vandals had returned to Africa with gold and silver by the ton.

Chapter 4

Urban administration

− The urban prefecture −

Although Italy had become part of the provincial structure in the time of Diocletian, the city of Rome stood outside these arrangements and came under the direct jurisdiction of the emperors. In 16 BC Augustus had given the city an urban prefect, with the task of representing him, and this prefecture continued to exist throughout late antiquity, lasting even under Ostrogothic royalty. Constantius II, following the Roman model, bestowed one on Constantinople in 359; but the fact that the emperors no longer resided in Rome conferred a more eminent role on its prefect than on the Constantinopolitan official, who was constantly under their eye. In the hierarchy of the imperial administration as presented to us in the *Notitia Dignitatum* early in the fifth century, the two urban prefects occupied the second rank immediately under the praetorian prefects. They were therefore personages of considerable status who held an enviable position.[1]

The vitality of the urban prefecture is remarkable. By means of various documents, researchers have been enabled to compile a list of the prefects for the period from 312 to 604, some 200 of whom we know, the last urban prefect, named Iohannes, holding office in 599.

The prefect of the city was appointed by the emperors for an indeterminate period which, in practice, was almost always less than two years. Nevertheless, although the mandates were brief, they could be repeated after an interval of time. For instance, at the end of the fifth century, Speciosus was called to the prefecture three times. This high-level official's authority was not confined to the city's fourteen administrative regions. The territory under him was much more extensive, comprising also Rome's ports, Portus and Ostia, as well as a zone of 100 miles (slightly over 140 kilometres) surrounding Rome. This territory escaped the jurisdiction of the governors of bordering provinces and, to a certain extent, that of the praetorian prefect of Italy. Answerable directly to the emperor, the urban prefect was often the recipient of imperial documents having the force of law, which he was obliged to apply in the areas coming under his authority. In the late fifth century, the decline of imperial power in the west placed him directly under the authority of the praetorian prefect at Ravenna.

A senator of *illustris* rank, the urban prefect was responsible for public order in the city and the 100-mile zone, a task in which until the reign of Constantine he was supported by a police force comprising the three urban cohorts. He had the task of publicising and applying the laws, and as such fulfilled the duties of judge. He was also responsible for the provisioning of the city, for Rome's ports, and for public works. In particular, it was his duty to monitor the drainage of the Tiber, the cleaning of springs and the beds of watercourses feeding the aqueducts, repairs to shops and Rome's public monuments. Inscriptions bear witness that they restored them frequently, and set up or moved statues within the city. Similarly, they had to keep an eye on the cemeteries to avoid burial violations.[2] The student population and trades guilds also came under the prefect's supervision.

The *vicarius* of the city of Rome was the city prefect's right-hand man until the 350s. Since the Augustan era two other prefectures had existed: the prefect of the *annona*, whose task was to keep the city supplied with provisions, ensured the safe transit of the grain cargoes to Roman warehouses. Evidence from 331 shows that he was subordinate to the urban prefect, as was the prefect of the *vigiles*, whose responsibilities were night policing and fire fighting. In addition, the prefect of the city had at his command a numerous and hierarchised staff, divided into some fifteen offices which collectively formed the urban bureau. From Constantine's reign onwards, it was the agents of these offices, and not the urban cohorts who had ensured public order in the city during the day, while firefighting was now entrusted to members of guilds of artisans.

– FOOD SUPPLIES –

While the office of urban prefect was a much desired dignity, as one of the highest posts in the upper imperial administration, the duties it imposed created many worries for its holder. The most burdensome, for it was continual, was to keep Rome provisioned. The prefect of the *annona* was, of course, responsible, but in the view of the Romans it was the urban prefect's duty to oversee it, not least because Constantine had reduced the powers of the prefect of the *annona* in his favour. The moment there was the slightest problem with the arrival or distribution of food supplies, the Roman population began muttering against him, so being urban prefect was a risky position and avoiding unpopularity a constant anxiety. Sidonius

Apollinaris realised this very shortly after his appointment to the prefecture of the city in 468. In a letter he urged his friend Campanianus to spur the prefect of the *annona* into action.[3] There had been rumblings among the plebs seated in the *cavea* of the theatre because there was a threat of food shortages. Sidonius, afraid that he would soon be the target of their outcry and see his reputation crumble, therefore announced that he was preparing to send the prefect of the *annona* to Portus to hasten the arrival in Rome of five ships from Brindisi, laden with grain and honey.

As in the late republic and the early empire, the chief characteristic of the Roman population was that it contained several tens of thousands of people with little or no income, dependent for their survival on free or low-priced distributions of essential foodstuffs. Neither Latium nor Italy had the capacity to feed the plebeian masses gathered in the city, so the authorities had to resort to massive imports of cereals, meat, oil and wine. Given that the slightest shortage was likely to unleash riots, the regularity, quantity and quality of the imports were the best guarantees of social order. The urban prefect therefore paid very special attention to the matter, and supervised supplies of provisions from their sources to their point of consumption.

– SCANDALS –

No less than at any other period, the exercise of such great power brought temptations of embezzlement and corruption. For the fourth century, the letters of the senator Symmachus and the history of Ammianus provide vivid accounts of scandals that assailed the reputations of several prefects. One such malefactor was Vitrasius Orfitus, twice prefect of the city in the reign of Constantius II, the first time between December 353 and June – or November – 356, and the second between April 357 and March 359.[4] Riots broke out in Rome during his first term because of a shortage of wine. According to what we know about it through his son-in-law, Symmachus, it is probable that Orfitus had dipped into the wine funds, the *arca vinaria*. Constantius had asked him to repay the sum, and he was replaced in the prefecture by Flavius Leontius. He was none the less recalled to the post in 357, during which he received the emperor in the spring of that year. Yet later he was accused of embezzlement by a master baker around 363–4: the charges went back to his prefectures. It emerged that Orfitus had repaid only part of the sum with which he should have reimbursed the *arca vinaria*, and had not been brought to court or punished. This time, his possessions were confiscated and he was sentenced to exile before benefiting from an amnesty some years later, at the request of a praetorian prefect.

The disturbances provoked by the affair of the wine fund had hardly died down when a new scandal erupted in 365–6. On several occasions the prefect Lampadius had sought building materials, iron, lead and copper, but failed to pay the suppliers. Such dishonest behaviour provoked several riots, and in the course of one of these the mob tried to burn his house down.[5]

Likewise, corruption of other officials in the urban administration could render the prefect quite powerless. Early in the 380s, the emperors Valentinian II and Theodosius I had entrusted the task of building a bridge and basilica in Rome to two *clarissimi*, the count Cyriades and the engineer Auxentius. This pair diverted to their own profit a large proportion of the gold allocated to these works. At that point Symmachus, as prefect of the city (384–5), intervened. An initial inquiry by the former prefect Anicius Auchenius Bassus resulted in a report in which praise was mixed with criticism. Cyriades then obtained, by means of an imperial rescript, the opportunity to defend himself and accuse those who, in his opinion, were the guilty parties. Following his accusations, Symmachus ordered a second enquiry, during which Auxentius disappeared. Having delivered a full report of the facts to the imperial administration, the prefect then received orders to take charge of the works himself, assisted by the deputy of the praetorian prefect of Italy. Another engineer, Afrodisius, replaced Auxentius, while a former governor, Bonosus, was given the task of pursuing the inquiry. However, to the great annoyance of Symmachus, who protested, Cyriades managed to get his offer to help in the work accepted.[6] In 384–5, two support piers were constructed, but an inspection of the work found that the masonry had not been jointed with mortar. The building of the bridge was considerably slowed down by this affair. We know from two further letters by Symmachus that it was still not finished in 387, six years after the work had been commenced.[7]

– THE SENATE –

The ancient assembly of the Conscript Fathers numbered 600 members until the reign of Constantine who in fact decided to bring the strength up to 2000. This was done gradually, between 312 and 326, by the promotion of heads of families of equestrian rank from Rome and the western provinces.[8] This extremely important political measure had the effect of suddenly widening an echelon of society which until then had not been very open, and bringing about the collapse of the old equestrian order. Indeed, after 324 to 326, provincial governors and praetorian prefects were recruited only from the *clarissimi*, whereas previously they had been selected from the *equites*.

The emperors of the late empire generally left the matter of co-opting new members to the senators themselves. To do this, they submitted a list from which the emperor chose those to be inscribed in the *album* (register). Nevertheless since the first century the emperor had had the power *adlectio*, which was to appoint directly individuals who were outside the senatorial order. He appointed them to either praetorian or consular rank. A new senator would receive his appointment in the form of an imperial codicil, and would then have to make a declaration of his property and income – the *professio* – before the Count of the Sacred Largesses, a principal official in the imperial finances. The honour bestowed upon him in fact involved his accepting onerous obligations. According to law, senatorial possessions were inalienable; their possible dispersal might, in fact, endanger the public benefaction system of the magistracies. The Senate was thus composed for the most part of rich and well-born personages who, in the words of Sidonius Apollinaris, were 'of respectable age and good counsel'.[9]

The Senate's ancient prerogatives had melted way like snow in sunshine since the foundation of the Principate. In the late period its powers were more or less those of the council of a large town, but since that large town was Rome the emperors maintained favoured relations with it and left it some honours. In the middle of the fifth century, in a metaphor on obedience which he slipped into his biography of Melania the Younger (c. 383–438), the monk Gerontios seems to indicate that the Senate's authority had survived: 'In the world, in the majority and the most important of cases, the wearer of the diadem [ie the emperor] takes no measures without first asking the Senate's opinion.'[10] Besides, as it contained representatives of the most powerful families in Rome and the west, its prestige remained intact throughout late antiquity, even during the Ostrogothic domination in the sixth century. Ammianus Marcellinus, who cannot be suspected of subservience towards them, wrote at the end of the fourth century that 'everywhere the hoary heads of the senators and their authority inspire veneration'.[11] Right up the sixth century, there are texts eulogising the Senate as the 'Most highly distinguished order', 'sacred order', or 'curia'. Therein lies a sign of the very strong attachment of the educated élite to the republican ideals which the Senate alone represented, since the *comitia*, Rome's ancient assemblies, had long since disappeared. Around 400, a writer produced the fake *Augustan History*, which in the guise of six different authors recounted the lives of the second- and third-century emperors. These *á clé* texts waver between pastiche and vicious criticism, denouncing the tyranny of authoritarian emperors and praising those who respected the Senate. Claudian, also writing between 395 and 405, pours out a stream of lyrical eulogies of the Senate, describing the noble sons of the Tiber, clad in patrician robes – the *toga praetexta* – and surrounding Honorius for the inauguration of his fourth consulate in 398. For the sixth, in 404, he mentions with joy the fact that Honorius refused to let the senators walk ahead of his chariot, asking them to proceed on a level with him thus indicating the esteem in which he held them.

Yet the history of the Senate was not unrelievedly happy. Between 369 and 371 the Roman senatorial circle fell victim to a serious dispute with emperor Valentinian I, who had hitherto shown himself to be very respectful of the order, appointing prefects from the Roman nobility. But in 369 an accusation of poisoning was brought before the prefect Olybrius. Being ill, he referred the matter to his deputy, Maximinus, and an inquiry rapidly led him to suspect some nobles of prohibited magic practices. That was the start of harassment which turned into the persecution of the senatorial circle. In fact, the report sent to Valentinian marked the beginning of a veritable period of terror. Maximinus and his second successor, the old grammarian Simplicius, showed themselves to be vindictive and pitiless. Some *clarissimi* were even tortured, despite traditional legislation which was temporarily shelved by Valentinian. Men and women were brought before the courts for adultery, incest and practising magic, and were imprisoned, banished or executed. Such was the case of the senator Cethegus, accused of adultery. The governor Hymetius, who was in touch with Amantius, the most renowned *haruspex* (soothsayer) in Rome, to whom he had made known complaints about the emperor's excessive harshness, was exiled to Dalmatia. Maximinus even ordered the execution of Lollianus, the young son of the prefect Lampadius, because he had made a copy of a book of magic formulae. Four *clarissimi* were accused of having practised magic to get their favourite charioteer to win, but were acquitted for lack of proof. During the vicariate of Maximinus, a cord dangled from a side window of the Praetorium to collect denunciations. Between 369 and 371, therefore, Rome lived in an atmosphere of informers, arrests, tortures, executions and suicides. Ammianus Marcellinus, who disliked Valentinian I and execrated Maximinus and Simplicius, accused them in his *History* of wanting to destroy the patrician families. The populist aspects of Valentinian's policies are known. Together with the fear of magic, a 'class hatred' may well explain some of the violence of the measures. These led the Senate to delegate some of its members, including the eminent Vettius Agorius Praetextatus, to go the emperor. The embassy succeeded in having the persecution halted, and the Roman nobility recovered its tranquillity. When Maximinus was indulging in his inquiries, interrogations and executions, a prodigy occurred in Rome. The brooms used to sweep the Senate house sprouted buds and blossoms. Ammianus interpreted this as a portent of the rise to Senatorial rank of 'persons of low birth'. Whatever credit one may give to the event, it shows the political aspect of the whole affair.[12]

With Valentinian's death, and the succession of his son Gratian, relations between the palace and the Senate became tranquil once more. In a letter to Ausonius, Symmachus recalls the session held by the Senate on 1 January 376. As on every New Year's day, many senators came to the senate house even before daybreak. By the light of torches a message from Gratian, which had arrived the night before by imperial messenger, was read out. Full of benevolence and affection, he well and truly put an end to the harassment of the senators. Symmachus does not fail to emphasise the assembly's prolonged applause and satisfaction when they heard these 'oracles of the new age' (*novi saeculi fata*).[13]

According to the Codex Calendar of 354, the Senate met twice a month. Certain sessions had an exceptional nature: for instance, when a new Augustus was proclaimed, or a particularly important law passed, or when a prefect of the city or consul took up office, the senators proceeded to chant acclamations. We know about those of a session which took place in December 438. The consul Anicius Acilius Glabrio Faustus opened the sitting by presenting the Theodosian Code. His speech was punctuated with acclamations such as 'What fresh eloquence! What true eloquence!' and 'That is just! It is pleasing! It is pleasing!' When the imperial document had been read, the senators performed some thirty separate chanted acclamations of praise and good wishes between ten and twenty-seven times each in honour of the emperors, the consul Faustus, the prefect of the city, Paulus, and the patrician Aëtius.[14]

– THE DECLINE OF THE SENATE –

In the middle of the fifth century, the Senate still enjoyed the emperors' respect. At the time of his proclamation in 458, Majorian addressed his first *novella* to its members, showing both deference and his wish to offer them protection. He declared that it was they and the army who had chosen him to be Augustus, and tried to restore the serenity of the 'conscript Fathers of the sacred order', assuring them that he would no longer tolerate slanders and accusations, declaring further that he loved the Senate and could not displease it.[15] In the late fifth century, senators still had reserved seats in the first rows of the Flavian amphitheatre. Their family names were carved in the stone and, when the Senate's composition changed, they were regularly recarved. Owing to this practice, we know the names of 195 of them in the time of Odoacer, that is, between 476 and 483. After that date, however, the Senate experienced a gradual loss of power.

In the mid-fifth century measures were applied in Rome that had previously been in force in Constantinople. *Clarissimi* and *spectabiles* – the two lowest ranks of the Senate – received permission to live in their provincial domains and were exempted from the praetorship, which effectively cut the link between senators of lower rank and Rome, leaving active roles in the assembly to the distinguished *illustres* residing in Rome and the nearby Italian provinces. Hence the praetorship became the prerogative of sons of the *illustres* resident in the city, while the number of senators, already reduced by the exodus of 410, began to dwindle.

The disappearance of the imperial office in the west in 476 had the consequence of isolating provincial senators still further and accentuated the Roman composition of the assembly. Odoacer tried to conciliate the city's powerful nobility and conferred privileges upon them, such as the right to strike copper coins and have a leader, the *prior* or *caput senatus*. For their part, the senators were torn between the desire to see the return of the emperor Julius Nepos, exiled to Dalmatia, and their Italian interests, which were dependent on Odoacer's goodwill.

During his reign, Theoderic kept the senatorial system in place and resumed the role formerly played by the emperors. Certainly, the Senate continued to co-opt its members, but the king appointed them, ordering the prefect of the city to inscribe their names in the *album*. Similarly, the holding of Palatine office continued to give access to the assembly. But all was not well. In his *Consolation of Philosophy*, written in 525, Boethius mentions several affairs in which he was involved, which reveal the senatorial habits of his time. He tried, he says, to apply Platonic principles in his public life, but came up against the intrigues of his colleagues. On several occasions he had to protect the weak against senators' attempts to seize their possessions, thus attracting their hatred. It was through one of their machinations that he fell into disgrace before being imprisoned and executed. Fraudsters sentenced to exile accused him of having expressed a wish, in his letters, for a return to Roman liberty. Boethius defended himself against the charge but was prevented from producing proof to the contrary. Theoderic mistrusted the Roman Senate, which was the subject of concern to Boethius. Shortly before his condemnation, he had supported the former consul Albinus against accusations of *lèse-majesté*. Theoderic had wanted to impute Albinus' crime to the entire Senate. Among other reasons, Boethius was therefore the victim of his devotion to the interests of the assembly; but he was also the victim of his colleagues, who wanted to see him vanish from the political scene, as he hampered their lucrative fraudulent practices.[16]

The long Gothic war, which devastated Italy for nearly thirty years in the mid-sixth century, delivered some hard blows to the Senate, leading to its inevitable decline. A number of senators left the city, which was captured and recaptured many times; others were killed or deported. Their heritage partly disintegrated, and eminent families were eclipsed. Yet even during the last third of the sixth century and the beginning of the seventh, the Senate was still meeting. In 573, under the presidency of the prefect Gregory, it held a debate and asked the eastern emperor for help against the Lombards. Twenty hears later, however, in a poignant homily, that same Gregory, now pope, had some bitter remarks to make: 'Where, then, is the Senate? And the people, where are they? . . . The Senate is enfeebled and the people have vanished, and Rome, henceforward empty, is prey to fire!'[17] The vast senatorial order of the fourth and fifth centuries had become a small assembly dominated by the figure of the pope. It was no longer any more than the civil counterpart of the clerical assembly surrounding the pope, to which it had lost every administrative and political prerogative.

– THE TRADITIONAL MAGISTRACIES –

In late Rome, magistracies still existed which had been inherited from the distant republic, and had survived under the Principate. Each year, quaestors, praetors and consuls were appointed, but the development of the Principate towards monarchy and the emergence of the urban prefecture had deprived them of real power. These magistracies had thus become basically honorific and, for that very reason, continued to be sought after and prized. For their holders they certainly presupposed colossal expenditure, but they formed unequalled steps in the climb to social and political eminence and conferred an undeniable prestige. In the *cursus* of Roman nobles, they constituted almost obligatory validating stages in attaining the heights of civil hierarchy. Involving considerable expense, they could be bestowed only on members of the wealthiest families, who in this way accumulated titles galore over the generations.

– THE QUAESTORSHIP AND PRAETORSHIP –

The aedileship and tribunate of the plebs had disappeared from the *cursus honorum* during the third century. In the late centuries of the empire the *cursus* comprised three essential grades: the quaestorship, praetorship and consulate. The quaestors, whose numbers we do not know, were appointed by the emperor from young *clarissimi* aged at least sixteen. Their role consisted in holding games when they entered office, on 5 December. The praetors were former quaestors, and in theory were aged twenty. In the fourth century there were three of them; they were selected by the Senate ten years in advance, and then appointed one year before they took up office. In practice, this magistracy involved the distribution of sums of money and presents as well as the sponsoring of costly games, and therefore implied an impressive fortune. It also gave access to the Senate. A law of 359 sets out the duties of the praetors, so the office was not purely honorific: they were guarantors for the emancipation of slaves, tried certain cases, such as matters of inheritance, appointed guardians and trustees and restored possessions when the guardianship or trusteeship was over.

– THE SUFFECT CONSULSHIP –

The consulship underwent some alterations in Constantine's time. Former Praetors aged twenty-five could be nominated for the suffect consulship and hold games on 21 April. It was not imperative to hold this consulate in order to accede to the more prestigious ordinary consulship. It was possible to obtain it, like the praetorship, from the age of sixteen. Starting from the time of Constantine or Constantius II, suffect consuls were designated by the Senate at the sitting of 9 January. They are attested until the end of the western empire, in 476.

– THE ORDINARY CONSULSHIP –

This post, which was held by two men each year, was the crowning point of a career, superior in the hierarchy to the urban prefecture. In fact, the emperors liked to invest themselves with it, which conferred an undeniable additional prestige on the magistracy; and when private individuals were appointed, for them it was the supreme honour. When Constantine reformed this consulship, he confirmed a trend that had already actually commenced. The Augusti had priority in holding the ordinary consulship; thus, out of forty ordinary consuls for the period 302–22, just under thirty were emperors, the scant ten remaining being private citizens. The members of Constantine's family held nineteen consulships in thirty years. This monopoly continued during the fourth century, but dwindled during the fifth. Statistics reveal that the emperors formed fewer than half the consuls between 284 and 395, around 36 per cent between 396 and 450, and barely 18 per cent between 451 and 541.[18] This very significant development, which was certainly accelerated by the disappearance of the western empire in 476, shows that, from the fifth century onwards, the emperors were less attracted to the consulship. That perhaps lowered its prestige, but nobles continued to be very keen to hold this office.

In keeping with tradition, ordinary consuls assumed office on 1 January and delivered a thanksgiving speech, before the emperors and consistory if possible. Ordinary consuls held games; that was their sole function, together with distributing liberal gifts, but it was no small matter in a city so passionately fond of the spectacles of circus and amphitheatre. Claudius Mamertinus, consul in 362, speaks of it as an *honos sine labore*, an honour free of the burdens associated with administrative positions.[19]

From 396, the division of the empire into discrete eastern and western halves, each with its own administration, is revealed by the choice of consuls: one was chosen for the east and the other for the west, so from that date onwards, until 527, there was only one consul annually in Rome, unless in exceptional circumstances. Yet, even in these later years, the office remained an honour of the highest distinction. Addressing Felix, consul for 511, through Cassiodorus, King Theoderic set out the extraordinary nature of this magistracy:

> Consuls must be generous. Do not worry about your personal fortune, since you have chosen to win public favour by your liberality. It is for this reason that we distinguish between your dignity and all the rest. Whatever they may do, the other magistrates, whom we appoint, have not asked to obtain their post. As regards the consulship, we appoint only those who have been candidates for this dignity, those who know that their wealth matches their ambition. Otherwise, it would be to impose a burden, not grant a favour. Therefore, in seemly manner, enjoy the honour to which you aspired. This way of spending money is a legal form of corruption. Be outstanding in the world, be prosperous in your life, and leave to posterity a fine example to be imitated![20]

– SOURCES ON THE CONSULATE –

Starting in the fifth century, it became the custom for consuls to offer the emperor and his friends an ivory diptych to commemorate the event of their assuming office, and some of these are still preserved today. Richard Delbrueck has listed forty-four, thirty-four of which can be dated to between 406 and 540. Among them, seventeen or eighteen are western.[21]

These diptychs, like the *missoria* – large engraved or carved dishes – are remarkable iconographic evidence, giving a fair amount of information on the consulate and its image. They took the form of two small ivory panels, of a maximum size of 40 x 5 centimetres, joined by hinges. Until the end of the fourth century, these objects were not peculiar to consuls, but became so from the fifth century. Of the thirty-four mentioning the name of the titular consul, nine belonged to western consuls who had taken up office in Rome; eight between 406 and 488, and the ninth dating to 530. The consul was portrayed wearing the richly decorated consular toga, the *trabea*, in the act that was recognitive of his dignity – the opening of the games he was offering to the populace. His raised right hand therefore flourishes the *mappa*, a piece of cloth which was thrown onto the sand of the circus as the official opening of the races.

Inscriptions are another of the major sources that we have on the consuls. For the period 311–410, 1104 are listed, 299 between 411 and 475 and 244 between 476 and 541 – a total of 1647 for the period from 311 to 541, the last consular date of the west. From this point of view, Rome is the place in the empire that has provided the most plentiful epigraphic dossier on consuls, and an examination of it enables us to draw several conclusions. In the first place, the majority of these inscriptions relate to private benefactions. Secondly, the inscriptions of the fourth century are for the most part the work of pagan consuls, whereas those of the fifth and sixth centuries were put up by Christian consuls. Lastly, it must be said that consular and senatorial inscriptions contain as many errors as the non-senatorial ones, so consular formulae were therefore not carved with the most scrupulous care.

– Decline of the traditional magistracies –

The suffect consulate and quaestorship disappeared in the second half of the fifth century, while the last mention of the praetorship, from the pen of Boethius, dates to 523. The one with the greatest longevity was the most prestigious, the ordinary consulate, whose last western holder, Mavortius, was in office in 527. He belonged to the distinguished Anicius family, which comes as no surprise, and is very symbolic. The gradual disappearance of the old magistracies reflects the enfeeblement of the Senate during the same period. However positive it had been, the republican heritage handed on by the empire did not manage to survive the ordeals experienced by the western empire. But rather than see it as twilight, which cannot be denied, should we not stress that extraordinary continuity to which the magistracies were the last witnesses? Their longevity cannot be regarded only in terms of relics or survivals, but as a sign of their vitality. To die at a great age is assuredly to die, but – above and beyond the trials and tribulations – does it not mean that one has enjoyed robust good health?

II

Plebs patresque: *Plebeians and patricians*

CHAPTER 5

The nobility, 'élite of the human race'

The existence of a rich and powerful nobility in Rome was nothing new – it went back to the earliest times of the republic and lasted throughout the imperial era. Generations succeeded one another, wealth and magistracies accumulated, simultaneously building the power and prestige of these great *gentes* (clans). Of course, certain families will have died out, but others replaced them. These families, whose political expression was the Senate, embodied the values of their milieu: culture, a rich way of life, holding high office, and religious rites. The repositories of ancestral traditions, the *mos maiorum*, they were by nature conservative. Moreover, no other social category in Rome was so conscious of its own worth, or inspired so much deference. For Symmachus, the most sacred order of the *amplissimi*, or most distinguished, was nothing other than the élite of mankind. In Prudentius' eyes, it was no less than the finest light in the world.

From the end of the third century, some innovations had been introduced. Senators were relieved of all military commands, and then witnessed the emperors distancing themselves, and only rarely spending time in Rome. Nevertheless, the administration set up by Constantine in the first half of the fourth century provided a new outlet for their ambitions in higher government posts, both palatine and provincial. What is more, Roman nobles saw in their midst the rapid growth of a process that had started long before: the rise of Christianity – which, if sometimes at odds with the *mos maiorum*, nevertheless failed to weaken the cohesion of this very powerful social group. Proof of this lies in the fact that they endured, without great mishap, through the periodic sacks of their city and, in the sixth century, the Ostrogothic domination.

– THE CLARISSIMI –

From the time of Constantine, this superlative designated the whole membership of the senatorial order, including their families, who were said to be 'of senatorial birth'. Valentinian I (364–75) then instituted three ranks in the clarissimate: the *clarissimi* strictly speaking, then the *spectabiles* and, lastly, at the summit of the honorific scale, the *illustres*.[1] This Roman élite certainly suffered some brutal ordeals during the fifth-century sacks of Rome, but these served only to initiate a remarkable social continuity, which persisted upto the seventh century. Marriages within a strictly defined group of families contributed to the creation of links, if not fusions, between the different family branches of the Roman aristocracy during the late empire. Between the fourth and sixth centuries, all senatorial families were closely interrelated.

– THE GREAT FAMILIES –

Biographical studies have shown that in the fourth and fifth centuries the city's most prestigious *gentes* did not come from very old stock. Those who could boast of a long line going back to the republic such as the Acilii Glabriones were exceptional. Whereas the majority did not possess senatorial roots dating to before the third century, the Acilii bear witness to a remarkable continuity. This family had had consuls in the second century BC, and in the first, second and third centuries AD (91, 124, 152, 186, 210, 256), while one of its members attained the consulate in 323, and another had the praetorian prefecture conferred upon him in 438.

Between the fourth and sixth centuries, the most prestigious and powerful family in Rome was indubitably the Anicii, to which Symmachus and Boethius belonged. Zosimus, who felt antipathy towards them because of their Christian sentiments, says that the Anicii 'on their own virtually possessed the wealth of the whole city'.[2] In comparison with the Acilii, the Anicii were parvenus, but they were already an old noble family. The earliest Anicius known to have held senatorial rank was a consul in AD 198, and they held governorships during the third century. It would appear that, around the middle of that century a close connection was established with the Nicomachi, bestowing great power on the new lineage. Later they merged with the Symmachi, Betitii and Neratii, and had links with the Pincii and Amnii.

The Petronii, who at each generation provided late antique Rome with consuls and prefects were closely connected with the Anicii and Caeionii. Petronius Probianus, consul in 322, was father of Petronius Probinus, consul in 341 and prefect of the city in 344, and grandfather of Petronius Probus, consul in 371. This last married an Anicia, Faltonia Proba. They produced three sons all of whom were consuls: Anicius Hermogenianus Olybrius and Anicius Probinus, consuls together in 391, and the western consul in 406, Anicius Petronius Probus. For that reason, an inscription describes

Petronius Probus as the 'most eminent personage of the house of Anicius'.[3] Moreover, in the first half of the fifth century, the Anicii became friends of the Acilii. One of the consuls of 438 was none other than Anicius Acilius Glabrio Faustus. The great Boethius belonged to the Anician family. Born around 480, and soon the orphan of a former consul, he was taken in and brought up by a Symmachus, the great-grandson of the prefect of 384, and whose daughter he married. He himself was consul in 510, and his two sons held office together in 522. Gregory the Great, prefect of the city, then pope between 590 and 604, was also an Anicius.

The Caeionii were landowners in Etruria – at Volterra – and Africa. Through the Nummii, their lineage went back to the late republic. In the fourth and fifth centuries, they had connections with the Turcii, Crepereii and the lineage of the Postumianus family, the Rufii and Festi.

Melania the Younger is a fine example of the link between two aristocratic families. Through her father, Valerius Publicola, prefect of the city in 375, she belonged to the family of the Valerii, itself connected to the Aradii and Brittii. Her mother Albina was the sister of Rufius Antonius Agrypinus Volusianus, a Caeonius who had been quaestor of the sacred palace, urban prefect and praetorian prefect. Daughter of a Valerius and a Caeionia, Melania married, in the person of Pinianus, the product of two families, the Aradii and the Valerii. They were therefore distant cousins.

In this way the great lineages of the Roman aristocracy were closely interconnected. Members of Roman senatorial families were cousins, near or distant. As water tightens the knots in rope, so each marriage in the milieu helped to fuse the different branches together a little more. Their relations thus formed a 'full circle', to use Arnheim's expression,[4] and this circle is clearly perceptible in the genealogical trees; the *stemmata* are in fact all closely interlinked. This is also noticeable in the names they bear. During the fourth century, the *tria nomina*, the traditional tripartite name that was the hallmark of a well-bred Roman, came to be extended. Besides their forename, important people had two, three or even four family names, ringing out proudly. Of course, this had become necessary for purposes of distinction from the others, but such accumulations were the product of a deliberate series of marriage alliances.

– Careers –

A *puer clarissimus* was destined for a senatorial career which, from adolescence, made him climb the ladder of traditional magistracies and, in many cases, caused him to be summoned to high governmental office. However, even if wealth and birth were equal, careers were by no means identical. Thus in the fifth century, Avienus and Petronius Maximus made a very rapid ascent: in contrast, Basilius made very slow progress. These differences were certainly related to personal talents, but had a great deal to do with family connections. Avienus was a Valerius and, according to Sidonius Apollinaris, supported only the members of his own family. Basilius, who was a Decius, was not averse from helping people who were outside his family.[5]

Besides strictly Roman magistracies, young people from senatorial circles could aspire to provincial governorships which would allow them to travel across the Empire in a succession of posts. After the most prestigious governorships, which were proconsulates, they could aspire to the top posts: *vicarius* of a diocese, the urban and praetorian prefectures, or, in the palatine hierarchy, palace quaestor, master of the offices or, at a lower grade, count of finances. The end of the western empire in 476 did not put an end to these prospects. In fact, first Odoacer and then the Ostrogothic kings preserved Roman administrative structures and continued to draw upon the city's senatorial breeding-ground to supply the holders of offices. Ambitions and careers therefore experienced no break in continuity. At the most, senators had to sharpen their sense of diplomacy, for they had to maintain good relations with both the king of Italy and the emperor of the east, whose interests and policies might be in conflict.

– THE WORKINGS OF PATRONAGE –

Friendship, protection and recommendation occupied a central place in the political and social sphere of influence of Roman nobles. Symmachus' correspondence swarms with examples; out of 198 letters in the first two books, 62 (in other words, very nearly a third) are letters of commendation.[6] The accession of Sidonius Apollinaris to the prefecture of the city in 468 is a good instance. In 467, this aristocrat, known for his poems, came to Rome as ambassador of the Arverni. There he stayed with Paulus, a noble versed in the liberal arts, who advised him how to set about gaining the ear of the powerful. As a result, he associated with two eminent senators who had both been consuls, Avienus and Basilius. Sidonius increased the number of his visits to the first, at the same time joining the loyal followers of the second. It was the latter who encouraged him to compose and deliver a eulogy of the emperor Anthemius, who was preparing to enter his second consulship. Sidonius took this advice, and his panegyric earned him appointment to the prefecture of the city.

Members of the great Roman families were surrounded by a crowd of followers and dependants, known as *clientes*, much as in the early empire. The distribution of *sportulae*, gifts offered by patrons to clients, and a key ritual in the structure of Roman patronage, continued during the fourth century. Ammianus Marcellinus reports it, stating that Roman nobles had themselves escorted by their clients in the streets of Rome.[7] Sidonius Apollinaris also testifies to this custom: the two nobles whose houses he frequented never left their homes unless preceded by their clients.

– WEALTH AND POSSESSIONS –

The Roman nobility's heritage was colossal. In no other place in the empire was so much wealth concentrated; not even in Constantinople, whose senatorial nobility, formed of *clari,* and promoted to *clarissimi* by Constantius II, consisted for the most part of parvenus. Thanks to a surviving fragment of the lost histories of Olympiodorus of Thebes, it has been possible to estimate that a great Roman family's annual income from landed property was in the region of 4000 gold *librae,* to which must be added the value of goods in kind, say some 1300 *librae.* This represented an income equivalent to 370,000 *solidi,* an immense sum, but slight in comparison with the total worth of the ancestral inheritance. These gold *librae,* whether as ingots, *solidi* or precious objects, could not be kept in their owners' houses, and, until the mid-fourth century, Roman *clarissimi* made use of safes situated in Trajan's Forum.

The emperors were not unaware of the gulf that separated these ultra-rich nobles from the vast number of needy plebs, so they were intent on creating and maintaining practices that would oblige the nobles to let the poor gain some advantage from their wealth. Of course, taxation was the first means. Since the time of Diocletian, they had been subjected to a land tax, the *iugatio,* on the basis of the larger the property the higher the payment. In addition, they had to pay in gold the *gleba,* in proportion to the lands they owned. For the purposes of imposing this tax, the senatorial lands were duly recorded. Senatorial families also had to pay oblational gold to the treasury on special occasions such as imperial anniversaries. Thus in 384, each family paid 1600 gold *librae* to Valentinian II for his decennial celebration. To these regular contributions were added exceptional payments in times of temporary difficulty, such as crises with the *annona,* or the siege of Rome by the Goths in 408–10.

The wealth of Pinianus, an eminent member of a branch of the Valerii family, is known to us through a text by Gerontios, relating the life of Pinianus' wife, Melania. It would seem that Gerontios heard him say that his annual income amounted to twelve myriads (120,000) of gold.[8] The immensity of this figure leads one to think that he was talking of *solidi* and not *librae.* One hundred and twenty thousand *solidi* a year indeed represented rather more than a considerable sum. The revenue from the properties of his wife Melania, equally large if not larger, had to be added.

And that was just their income, modest by comparison with the value of their ancestral inheritance in land, buildings and furniture, which Gerontios judges to be incalculable. When the couple began to divest themselves of their Roman possessions in order to distribute the proceeds to the poor and the churches, they raised the staggering amount of 45,000 gold *librae*, or 3,240,000 *solidi*, which they sent to various provinces in the empire.

In addition to this monetary wealth, the élite also possessed extensive properties. The most ostentatious properties of noble Roman families were great *domus* on the city's hills. These rich dwellings of palatial scale were adorned with marble, mosaics and paintings, and were set in carefully tended gardens. In addition, Roman nobles owned other villas in the countryside, as well as immense tracts of agricultural land scattered throughout the empire, which caused Ammianus to remark that vain nobles could boast, as Trimalchio once did, that their estates stretched from sunrise to sunset. They were populated by tenants and slaves, who worked under the supervision of *actores* (stewards) or *conductores* (tenant farmers). In the fourth century, the agronomist writer Palladius advised landowners to have their own artisans on their estates; their presence could relieve the peasants of the necessity to go into town to buy manufactured products. Ammianus Marcellinus reports that Petronius Probus owned lands throughout the entire empire, while Symmachus, a senator with a fairly moderate lifestyle, owned fifteen estates in Italy, and numerous others in Sicily and Mauretania. Melania and her husband, Pinianus, possessed property in Campania, Sicily, Spain, Africa, Mauretania, Numidia and Britain. Melania recalls the charms of one of her properties, probably situated in Sicily, as follows: its sumptuous swimming pool lay between the sea and a wood of various species of trees, so that while bathing one could see on one side boats driven by the wind and on the other wild animals browsing. There were sixty-two dwellings around this villa.[9]

It seems that land ownership could lead to favoured relations between Roman nobles and certain cities and provinces. Such links have been discovered between Roman families and the African provinces. In the fourth century, the Aradii were patrons of Bulla Regia, and one Aradius received the governorship of Byzacena. Similarly, of the twenty-four consular governors who administered Numidia in the fourth century, four belonged to the family of the Caeionii. In the same period, thirteen of the sixty-four proconsuls of Africa, and five of the ten known *vicarii* were Anicii, Caeionii, or collaterals of these two prestigious lines.

The geographic vastness of the Roman nobility's landed property is therefore not only an indication of wealth, but serves also to denote the considerable sphere of authority of some families. This was further ensured by the establishment in some regions of veritable dynasties, for whom the occupation of governors' posts increased the influence exerted by riches. This state of affairs helps to explain how, even though deprived of a resident emperor, Rome continued to make its presence felt during the fourth century. It also gives us a better understanding of how the severing of provinces by the Goths and Vandals separated the Roman aristocrats from a good number of their domains. Some owned lands in eastern provinces, a fact which, in the wake of 410, made them resolve to go and establish themselves in the *pars orientalis*.

– ÉLITE LIFESTYLES –

– HOUSES –

Rich Roman families owned beautiful *domus* in Rome's green areas. Texts mention some of them, and archaeological excavations have enabled them to be brought to light. We know that in Rome or its environs Symmachus owned three such *domus*. Literary and epigraphic evidence shows that the great senatorial *domus* were situated mainly on the hills surrounding the Capitol and Palatine. On the Aventine was the only one belonging to Marcella, the matron in whose home Jerome assembled pious women, such as the wife of Praetextatus, in order to teach them. The Caelian Hill housed Symmachus and some Valerii. The Nummii and the prefects Lampadius and Junius Bassus lived on the Quirinal.

These superb residences could arouse jealousy. For example, in 440 an *illustris* named Auxiliaris complained that he had been dispossessed of his Roman house, during his absence, by the *illustris* Apollodorus. The prefect of the city, Pierius, informed the emperor, Valentinian III, about this invasion of property, and a response was given in his eighth *novella*, drawn up on 9 June 440. Valentinian ordered Pierius to see to it that Apollodorus restored the usurped property to Auxiliaris and, in addition, paid damages of a sum equivalent to its value, at the same time renouncing any idea of seeking court action.[10]

Certain aristocratic *domus* had an incalculable value, for instance that of Pinianus on the Caelian Hill. Early in the fifth century, when he wanted to sell it, he could find no buyer among the Roman *clarissimi* able to pay the fair price. His wife, Melania, then asked Serena, niece of the emperor Theodosius I, to purchase it, but she told her that she could not afford the price. So it remained unsold, and was partially burnt when the city was sacked in 410, at which time, allegedly, it could have been sold for a mouthful of bread.[11]

– TOWN AND COUNTRY –

Town and country were very distinct from each other in mental attitudes, representing the opposite poles in the Roman nobles' system of values. The city was the focus of attention for political and social activities. It was the *forum*, in other words, the place where the nobility discharged their responsibilities: connections between patrons and clients, family duties, participation in the sessions of the Senate, magistracies and expenditure on public benefaction. The other side of the coin, sojourns in the country, represented relaxation, the pleasures of a peaceful and studious life and a retreat from public life. Even in republican times, rich Romans had liked to withdraw to their holiday homes, and this was still the case in the late Empire. Senators were happy to absent themselves from Rome to stay in their peaceful rural properties. It was probably for that reason that a law of 356 laid down a quorum of fifty for the Senate's sessions. In the course of the fifth and sixth centuries, Roman *clarissimi* tended to spend increasingly lengthy amounts of time on their rural estates, and elderly senators certainly retired there. When Mallius Theodorus was appointed consul for 399 and had to return to Rome, from retirement on his country estates with his books, his military and political career seemed to have reached its climax.[12] But young *clarissimi*, doubtless tired of the burden of their duties, copied their elders, to the point where Cassiodorus, Theoderic's praetorian prefect, urged them to come back to the Forum and assume the responsibilities incumbent on their rank, rather than live cosily retired in a political no man's land.[13]

The 'better part of the human race' (*pars melior humani generis*), as Symmachus called it, was thus torn between its urban duties, which entailed at least as much harassment as glory, and the pleasures of the man of private means who, between hunting and reading, turned country life into an oasis of tranquillity. That choice is certainly one of the outstanding characteristics of aristocracies in late Roman society, when they were both disheartened by the harsh realities of political tasks and yet pledged to them by centuries-old tradition.

– DEPORTMENT –

Roman *clarissimi* were the custodians of a tradition as rich as it was ancient, that of the senators of the republic and the empire. Wealth was its primordial element, since it allowed them to hold a rank that presupposed enormous expenditure. Yet wealth was not the only qualification, and since

Augustus' time emperors had formed the habit of subsidising financially embarrassed senators to help them meet the expenses they had to bear. Education was also essential, by which *clarissimi* were recognised and recognised one another. Children received instruction in Latin and Greek, while the *domus* of Roman *clarissimi* had well-stocked libraries. Education and upbringing aimed to prepare the young nobles for their future: the Senate, praetorship and the consulate, but also high posts in the administration, culminating in the urban and praetorian prefectures. Emphasis was therefore placed on learning the liberal arts, among which grammar and rhetoric played a dominant role, for the young *clarissimi* had to know how to make speeches within the rules of the art, with appropriate accompanying gestures.

Ammianus Marcellinus paints a bitterly critical picture of the Roman nobles' mindset and lifestyle. He makes it quite clear that not all nobles were at fault, but that a disorderly and irresponsible few were exasperating, turning the traditional values of the senatorial rank upside down and marginalising the cultured men of their rank, who were regarded as useless or bringers of bad luck. In his opinion, these rich Romans behaved with great self-importance, arrogance and vanity, in their desire to see statues of themselves erected, covered with gold leaf. He depicts them, clad in sumptuous garments and sweating under their silk robes, boasting exaggeratedly about their rich estates and their harvests. They paraded through the town in higher than customary carriages, or dashed around in vehicles with swift horses, whether over paved or unpaved roads, always accompanied by an army of slaves. For example, one senator who, in Julian's time, had managed to extricate himself from an affair involving magic, was later to be seen, escorted by a cohort of servants, strutting around the town, going up and down the paved streets on a horse adorned with metal trappings, 'with an air of a man who believes no one but himself can go about with his head held high'.[14] Such vanity is to be found also in Lampadius, urban prefect of 365-6. When he restored buildings, he added inscriptions ascribing the foundations to himself. Moreover, his vanity showed itself in petty details; according to Ammianus, he would fly into a fury if people did not admire everything about him, even his way of spitting, for 'he claimed to imbue this act with a refinement that was his alone'.[15] As for the matrons, they went around Rome in closed litters, hiding, so Ammianus alleged, their debaucheries from the public gaze. They doubtless used silver toilet accessories like those presented in 379-82 to the young married couple, Secundus and Proiecta. They were Christians, but their small treasure casket was decorated with pagan motifs.

A few great houses, formerly with a serious and dignified reputation, resounded with entertainments when interminable and indigestible banquets were held. The sound of voices mingled with that of wind instruments, lyres, hydraulic organs and flutes – the bigger, the better. The preferred guests were singers rather than philosophers, theatrical producers and stage players rather than orators, and, above all, charioteers' bodyguards, who were notorious as dice-players and magicians. As patrons, the wealthy received their clientele and handed out the customary *sportulae*, but, according to Ammianus, the nomenclators, or those who drew up the lists of clients, were involved in trafficking. In return for bribes, they let in to the distribution and the meals 'pseudo-clients who were not known and were of low birth'. Ammianus also accuses them of being turncoats; obsequious to you one day, and ignoring you the next.[16]

– THE CULTURE AND RELIGION OF THE ÉLITE –

Roman nobles were highly conscious of belonging to an élite, not only of the city but also of the empire. Their arrogance, accentuated by displays of the *imagines* (portraits) of their ancestors, irritated Ammianus Marcellinus, who mentions it the better to censure it. But satire could not conceal the fact that men and women steeped in literary knowledge were to be found in the heart of the Roman nobility, as well as those who liked to write. We know, for instance, that Petronius Probianus, urban prefect in 329, wrote poetry. The Symmachi family were particularly bright stars in the literary firmament. The great Symmachus, prefect in 384, reveals in an inscription that his father was a prolific historian, and several of his epigrams on former urban prefects are also preserved. For his own part, Symmachus composed reports – *relationes* – and an abundant correspondence which was published shortly after his death by his son. He also undertook the re-editing of Livy's works; annotations show that he was aided in this task by his relative, Nicomachus Flavianus.[17] Some people attribute the much-disputed authorship of the *Historia Augusta* to the latter, although the hypothesis cannot be proved. It is quite certain, however, that the *Historia Augusta* is a product of the Roman nobility of the Theodosian era, and reveals a good knowledge of literature and history. Another Symmachus, the adoptive father of Boethius, 100 years later, knew Greek and was the author of a history in seven books. Boethius himself, before writing his famous *Consolation of Philosophy* when he was in captivity, had written numerous works. He was a true protean scholar of the kind that a liberal arts education could produce when given to gifted children. Boethius wrote an abridged Latin version of the *Introduction to Arithmetic* by Nicomachus of Gerasa, an *Introduction to Music*, and treatises on astronomy and geometry. He was unable to conclude his enterprise of translating Aristotle's works on logic into Latin.

In the midst of this scholarly nobility, women were not to be outshone. Faltonia Proba, daughter of Petronius Probus, had an extensive knowledge of Virgil, to the point of composing a work in praise of Christ using lines borrowed from the *Aenied*. In the *domus* of Marcella, on the Aventine, before his departure for the east in 386, Jerome regularly gathered together the women of this circle, such as Paula, Blesilla and Eustochium. He taught them Greek and the rudiments of Hebrew and explained passages from the Scriptures to them. We know, too, that Melania, a Roman aristocrat convert to the ascetic life, consigned her thoughts to little notebooks faultlessly and with talent. During her sojourn at Thagaste in north Africa, she always had her Bible in her hand. Her biographer Gerontios recounts that she read it through three or four times a year, and wrote fair copies of certain passages. She also assiduously read the treatises of Christian writers, and there was no known book, Greek or Latin, that this bibliophile did not seek to purchase or borrow.[18]

− ATTACHMENT TO TRADITION −

Loyalty to tradition which, if one wishes, may be construed as conservatism, was not merely a matter of hanging onto privileges. It was bound up with Rome's senatorial aristocracy by the very nature of their role in history and Rome's institutions. Through the Senate, the nobles had always been invested with the maintenance of ancestral customs, the *mos maiorum*. At the end of the fourth century, the Symmachi and Nicomachi were the most conspicuous for their loyalty to tradition. It was perhaps in the hope of restoring paganism that they upheld the usurpation of Eugenius between 391 and 394. Among Symmachus' friends was Publilius Caeionius Caecina Albinus, who had been governor of Numidia in the time of Valentinian I, and who is presented in Macrobius' *Saturnalia* as the paragon of the old classical culture.[19] He had been a priest of the pagan religion, but his daughter, Laeta, one of Jerome's correspondents, was a convinced Christian ascetic. This is eloquent testimony to the changes that took place in Rome between 370 and 420, a most decisive half-century.

Devotion to the religious rituals of Rome was not the least aspect of the conservatism of some Roman nobles. Several forms of this conservatism must be distinguished, and André Chastagnol has made clear the difference between the traditionalism of a Praetextatus and that of a Symmachus. Whereas the first was open to so-called 'oriental' or 'mystery' cults, the second turned towards the old Latin religion. In this sense, Praetextatus was rather the heir of Hadrian, and Symmachus of Augustus. Symmachus' religious tendencies were more archaistic than conservative, but he was not totally consistent. In his third *relatio*, asking for the return of the altar of

Victory to the Senate house, he reveals a religiosity stamped with Neo-platonism:

> We all look at the same stars, a sky that is common to all of us, and the same universe envelops us: so it matters little by which philosophy each of us seeks the truth: one single path does not suffice to lead to such a great mystery.[20]

In the view of such pagan Roman nobles, Christianity represented a religion and culture for the masses, somewhat weak in its thinking and expression. Stubborn and pugnacious, Symmachus none the less preached intellectual tolerance and religious pluralism, from which he intended that Roman religion should benefit. His ideological opponents, Ambrose of Milan and the Spanish poet Prudentius, however, rejected his opinion. In their eyes, there existed only one revealed truth and one single road to God, and those belonged to Christianity.

– THE EVIDENCE OF THE *CONTORNIATES* –

Contorniates (coins or medals with a deep groove round the disc) are a specifically Roman source, providing valuable information about the ideology of the city's aristocracy between the middle of the fourth century and the later fifth. They were medals issued in Rome; the first on 1 January 358, during the second urban prefecture of Vitrasius Orfitus. Subsequently they were struck, cast or engraved at the new year, until 472.

The first *contorniates* were issued just after the visit by Constantius II to Rome in the spring of 357, and thus after the measures taken by this emperor against sacrifices and temples. This context may partly explain the most characteristic feature of *contorniates*, which is the total absence of any Christian iconography. There is no doubt that these commemorative medals expressed the disapproval of some of the aristocracy in the face of measures that were inimical to traditional rites. They may perhaps be placed among the manifestations of the 'pagan reaction'.

Before Theodosius, these *contorniates* bore no representations of living emperors, but the effigies of former Augusti; for example, Caesar, Augustus, Nero, Vespasian, Trajan, Antoninus. Alexander the Great also appeared, and other representations were of deities, such as Dea Roma, Sol, Cybele, Hercules and Bacchus, Isis and Serapis; or the effigies of great writers and philosophers, such Homer, Solon, Horace, Sallust or Apollonius of Tyana.

These representations reveal a strong attachment to classical culture, still dispensed in the fourth and fifth centuries by grammarians and rhetors. It must be stressed that it is the culture of a *koiné*, a Graeco-Roman community still lively in the fourth century but starting to crack during the fifth. In it are amalgamated Greek and Hellenistic components, and those of the Roman republic and Principate. The magnificent reverse sides of the *contorniates* serve only to confirm this. There are representations of the story of Hercules, Ulysses and Alexander, but also of the she-wolf and episodes from Roman history. As for deities depicted, it is noteworthy that they represent both pure Latin tradition, with *Dea Roma*, and also eastern soteriologial cults of more recent origin.

In short, the *contorniates* defined the Roman cultural heritage, in its mythological, religious, historic and political components, a heritage such as Roman nobles wished to accept and hand on. The product of culture, *contorniates* also served as an instrument of propaganda, intended to challenge the rising tide of Christianity, certainly, but also possible changes in patriotism and attainments. Starting with Theodosius, the emperors became aware of them and began to have the likeness of the reigning Augustus portrayed, but, however Christian they themselves may have been, the essentially pagan symbolism remained the same.[21]

– CHRISTIANITY AND THE ÉLITE –

Because of its culture and attachment to traditions, the Roman nobility is often presented as the last bastion of paganism in the second half of the fourth century and throughout the fifth. That is undeniable, but should not conceal the fact that Christianity had found followers among the Roman nobles before the fourth century. Besides, the conversion of senatorial circles was a very gradual process. It was only at the close of the fourth century that Christians had a majority in the Senate; furthermore, these Christian *clarissimi* preserved and passed on a culture and social customs that had emerged from pagan tradition, so misleading simplifications on this question are to be avoided.

The impressive public conversion of the urban prefect Furius Maecius Gracchus, and Pammachius' entry into the Senate dressed in a monk's habit were among the most sensational indications of the progress of Christianity among the élite of Rome. Gracchus' ancestors had been pagan, but he had converted. Although he was a Christian when he was appointed prefect of the city in 376, Jerome and Prudentius report that during his term of office he had himself baptised, at the same time as his lictors. To this spectacular act he added anti-pagan measures, such as the destruction of gods' statues, and the closing of one – or several – sanctuaries of Mithras.[22] Following him, his descendants are attested as having been Christian. Also through Jerome we know about Pammachius' startling fact, which probably occurred in the 380s: 'Who would have believed it?' he exclaims, showing that even in his time it was hard to imagine. But in the time of Valentinian

II Ambrose said that the Christians had reached a majority in the Roman Senate. The same echo is to be found in Prudentius around 400; in his view, the die was cast: 'there are hundreds of houses of old noble blood', he writes in his poem against Symmachus, 'who have been marked with the seal of Christ, thus escaping the vast abyss of shameful idolatry'. And, a little farther on: 'Rome serves the God-Christ and rejects its old cults.'[23] The reality was probably somewhat more complex. A few years after the death of her husband in 432, Melania in Jerusalem received a letter from her uncle Volusianus announcing his arrival in Constantinople, and she went to join him there. Her uncle was a pagan, and, taking the opportunity of his illness, Melania resolved to convert him, at first through fear, threatening to reveal his paganism to the emperors Theodosius II and Valentinian III, and then choosing persuasion, sending Proclus, the city's bishop, to visit him. The bishop achieved his goal, prompting Volusianus to say, 'If we had three men like the lord Proclus in Rome, there would not be a single pagan left.'[24] This eloquently reveals that the Roman population was not yet unanimously Christian.

When adherence to the new faith followed evangelical precepts most closely it had profound ramifications for the passing on of inheritances among the Roman aristocracy. In the first place, nobles handed over their monetary wealth, properties and possessions to charities in aid of the poor. In extreme cases, such care for the poor led nobles like Pinianus and Melania to shed their entire fortune, bit by bit. Hence wealth no longer remained within the family. In the second, the increase in consecrated virginity, as attested by Jerome in his late fourth- and early fifth-century letters, deterred a good number of *puellae clarissimae* from marriage and childbearing. Fortunes both dwindled in size and became concentrated in the hands of the married non-religious members of families, and this contributed more than a little to breaking up the coherent organisation of family lines and the passing on of hereditary wealth.

Pammachius was the archetypal noble Christian benefactor of the late fourth and early fifth century. A senator, he had converted to the ascetic way of life and used his wealth for ecclesiastical foundations. In 398 he founded a *xenodochium* at Portus for the benefit of pilgrims, and in 410 he financed the building of a large basilica in honour of SS John and Paul. Some time between 401 and 417, a lady of *illustris* rank, Vestina, died. In her will she had ordered the construction of a basilica with the proceeds of the sale, at a fair price, of her jewellery. Built shortly afterwards, this was dedicated to SS Gervasius and Protasius. Pope Innocent I made it a *titulus*, to which he gave a substantial donation, the details of which we know from the *Liber Pontificalis*.[25]

Pinianus and Melania are one of the most astonishing Roman couples in the early fifth century. Cousins – they both belonged to the *gens* Valeria – they were married when Melania was fourteen and Pinianus seventeen. Each kept control of his or her own fortune, and together these assuredly constituted the most enormous aristocratic inheritance in Rome. According to Gerontios, Melania's biographer, they were the first people of senatorial rank to 'trample underfoot the vanities of worldly glory'. This withdrawal began with the abandonment of silken garments, so characteristic of the clothing of Roman *clarissimi* in late antiquity. Melania replaced them with coarse wool, asking her aunt not to reveal the fact to her parents, who were hostile to the ascetic life. After her father's death, Melania wore only old or cheap clothes, while Pinianus adopted the characteristic Cilician habit made of goats' hair.

They then embarked on the sale of their possessions, provoking a certain agitation among their slaves, who did not want to be sold to anyone but Pinianus' father, Severus. Thanks to the intervention of bishops, the couple were received by Serena, niece of Theodosius and cousin of Honorius. Contrary to customary protocol, Melania kept her head covered in the presence of Serena, to whom she made a gift of luxurious clothing and crystal vases. Fearing that everything would be squandered, the couple's close relations tried to repossess the possessions they had inherited; others made plain their intention of taking advantage of the situation to get rich. At Melania's request, Serena, who admired her, asked Honorius to ensure that in each province their property would be sold under the supervision of governors and magistrates, and that the proceeds should be sent to them. They were immediately given the necessary decrees. The fact that Pinianus and Melania sought imperial aid reveals much. Their behaviour was regarded as madness, and the rumour that they were liquidating their gigantic heritage doubtless caused a serious stir among Roman nobles, whose whole system of values was being turned upside down. So great was their wealth, in quantity and geographical widespread location, and so widespread was the greed to gain some of it, that the couple had to cope with numerous plots, which is why they sought imperial support and protection. Christians themselves, Serena and Honorius agreed to have the sales protected by the apparatus of state. But this created a precedent: up till then, one of the prime concerns of emperors had been to preserve the fortunes of senators, who were the guarantors of the continuance of public benefaction and costly magistracies. From many points of view, then, this episode represented a small revolution in Rome's political and social customs.

As we know, they did not manage to find a purchaser for Pinianus' sumptuous mansion on the Caelian Hill. It would seem that no senator possessed adequate means; nor, even, did Serena, to whom the purchase was suggested through the intermediation of bishops. The couple presented her with its precious marble fittings. Just before 410 they had amassed the considerable sum of 45,000 gold *librae*, or 3.2 million *solidi* from the sales, the equivalent of thirty years of land revenues from Pinianus' estates. Not everything was sold, however: islands – useful as retreats from the world – and quantities of gold were presented to monks and monasteries, while silk and silverware were given to decorate churches.

Early in 409, Rome was besieged by the Goths. Anxious to get together enough money to buy them off, the prefect of the city, Pompeianus asked the Senate to declare the confiscation of the couple's wealth by the public treasury, but soon afterwards he was killed during a riot. Pinianus and Melania took refuge in Africa, where they began to sell their estates in the provinces of Numidia, Mauretania and Proconsularis. On the advice of Augustine and other bishops, they made a gift of premises and revenues to the monasteries. But such generosity could be divisive: the church of Thagaste was so showered with offerings that its bishop, Alypius, was envied by his colleagues in other cities.

Pinianus and Melania then left for Jerusalem, where they continued to bestow gifts. The upheavals caused by the various Gothic invasions had prevented the sale of some western estates, but after the *foedus* of 418 that settled the Goths in Aquitaine, Melania was able to go ahead with the sales. Thanks to intermediaries who brought her the proceeds, she also sold her Spanish estates. Following her husband's death, she travelled to Constantinople, at imperial expense, there to convert her uncle Volusianus, who had been prefect of the city in 421. In spite of her efforts, her wealth seemed inexhaustible, and at the end of her life, around 440, Gerontios says she still had fifty gold coins and the sums she distributed were from gifts that she continued to receive.

The story of Pinianus and Melania is unique because of the sheer size of the wealth involved, but not because it is the only example. Other Roman nobles followed the same path, mainly from among Jerome's friends. We have seen the instance of Pammachius, and matrons like Paula, Fabiola, Lea and Blesilla also sold their properties. This was the climax of an ascetic trend in Roman Christianity, as preached by Jerome, and it was to be a considerable shock to both the Roman nobility and the state. By such means, the primacy of material wealth, which had been one of the pillars of senatorial power, was being obstinately and methodically rejected. But the adventure of Pinianus and Melania was very much a product of its time, since it could not have been accomplished without the support of the imperial family, who by the beginning of the fifth century were won over to respect for a more radical Christianity, and an admiration for saintliness.

CHAPTER 6

Tradesmen and plebs

In Rome, trades were structured in professional bodies, the *corpora*, whose management was regulated by imperial legislation. These *corpora* had patrons, chosen from among the great Roman notables. Several were in the service of the city of Rome, and hence enjoyed special privileges. Furthermore, in those corporations deemed to be most useful to the public good, it was obligatory for offices to be hereditary. The members of these corporations were unable to dispose freely of their possessions, as these were used as security against the fulfilment of their duties.

– FEEDING THE CITY –

The size of the Roman population created an acute problem of food supplies. The old public system of the *annona* still survived in late antiquity, consisting of taxing the provinces in kind for a certain quantity of wheat, wine, oil and pork. This amount, fixed each year by the praetorian prefecture, had to be collected under the direction of the prefect of Rome and his assistant, the prefect of the *annona*. Rich Romans, formed into corporations, had the task of collection and transport.

The *navicularii* did not form a professional body strictly speaking.[1] The office of shipowner was a burdensome one laid upon landowners, whose estates, which were subject to the *munus navicularium*, served as a guarantee. It was their duty to build, equip and repair the boats used for transporting the food supplies, and holding this office exempted them from other taxes and municipal duties. The boats' capacity ranged from 2000 to 10,000 *modii* – between 6 and 30 tonnes. They had two or three masts on which square or rectangular sails were hoisted. When the sea was declared open to traffic, between March and November, the supply convoys left from Africa, Sardinia and Sicily, laden with the amount of wheat fixed by the praetorian prefect of Italy, to bring it to Rome where, after being weighed, it was placed in sacks or amphorae. Furthermore, the ships' captains had to make an official declaration that they had taken charge of undamaged goods.[2] They also had to take the shortest possible route: the African convoys generally managed the distance between Carthage and Rome in a week, but were capable of covering it more quickly, at best in two days. Any diversion or misappropriation of the merchandise, or any illicit sale on the occasion of a landfall, were punishable by death.[3]

The emperors regarded the shipmasters as an essential link in Rome's food supply. Valentinian III's 29th *novella*, dated 24 April 450, is evidence of this concern. According to this law, the emperor ordered the prefect of the city to compensate the shipowners for losses they had suffered. Another problem could be the increasing scarcity of holders of this office. The *novella* commanded shipowners who had left their *corpus* to rejoin it and claim the possessions of colleagues who had died without heirs. Furthermore, so that their efforts should be directed to vessels of large tonnage, they were prohibited from repairing or building ships with a capacity of under 1040 *modii*. In the fifth century, there were seldom enough shipowners to ensure the service of the *annona* by themselves, so the help of private shipowners was needed to carry out the transport, but they were less well paid.

The harbour at Portus was the scene of considerable activity. There were several trade corporations assigned to the unloading of goods. The *saccarii* were the dockers, and it was the task of the *mensores* to measure the quantities of grain, which were noted by the *tabularii* (record clerks) of the prefecture of the *annona*. These quantities could then be compared with those that had been loaded. It appears that a 4 per cent loss was permissible, but beyond that there had to be an inquiry. A certain amount was deducted for the payment of the crews. The wheat was then stored in the port's warehouses, under the responsibility of the warehouse managers, who were Roman bakers elected to this post for a five-year period.

The *caudicarii* were responsible for transporting the grain from the warehouses of Portus to those of Rome. This was effected in barges without oars or sails which were towed along the 35 kilometres of the Tiber that separated its mouth from the city, a journey that took some three days. In the sixth century, towing was done by oxen, which was a fairly recent practice. Before then, it seems that it had been carried out by human strength alone, but the meanders and current of the river, together with a lack of slaves, eventually meant the use of animals to haul the boats. As the convoys arrived in summer, the Tiber had its most intensive traffic in autumn, October and November. In the fourth century, the *caudicarii* alone were not always enough for the job. A law of 8 October 364 ordered the requisitioning of Tiber ships to assist them.[4] In 400, this important *corpus* incorporated that of the Tiber's fishermen, the *piscatores*.

Once the boats were alongside the city quays, the wheat was unloaded by the *saccarii*, then re-measured, before being placed in the warehouses. Opportunities for fraud and embezzlement were rife: an inscription of 389 tells us how the perfect of the *annona*, Ragonius Vincentius Celsus, was called upon to intervene in a long-standing dispute involving the *caudicarii* and *mensores*.[5] In 417, a law compelled the *caudicarii* to appoint one of their number to watch out for frauds committed against the *annona*.[6]

There were around 300 of these stores in Rome, situated mainly in the XIIIth district, in the area of the *emporium*. The *horrea galbana* storehouses measured 167 x 147 metres and had three porticoed courtyards. Excavations have shown that the buildings comprised between 130 and 140 rooms of modest dimensions – 13 x 5 metres for the largest – in which wheat was stored. Fire, humidity, theft and length of storage were the main dangers which the prefectural services had to combat, the first two being the hardest to avoid. An excess of heat or humidity – over from 14 to 16 per cent – brought about a microbiological process that damaged the grain, so it was necessary to ventilate the granaries, and there was a ban on storage in the lower parts.[7] A law of 365 ordered that old rations were to be finished before starting on new ones. Likewise, if a large amount of poor quality grain was found, it was mixed in with the good stuff. Dispatching the grain to the mills came under the control of a magistrate appointed by the prefect of the *annona*, the *custos ac mensor*. The law indicates that the choice should fall upon a noble, scrupulous and conscientious man.[8]

The wheat was next carried on yoked carts by *catabolenses*, after prefectural authorisation, to the 250 public bakeries in the city, each district having between fifteen and twenty. Baking the bread was entrusted to the *corpus pistorum*, the bakers' corporation. In the service of the *annona* and considered to be a public utility, this *corpus* was closely supervised. Membership of it was hereditary and the law prohibited anyone from avoiding his obligation. In the same way that the shipowners were not sailors, Roman *pistores* did not actually put their hands in the flour. Rather, they were landed property owners of high rank: a law of 364 indicates that they could become senators.[9] Each bakery had a least two *pistores*, so the city must have had over 500. From their members they elected a *prior* whose task over a five-year period was to combat the fraudulent practices of the *caudicarii* bosses. To do this, they took samples of wheat at Portus and passed them to Roman colleagues for use as evidence in case poor quality wheat was substituted for good during transport. As recompense for their obligatory office, bakers, like shipowners, were exempted from the other duties to which their social class was subject.

The bakeries themselves were entrusted to managers, with millers and bakers' boys, often of slave status, working under their command. The grinding was done either in the bakeries, by millstones turned by donkeys, or in the town's watermills. There were some of these on the slopes of the Janiculum, to the west of Rome, where the waters of Lake Bracciano were channeled through the *aqua Traiana*. The flour obtained was sieved through several riddles, and mixed with water and salt; then yeast was added; the dough was kneaded and put in the ovens. Several indications in texts lead one to think that there was a shortage of labour in Roman bakeries. In 319, for instance, the governor of Sardinia was entreated to send criminals to Rome to work in the bakeries.[10] Moreover, certain crimes could be punished by a life sentence of bakery work.

The heredity of the office of master-baker, and the use of slaves and convicts as a large part of the staff of bakeries, show that, more than any other trade, breadmaking was subject to a certain fixedness, under strict state control. In this trade which was deemed indispensable to Rome, a shortfall in the workforce had to be avoided at all costs, so efforts were made to maintain and enlarge the *corpus*. According to laws of 370 and 380, the proconsul of Africa had to send new bakers to Rome every five years.[11]

Legislation was concerned almost entirely with what came under state control, namely the duties and trades connected with the *annona*. Until fairly recently, historians included these as indication of the later Roman empire's planned economy under state control; but this was an unwarranted extrapolation, ignoring the existence of the free and private exercise of trade outside the framework of the *annona*. It was not a sign of oppression exerted by heavy-handed, exacting or implacable legislation over the whole of society's workforce; rather, it should be seen only as the emperors' concern to achieve the best possible management of those things necessary to the smooth running of the state.

More of a luxury than bread, the meat consumed was mostly pork, for which Romans had a great liking. According to the *Historia Augusta*, the emperor Aurelian (270–5) is supposed to have been the first to set up free distributions of pork in Rome. It seems, rather, that he was the first to regularise them, since there is evidence of occasional meat distributions before his time, chiefly under the Severi. Alongside a free market, with its main outlets in the *forum boarium* and the *forum suarium*, there existed a pork *annona*. This was provided by the corporation of pork butchers, the *corpus* of the *suarii*. Like shipowning and bakery, it was not a profession but a service, a *munus* weighing on landed property owners. Each year, the prefecture established a quantity of pork meat, the *canon suarius*, which had to be supplied to the Roman butcheries, and provided by landowners in the provinces of southern Italy, such as Campania, Lucania, Bruttium and Samnium. It was the task of the *suarii* to see that it reached its destination, and to do this they hired the services of herdsmen, who drove the herds of pigs from the Italian provinces to Rome. Following a measure taken in 324–6, landowners who were obliged to provide the *canon* could do so in money, in which case the *suarii* had to buy pigs at the going rate with the sums levied; thus the *canon* could be expressed in pounds of meat or in *solidi*. From the figures available to us, the *canon* was the equivalent of 14,700 *solidi* per annum, four-fifths of which were supplied by Lucania and Samnium. At the price of one *solidus* for 240 pounds of meat on the hoof, the *canon* was therefore equivalent to 3,528,000 pounds of meat in the fifth century. From this quantity of pork about 15 per cent was deducted for the *suarii* by way of remuneration, so that the carcasses destined for distribution thus represented about 3 million pounds. It could happen that the quantity of pork failed to match the *canon*, not least because during the journey the pigs lost weight. A law of Valentinian I devised a scheme for compensating the *suarii* for this shortfall and the losses that they would therefore incur. The *suarii* were paid with amphorae of wine drawn from Rome's *vinarius* canon, together with a contribution from the town councils of the Italian provinces that had provided the pigs in the first instance.[12]

Legal documents mention other butchery corporations. The *pecuarii* sold meat from sheep and the *boarii* meat from cattle. They were annexed to the *corpus* of the *suarii* during the fifth century, which suggests that on their own they were not adequate for the task. Valentinian III's 36th *novella*, dated 452, gives similar evidence: the offices of the praetorian prefecture could be requested to take part in levying the *canon*, in which case they would receive an emolument of five additional civil servants.

Once they had arrived in Rome, the pigs were gathered in warehouses. Like the cereal stores, they were placed under the supervision of a man belonging to the corporation, elected by his colleagues for a five-year period. On leaving office, he would receive the dignity of count of the third rank. After being kept without food on the eve of their slaughter, the pigs had their throats cut by the *confectuarii* or *porcinarii*. The carcasses were put on scales to be weighed, then handed over to the *suarii* for distribution.[13]

– MERCHANTS AND OTHER OCCUPATIONS –

The Roman corporations are know to us from two types of evidence: on the one hand, the laws that regulated them, which were collected in the Codes of Theodosius and Justinian; on the other, the dedicatory inscriptions they had carved in honour of the patrons whose benefaction they had enjoyed.

Wholesalers belonged to the corporation of the *magnarii*. Numerous Greek merchants, the *pantapolae*, lived in Rome. They aroused the jealous enmity of the city's shopkeepers, and were the victims of banishment in the first half of the fifth century. On 3 March 440, in his fifth *novella*, Valentinian III let it be known to the people of Rome that he would no longer tolerate such actions. The law permitted the banished *pantapolae* to return to Rome and resume trading. According to the emperor, they would be a guarantee of plenty and repopulation should circumstances become difficult.

A whole crowd of craft trades existed in Rome. The *fabri tignarii* were the city's builders and carpenters, the *corarii* its leatherworkers. It is known that the prefect of 334–5, Anicius Paulinius Iunior, had their workshops repaired.[14] Also connected with building were the marble-workers, stone-cutters, brick and tile-makers. Artistic craftsmen, such as mosaicists, painters, sculptors and goldsmiths worked on the decoration of public buildings and aristocratic residences, and for the churches.

Some jobs were considered ignominious, including those of charioteers, procurers and prostitutes, innkeepers and actors, who were the subject of particular surveillance by the urban prefecture. If they became Christian and received baptism, they could not continue to follow their old job: hence an actor who received the last rites on the point of death and then recovered could not return to the stage. In contrast, intellectual professions enjoyed the respect of the state; doctors, teachers and public orators, like civil servants, were paid by the state straight from the *annona*, and enjoyed fiscal immunity.

In 440, Roman citizens and members of the trade corporations were exempted from military service, and would henceforward be assigned only to guarding gates and walls should the need arise, under the direction of the urban prefect. Moreover, limekiln workers and carters, on whom materials for repairing the defensive walls depended, were exempted from land tax.[15] But every occupation involving commercial transactions was subject to the quadrennial payment of a tax, the *chrysargyron*, created around 318 and abolished in 498. Although modest, this tax was particularly unpopular, and certain Christians were indignant that the treasury of Christian emperors should be enriched by sums paid by prostitutes and their pimps, the *lenones*. But, after all, had not their predecessor, Vespasian, declared in the first century that money has no smell (*pecunia non olet*)?

– THE ROMAN PLEBS –

Rome had a very varied population. Not only did contrasting social categories rub shoulders, the poor and the needy with ultra-rich senators, but also people coming from every region in the empire, whether they were students or merchants. These residents were kept under the eye of the urban prefecture. We read in Ammianus Marcellinus, who doubtless harboured some personal grievance, that foreigners in Rome were regarded with mistrust, not to say disdain.

– XENOPHOBIA –

During the food shortages in the fourth century, foreigners in transit were expelled from the city by the prefects, Orfitus in 353–6 and Symmachus in 384. By foreigners we mean *peregrini*, or residents not possessing Roman citizenship, although Roman citizens originating from other cities must probably be included. They had no right to the public food distributions but, when shortages struck, they put a strain on the free market. At the time of the food shortage in 384, Ammianus Marcellinus was perhaps one of those expelled, which would explain the virulence of his diatribe against this measure, and against the vices of the Romans. His indignation was at its peak because, according to him, a small number of men devoted to the liberal arts were expelled, while mime actresses and their entourages were kept in Rome, as well as three thousand female dancers and as many dancing teachers, with their choruses.[16]

By a law of 12 December 416, Honorius and Theodosius forbade the wearing of long hair and garments made of animal skins in the most sacred city, by both free citizens and slaves.[17] This measure was of course introduced to deal with a long-established trend and testifies to the existence in Rome of a whole population of barbarian origin who had preserved their customary hairstyles and clothing; it also shows that a proportion of the slaves shared the same origins. Six years after Alaric's sack of the city, this legal measure was a reaction against barbarisation. Barbarians living in Rome were therefore obliged to get their hair cut and wear clothes made of cloth. Slaves who did not comply would be sentenced to do public work. It is noteworthy that the prefect of the city, Probianus in that year, was expected to have this law publicised and observed not only in the city itself but also in the neighbouring regions, that is, in the area of 100 miles around Rome which came under his jurisdiction. Indeed, since the reign of Valentinian I, mixed marriages between Romans and barbarians had been prohibited – even so, this did not prevent the birth of half-barbarian children.

– ASSISTANCE FOR THE PLEBS –

The existence in Rome of a large population of plebs who were dependent on the state and receiving assistance goes back to the second century BC. They eked out a living not only from a variety of jobs but also from free, or cost price, distributions of food. They might also obtain some income from one or more patrons.

This mass of poor Romans, or those of modest means, formed a mob whose way of life Ammianus Marcellinus deplores. In his view, the common people spent the night drinking in the taverns, quarrelling over dice games and complaining noisily. During the day, they passed their time watching mime shows at the theatre or conducting a careful examination of the respective merits of charioteers and horses before the chariot races began. If we are to believe a scornful Ammianus, that was the Romans' burning and dominant passion. In his view, the plebeian way of life contaminated the city to the point where, even among the nobility, it corrupted and effaced intellectual culture and the taste for study.[18] Assiduous spectators at shows, the Roman plebs expressed their opinions without ceremony. We gather from sources that this freedom of speech, which might be directed at the prefect or even the emperor, was a constant feature of the arena and was tolerated.

Around 368, Valentinian I instituted the *defensores plebis*, who in each city were given the task of protecting the humble from abuse by the powerful. They had the authority to settle small legal cases, thus exempting the more modest citizens from the expense of the usual procedures.[19]

– SLAVES –

The slave population was less numerous in late antique Rome than in the time of the republic or the early empire. Some have at times connected this reduction with the rising social influence of Christianity, which would have favoured their emancipation, but one must remember that the tendency had begun before Christianity started to prosper in the city. Foreign conquests had finished with Trajan's acquisition of Dacia, and with them the chief source of renewing the slave population had dried up. Besides, Christianity did not make an issue of the status of slavery; at most, churchmen exhorted masters to treat their slaves humanely. Beginning in the fourth century, the state alleviated their condition slightly and favoured sporadic emancipation. In 316, for example, Constantine prohibited branding with a redhot iron, which it was customary to inflict on slaves' faces. Thus the use of collars developed, inscribed with the name and address of their master. Anyone sheltering and helping a fugitive slave was liable to a fine equal to the price of the slave. A law of 319 punished masters who beat their slaves to death, unless it was a matter of chastising an acknowledged misdeed. Two years later, Constantine authorised emancipation in church, before the bishop of the city.[20]

Romans of senatorial rank would have had large crowds of slaves and servants in their service, both in their houses and on their country estates. Ammianus Marcellinus says that in the noble carriages in the streets of Rome the stewards of household staffs could be recognised by the batons of office they brandished in their right hands; there would follow also the servants employed for weaving, and the smoke-blackened slaves who toiled in the kitchens. Some nobles did not go anywhere without a large number of slaves, whom Ammianus accuses of pilfering and looting with impunity. Escape, however, was severely punished by law. A fugitive slave might be sentenced to hard labour in the mines, or even to having a foot amputated. In the fifth century, many slaves took advantage of the disorder created by the sieges and sackings of the city to make off; but slavery by no means disappeared, and there is still evidence of it in the late sixth century.

1. *Western end of the Roman Forum. Left foreground, platform of the Rostra, extended northwards c. 470; behind, the arch of Septimius Severus (203). Right, the Senate house (curia) as rebuilt in the late third century after the fire of 283. Photo B. L.*

2. *Roman Forum. Base of the column for the* decennalia *of Galerius and Constantius Chlorus (303). Bas-relief showing the procession of senators. Photo B. L.*

3. Roman Forum. Surviving part (north wing) of the building known as the 'Basilica of Maxentius' begun by him but completed by Constantine. Photo B. L.

5. Foreground: the arch dedicated to Constantine in 315. Background: the Flavian amphitheatre. Photo B. L.

4. (opposite) Colossal head of Constantine (height 2.60m; Capitol, courtyard of the Palazzo dei Conservatori). It was part of the colossal statue situated in the Basilica of Maxentius. Photo B. L.

6. *Bust of Constantius II as a young man (Capitol, courtyard of the Palazzo dei Conservatori). Photo B. L.*

7. Roman Forum. Base of a statue. Inscription in honour of Constantius II, dedicated by Vitrasius Orfitus during his second urban prefecture (357–9). (CIL, VI, 31395.) Photo B. L. Inscription reads: 'To the propagator of Roman power. Our Lord Flavius Julius Constantius, the greatest, victorious and triumphant over the whole earth, forever Augustus, Memmius Vitrasius Orfitus, vir clarissimus, *prefect of the city for the second time, judge of the sacred hearings for the third time, devoted to his emperor's divinity and majesty, set this up.'*

8. *Roman Forum. Base of a statue transferred by Petronius Maximus during his second urban prefecture (before 433). (CIL, VI, 36956.) Photo: B. L. Inscription reads: 'Petronius Maximus, vir clarissimus, urban prefect for the second time, restored this.'*

9. *Colosseum. Inscription of Decius Marius Venantius, clarissimus and illustris,
prefect of the city,* patricius *and ordinary consul (484), who at his own expense
restored the arena and balcony which had been destroyed by an earthquake. (CIL,
VI, 32094.) Photo: B. L. Inscription reads: 'Decius Marius Venantius Basilius, vir
clarissimus and illustris, prefect of the city, patrician and ordinary consul,
restored at his own expense the arena and the balcony which the destruction of
a terrible earthquake had destroyed.'*

10. *Fourth-century mosaic representing gladiatorial combats. The names of famous gladiators are mentioned. Rome, Galeria Borghese. © Fratelli Alinari/Giraudon.*

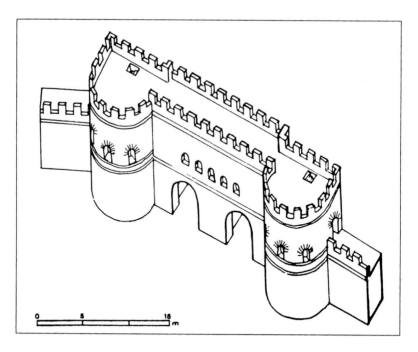

11. *Aurelianic walls. Porta Appia, after the modifications carried out at the beginning of the fifth century.*

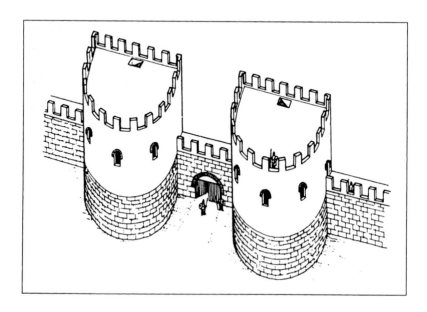

12. *Aurelianic walls. Porta Ostiensis.*

13. *Ivory diptych presented to Honorius by Petronius Probus, ordinary consul in 406. The emperor is pictured as a soldier victorious in Christ's name. Treasury of the Cathedral of Aosta. © Alinari/Giraudon.*

14. *Mosaic in the nave of Sta Maria Maggiore (fifth century). This Old Testament scene depicts the appearance of the three men to Abraham at Mamre. The three angels are dressed in Roman style, in this instance the* toga praetexta. © *Fratelli Alinari/Giraudon.*

15. *Marriage chest of Secundus and Projecta. (Rome, late fourth century.)*
London, British Museum. © British Museum.

16. *Allegorised as a seated woman, wearing a plumed helmet, Rome possesses the attributes of power (the spear), victory (orb, surmounted by a winged victory presenting the palm and the crown, the symbols of victory) and wealth collected and dispensed (the bag and amphora of coins). Seventeenth-century copy from a ninth-century manuscript, itself copied from a fourth-century original. Rome, MS Romanus 1, Barb. lat. 2154, fol. 2.* © *Vatican Library, Rome.*

III

Religio: *Religion and religiosity*

CHAPTER 7

Ancestral cults

Religion offers an additional element of variety in the Roman population up to the middle of the fifth century, the time when Christianity may be judged to have really triumphed over the other religious elements in the city. What Christians belatedly termed 'paganism' was in fact a mosaic of cults adopted by Rome since the first centuries of the republic. The word they chose should not mislead us; it would be a mistake to think that paganism was then no more than a characteristic of the *pagani*, the peasants inhabiting the *pagi* (villages). It merely bears witness to the fact that Christianisation first took place in towns. There was nothing at all rustic about the pagans of the great Roman aristocracy in the fourth century, apart from their luxurious villas. Paganism at that time presented many faces, but was none the less coherent. In Rome, its leaders were *illustres*, of the highest social rank, and prided themselves on bearing titles and priesthoods steeped in tradition.

Similarly, Roman Christianity should not be regarded as monolithic, in any case not before the end of the fifth century. In fact, although the Roman Church was chiefly Nicene, dissident minorities continued to exist who resisted conciliar condemnations: Manichaeans, Arians and Novatians.

– ROMAN RELIGION –

Throughout the whole of the fourth century Roman religion preserved its traditional framework: places of worship, priesthoods, rites, festivals and games. This is clear, in the first place, from architectural evidence. Temples remained open and attended until their legal closure by Theodosius in February 391.[1] Pagan urban prefects had them restored all through the century; for instance, Praetextatus, one of the prominent figures in the pagan reaction, had the portico of the temple of the *Dii consentes* restored during his prefecture.[2] After a fire, the temple of Saturn in the Forum was restored between 360 and 380. Moreover, statues of the Vestal Virgins continued to be erected in their house in the Roman Forum. Secondly, the Calendar of 354 mentions the great pagan festivals, encompassing those of the imperial cult and of more than thirty deities.

Aristocrats' funerary inscriptions provide an invaluable body of evidence testifying to the lasting nature of priestly dignities and the variety of pagan cults in fourth-century Rome. It should be pointed out that they existed in a perfectly legal setting, and that emperors continued to hold the title of *Pontifex Maximus* (that is, the chief priest of Roman religion) until Gratian and Theodosius rejected it. Zosimus notes that, in theory, emperors received the 'mantle' of *Pontifex Maximus* upon their appointment;[3] but as it was now exceptional for emperors to reside in Rome, it is likely that pontiffs at Rome did not bestow it upon them until the first imperial *adventus* to the city. So it was probably in 379, on his only journey to Rome, that Gratian gave back to the disappointed pontiffs the mantle they had brought him. From Constantine to Gratian, therefore, Christian emperors had remained heads of the Roman religion.

Paganism was nothing more than a syncretic group of cults among which it is possible schematically to distinguish two strata which, in the late period, were no longer compartmentalised. First there was the Roman religion itself, which had long been Hellenised, and in which reverence was paid to the gods of Rome. In the view of traditionalists like Symmachus, it was indissolubly linked to the state. The other level belonged to the so-called 'oriental' religions which, transported by soldiers, administrators and traders, had established themselves in Rome since the late third century BC. Besides attractive rites, they offered an eschatological perspective and enjoyed vast success in the early Roman empire, while Christianity remained a minority religion.

In the fourth century, the inscriptions of pagan dignitaries reveal a multiplicity of religions, but the fact that they were named together indicates that in the eyes of their holders they formed some kind of unity. Formerly competitors, these cults were henceforward reconciled. Since the late second century, reflection and sensitivity had led religious feeling to a sort of monotheism. The cult of *Sol Invictus* – the unconquered Sun – established by Aurelian around 274, with a temple on the Campus Martius, a priestly college and quadrennial games, bore remarkable testimony to this. In his writings, the emperor Julian reveals himself as the paragon of this syncretic religiousness. Sol, Mithras and Apollo are the names of the same deity. In Franz Cumont's words, at the time the gods were regarded as 'cosmic energies whose providential action is regulated in a harmonious system.'[4] For fourth-century pagan intellectuals, who were often brushed with Neoplatonism, the universe was ruled by a single, omnipotent God, the master of fate and time, a father known by various names and honoured in a thousand different ways.

The epitaphs of several Roman nobles, including urban prefects, mention their priestly dignities. For instance, in that of Agorius Praetextatus, prefect of the city in 367–8, then praetorian prefect,[5] the list of titles begins with strictly Roman priesthoods: he was an augur, priest of Vesta, pontiff of Sol, *quindecemvir* (reader of the Sibylline Books) and *curialis* of Hercules, initiate of Liber and the Eleusinian mysteries. Then the dignities in 'oriental' religions are mentioned: hierophant (initiator into the Eleusinian mysteries), *neocorus* (in charge of sacrifices), initiate of the *taurobolium* (Cybele) and was Father of fathers (Mithras). His wife, Fabia Paulina, was an initiate into the mysteries of Ceres, Hecate and Eleusis, had been initiated into the *taurobolium* and was a *hierophantria* (high priestess of Hecate). The couple had thus been initiated into the best-known mysteries in the Roman world. In what might be called his religious titles, Agorius thus epitomises all the components of paganism in his period. Among his predecessors, Lampadius, prefect from 365 to 366, belonged to the Caeionii family who remained mostly pagan. His wife, Lolliana, was a priestess of Isis; of their six children, we know that Publius Caecina Albinus was a pontiff of Vesta, Caeionus Rufius consecrated an altar at the temple of Magna Mater known as the *Phrygianum* on the Vatican on 23 May 390,[6] and their two daughters were also initiated into the *taurobolium*.

Until the Theodosian era, the flower of pagan aristocracy in Rome donned the mantle of Roman priesthoods; the titles of augur, the major pontificates and *quindecemvir* are those which occur most frequently in the inscriptions. Although religious, this fidelity was perhaps more political and cultural. To quote Cumont again, 'These archaic priesthoods were as lacking in real influence on religion as republican magistracies were on the power of the state.'[7] Even so, they revealed the continuity of the ancestral *mos maiorum* and, in this sense, played a far from negligible role. In contrast, from a personal viewpoint, the cultured nobility turned to mystery religions which offered initiations and salvation.

– THE CULT OF ISIS –

The cult of Serapis and Isis, very much in vogue in Rome in the late empire, is attested throughout the fourth century. Having become a great pantheistic goddess, Isis was honoured daily in her temples by colleges of priests who had shaven heads and dressed in linen. Each day at dawn they opened the temple gates, lit a sacred flame and went on to offer libations, singing hymns to the accompaniment of flutes and sistra. They then attended to the toilet of the goddess's statue, which was adorned with rich garments and jewels. At sunset, the temples were closed with the same ritual solemnity. The high point in the cult of Isis, mentioned in the Calendar of 354, was the festival of *navigium Isidis* – the vessel of Isis – which was celebrated on 5 March. It was the day of the reopening of seaborne traffic after four and a half months of *mare clausum*, when the sea was closed to navigation. A great procession went to the river bank, where a boat dedicated to Isis was launched. The highly colourful procession included a group in fancy dress, women in white garments strewing flowers on the ground, torchbearers, hymn-singers and, of course, priests. In Isiac mythology, the quest for Osiris promised salvation similar to that which could also be found in the cults of Cybele or Mithras. Isis had restored life to Osiris by seeking and reassembling the scattered parts of his body. This 'discovery' by Isis gave rise to several days of exuberant rejoicing at the end of October. Was it not the guarantee of a new life? To reach it, followers of Isis went through an initiation that led them to ecstasy. Moreover, Roman epigraphy reveals that in their view, as the pledge of a new life, Osiris brought cool water, the *refrigerium*. This term was re-used later by Christians at their funeral banquets.

– Mithraism –

Excavations at Rome have revealed the existence of several *mithraea*, which were frequented by devotees of Mithras in the city in the fourth century. The best known are those discovered under the church of S Clemente, not far from the Colosseum, and under the church of Sta Prisca, on the Aventine. Persian and Mazdean in origin, Mithraism enjoyed great popularity in the empire during the second and third centuries, reaching its apogee in the era of the Tetrarchy. The original feature of Mithraism was its dualism: in the face of gods of evil, Mithras was the god of justice and truth. The *mithraea* were small and were used for rites of a sober character. Followers of the cult wore a simple garment. The *chryfi* – uninitiated – could be admitted to follow an initiation in seven grades, with seven corresponding dignities. The Latin terms revealed in the epigraphy show that they formed a *militia* and pronounced an oath (*sacramentum*). Initiates had tattoos on their hands or forehead. Those who reached the highest ranks were known as Lions, and were the ones who carried the incense before the stele where the god was portrayed in the act of killing a bull. The highest

Mithraic dignity was that of *pater patrum*, Father of fathers. Communal meals and initiation were intended to lead to the expiation of misdeeds and purification.

At the end of the fourth century Theodosius banned the *taurobolium*. The frescoes of the Aventine *mithraeum* were partly defaced by the Christians, who built the church of Sta Prisca on its site. This destruction resulted in revealing lines of verse, written with a paintbrush, on an underlying layer of plaster. They comprised elements of the doctrine, as well as rules of conduct praising loyalty, fraternity and the courage that each individual needs to bear his burden. I will quote three examples, in the form of aphorisms:

> You must spend cloudy days together, and in the accomplishing of rites.
> Sweet are the livers of birds, but anxieties prevail.
> Here, Aries runs in front exactly on his course.[8]

They bear witness to a sense of community and, despite the hierarchy, a community spirit among its followers. Life is a burden, but brotherhood and piety must be preserved for they will lead to salvation.

– THE CULT OF THE GREAT MOTHER –

The Phrygian cult of Cybele, the *Magna Mater*, which had been introduced in Rome in 204 BC, still had pious followers in the fourth century. They gathered in sanctuaries like the Vatican *phyrgianum*, or the temple on the Campus Martius. Seven such sanctuaries have been found with an altar, and they were in use in the fourth century. Like that of Mithras, this cult had a soteriological nature. At the end of an initiation covering several grades, it in fact offered a rebirth akin to salvation. This was obtained by a kind of baptism, the *taurobolium*. Stretched out beneath a hurdle on which a bull had its throat cut, the initiate was drenched in its blood as the pledge of a new life. This ceremony, regarded by Christians as an idolatrous and disgusting rite, was described by the poet Prudentius. Moreover, those who had gone through the *taurobolium* ate food from the tambourine and drank liquor from the cymbal which were used in the cult of Attis, Cybele's partner. Because of the taurobolic 'baptism', the feasts , and the 'holy' week in spring, followers of the cult maintained, in the fourth century, that Christians had imitated their own rites with baptism, the eucharist and Easter week.

THE OFFICIAL ABANDONMENT
OF TRADITIONAL RELIGION

A series of laws issued by the emperor Gratian and then Theodosius interrupted the course of traditional religion in Rome between 382 and 394. Having put an end to the usurpation of Magnus Maximus, Theodosius went to Rome in 389 where he convened the Senate, some of whom remained loyal to religious traditions, and exhorted them to renounce paganism. As he received only a poor response, Theodosius appears to have suspended state subsidies to the cults; from then on, since their rituals could no longer be observed, the cults fell into decline. Zosimus dates this episode to 394. It is true that at this time Theodosius, having defeated Eugenius, put an end to several months of attempts at pagan restoration, but probably did so in Milan. According to François Paschoud, Zosimus must have transposed by several years a scene that took place in 389.[9]

– THE SURVIVAL OF PAGAN RITES –

The rites of pagan religions were hardly troubled at all during the fourth century. At the most, the Christian emperors stopped a few sacrifices here and there and closed some temples, but no systematic policy was undertaken. In certain instances, they retreated; for example, at the beginning of his reign, Valentinian I had wanted to do away with nocturnal sacrifices. Praetextatus, who at the time was proconsul of Achaea, pointed out to him that such a measure ran the risk of disturbing public order and it was revoked.[10] It must be said that until 379 the emperors remained the chief priests of Roman religion, and that traditional cults were subsidised by the state until 382. In that year, Tamenius Augentius had the *mithraeum* on the Campus Martius restored. The grandson of Victor Olympius, a *pater patrum* in the middle of the fourth century, had a dedicatory inscription carved on it. This specifically stated that Rome had played no part in its cost, which means that the state was no longer subsidising the restoration of temples. A law of 27 February 391 prohibited all public pagan cults in Rome and all visits to temples; the following year, a law extended the ban to private cults. Was this law defied? Very probably, if we can believe certain indications. In 394, if this date can be taken as accurate, there was an Isiac procession in Rome. As Isis was the patron goddess of sailors, and the *navigium Isidis* was linked with the re-opening of seaborne traffic, it is possible that the authorities did not want to hinder a rite of good omen. Other, better-known episodes bear witness to pagan defiance.

– THE AFFAIR OF THE ALTAR OF VICTORY –

This affair is the most famous episode in the conflict that set paganism against Christianity in Italy during the second half of the fourth century. Begun in 357, it was to have repercussions until 401–4. The object of the dispute was the statue of Victory in the Senate house. After his victory at Actium in 31 BC, Octavian had placed there an ancient statue of Victory, allegorised as a winged woman, with a small altar at her feet. For almost four centuries, senators coming into a session had been accustomed to burn a few grains of incense on it. Before this statue they swore loyalty to the new emperors and, every three years, on 3 January, expressed their wishes for the emperor's wellbeing and the empire's prosperity. Visiting Rome in the spring of 357, Constantius II, who was a haughty Arian, had the altar removed, but after his departure it was put back in place. Gratian had it removed again in 382, at the same time taking measures against traditional Roman religion, such as suspending the remuneration of priests and Vestals, ending their tax exemptions, and confiscating lands belonging to temples and priestly colleges. When Gratian died the following year, Symmachus asked for an audience with the young Valentinian II. He went to Milan and passed on a request to the emperor, though without obtaining an audience. This asked for the statue and altar of Victory to be preserved within the Senate house and, moreover, that the temples and priests should recover their possessions so that the ancient rites could be fulfilled. At the same time, the bishop of Rome, Damasus, had sent a memorandum to his Milanese colleague Ambrose, in which the Christian senators dissociated themselves from Symmachus' actions. So, to forestall a possible reversal of the situation, Ambrose wrote to the emperor asking for the text of the *relatio* (report) which Symmachus had given him. His request was granted and, after reading the text, he composed a second letter in which he refuted Symmachus' arguments point by point. Although Valentinian had not acceded to his request, Symmachus did not lose heart. Delegations repeated the same request to Theodosius in 389 and Valentinian II in 392. After the latter's death in the same year, two new approaches were made to Eugenius. To Ambrose's outrage, and running with both hare and hounds, Eugenius personally gave the members of the delegation a sum of money to fund the cult that was dear to them. Had their stubbornness paid off? A passage from Claudian could imply that the statue and altar were replaced in the Senate house around 400, but it is only a supposition, difficult to sustain. In contrast, it is certain that the controversy had not died down, as we can see from the versified polemic in two books written in Rome around 402–3 by the Spanish poet Prudentius, *Contra Symmachum*. His verse aimed to show

how ridiculous the gods were, at the same time praising Theodosius for having abandoned old cults. The poet certainly paid homage to the eloquence of Symmachus, but more to underline the bad use to which he had put it: does one use a golden hoe to work in mire and swamp? For Prudentius, neither Victory, nor the gods, nor tradition had made Rome great: this had been achieved, rather, by armed might and God's plan. Meanwhile, Ambrose had died in 397. Symmachus probably died around 402–3, but there was no Roman senator to take over from him.[11]

– THE YEARS 408–10 –

According to Zosimus, Serena, niece of Theodosius and wife of Stilicho, visited the temple of Cybele in Rome. From the statue of Rhea which stood there she took a necklace and placed it around her own neck. An old woman, a survivor of the former college of Vestals, reproached her, receiving in exchange a flow of insults and was driven from the temple, whereupon the old woman apparently uttered a stream of condemnations against such sacrilege.[12] If it is true, the episode shows that a Christian noblewoman could wish to enter a pagan temple in order to admire it. The presence of the old woman shows that members of the priestly colleges still frequented them privately. Zosimus ascribes this sacrilege to the Theodosian measures which, in his view, precipitated the city's misfortunes. He is equally indignant when recounting that Stilicho had given orders for the layer of gold covering the gates of the Capitol to be scraped off.

In December 408, Alaric laid siege to the city for the first time. The new prefect of the city, Pompeianus, received some men from Etruria who had succeeded in driving the Goths from the town of Narni. They were said to have achieved this glorious feat thanks to the celebration of ancestral rites. That most probably meant *haruspices* (soothsayers or diviners) whom Pompeianus invited to repeat their rites in Rome.[13] But first he asked the bishop of Rome, Innocent, for his agreement. Was this a case of a Christian prefect's deference towards his bishop? Or was it political caution on the part of a pagan prefect? At all events, the prefect's request shows that the rites of Roman religion were no longer in current use in Rome and that, when a very grave crisis occurred, it was thought that no attempt should be spared to reverse the situation. In fact, Innocent agreed that the *haruspices* could sacrifice in secret, but they demanded that the rites should be performed at the state's expense, and by the senators, at the Capitol and in the city's open squares. According to Zosimus, no senator dared to do so, thereby demonstrating that only a few years after Symmachus' death, no senator was prepared openly to declare himself a pagan. A little earlier, to be sure, a law of 14 November 408 had prohibited non-Christians from attaining the higher offices in the imperial Palace.[14] Very probably there were still pagans among the senators, but none seemed ready to sacrifice possible career advantages to defend ancestral rites. In any case, pagans still held high administrative posts. In 410, the praetorian prefect, the prefect of the city and the western consul were all three of them pagans.

– 494: THE AFFAIR OF THE LUPERCALIA –

This affair is very revealing of Christian viewpoints in Rome at the end of the fifth century, and bears witness to the differences that could set the pope and certain Christians at odds. We know about it from a letter which, during the winter of 494, pope Gelasius I (492–6) addressed to a Christian noble of Rome, Andromachus. The letter was a response to criticism directed against Gelasius: his initial prohibition against Christians participating in the Lupercalia had drawn the wrath of the aristocracy, who were already angry at the pope because of his feebleness in passing judgement in a case of adultery involving a cleric. Why, they reasoned, should they abide by the pope's directive on the Lupercalia, when he could not even set the affairs of the Church and its clergy in order? This fertility festival was one of the oldest in the Roman calendar. It took place every year on the 15th of the kalends of March (15 February), in honour of Februus and Faunus. In his *Life of Romulus*, Plutarch describes its ritual: after the sacrifice of a goat in the Lupercal (the cave on the Palatine where traditionally the she-wolf had suckled Romulus and Remus), the members of the college of the Luperci, who were theoretically nobles, performed the ritual of running round the Palatine. They were nearly naked, and with strips cut from the hide of the goat they struck any women who crossed their path, thus ensuring their prosperity and fertility.

Now, a century after Theodosius' anti-pagan laws, the rite had survived, and important Christian people wanted it to be preserved. The shameless immodesty of this faunlike race, where laughter mingled with the cracks of the hide-strips, had driven Gelasius to ban Christians from taking part. That brought protests, and a swift retort from Gelasius. In his view, Christians who demanded the Lupercalia were committing spiritual adultery and defending a festival without understanding its significance or carrying out its true ritual. Thus, according to Gelasius, the Roman nobles did not celebrate it themselves, but had people of low birth run around the Palatine in their place. Moreover, according to the supporters of the Lupercalia, the festival had the power of averting epidemics. Gelasius gleefully set about the proponents of this argument: first, he reminded them, the festival was not aimed against epidemics but sterility; secondly, its performance had not prevented Italy from experiencing grave *pestilentiae*, including those in Livy's era.

As Gelasius points out, this picturesque episode shows that pagan rites in Rome were discarded only very gradually. According to him, his predecessors in Peter's chair had asked emperors to do away with pagan rites, but that had not been done, and Gelasius reads into the absence of measures an explanation of the imperial downfall in the west. When he wrote his letter attacking the Lupercalia, the west had been without an emperor for eighteen years. Moreover, some Christians not only considered the performance of old pagan rites compatible with their faith but also showed a great attachment to them. For that reason Gelasius, anxious to bring some semblance of order to Rome's Christian community, excommunicated those who took part in the festival, judging them to be 'everywhere renegades and nowhere believers'.[15]

– MAGIC AND ASTROLOGY –

The sources are especially rich in references to magic and astrology. In the fourth century people took a passionate interest in these practices, and the abundance of information is due to the fact that the emperors tirelessly reiterated edicts suppressing them. The Romans were convinced of the powers of magic and the significance of portents. They believed in spells and curses, favourable and unfavourable signs. They also believed in the influence of stars and planets on their lives. Nature worked on men and, by magic, men could take action in return and alter their destiny. So they assiduously visited diviners, magi and astrologers in order to lift curses, know the future or read their horoscope.

Constantine condemned magical practices that were not beneficial, authorising only those that could improve health or crops. Under Constantius II and Valentinian I, between 337 and 375, a veritable witch-hunt followed. These two emperors showed remarkable fear and aversion for anything pertaining to magic, and took draconian measures. Ammianus Marcellinus reports a long train of enquiries, denunciations, cross-examinations and tortures, executions and *auto-da-fés*, carried out by notaries and agents of the state.[16] There were some cases in Rome itself. The prefect for 362-3, Apronianus Asterius, waged a bitter battle against the *mathematici*, the city's diviners and astrologers. According to Ammianus, he had developed a hatred of them because he had lost the sight of an eye when coming to Rome to take up his prefecture. He ordered searches, arrests, and executions which were carried out even in the middle of the circus. He had the charioteer Hilarinus accused of having entrusted his son to a magician to instruct him in the occult practices likely to make him win chariot races. Arrested, Hilarinus managed to escape and take refuge in a Christian church, but he was dragged from it and beheaded. After Asterius' prefecture, so Ammianus says, there was a return to laxity in these matters.[17] But Valentinian I resumed the repression. In 372, the young Lollianus, son of the former prefect Lampadius, was executed for the crime of practising magic. Yet even in the mid-fifth century, in his sermon on the Nativity, pope Leo the Great was still vituperating against Christians who lent any credence to astrology and asked diviners for predictions.

CHAPTER 8

The expansion of Christianity

– THE CHRISTIANS –

In the fourth century the Christian community was well established in Rome, and had been so for a long time. As early as the beginning of the third century, when addressing the pagans, Tertullian had been able to say not without some boastfulness, 'We are foreigners, but already we fill the earth and all your places – towns, buildings, palaces, Senate, Forums. We leave you nowhere but your temples!'[1] In the course of the fourth and fifth centuries, however, Roman Christianity experienced some divisive arguments, which, even if of small importance when compared with the conflicts raging in the eastern churches, nevertheless allowed certain minorities – such as Manichaeans, Arians and Novatians – to maintain a presence in the city.

The Novatian community in Rome had their own bishop and met in several churches. The sect developed from a disagreement at the time of an episcopal election in the mid-third century, and was distinguished from the Nicene church by a very special severity with regard to penitence. In the end, however, the Novatian church was suppressed, shortly before the Manichaeans, by Pope Celestine (422–32).

Manichaeism had been born in the third century in Persia, from the preaching of Mani. It was a derivative of Zoroastrianism, the official religion of that empire. Its dualist thinking influenced eastern Christians to the extent of spawning a sect which spread as far as Africa, where Augustine was a follower for nearly ten years. At the end of the third century, Diocletian had embarked on their persecution, but they subsequently benefited from the 'Edict' of Milan's call for toleration of all religions. The Vandals' conquest of Proconsular Africa had doubtless caused an influx of Manichaean refugees to Rome in the fifth century. At all events, in 443 Pope Leo became aware of their influence, and had them and their leadership arrested. The inquiry enabled lists of followers to be seized, bringing new arrests. After the trials, those who repented had to do penance, whereas those who persisted were sentenced to perpetual banishment.

Confronted by a Roman episcopate anxious to root out such sects, Arianism, as elsewhere, proved one of the toughest. Arians had been in a minority in the west until the settlement in the fifth century of the Goths and Vandals, who had been evangelised by Arians. For example, the patrician Ricimer, who dominated the western empire in its last twenty years, was an Arian. Around 470, he had the church of S Agata dei Goti built on the Viminal for his co-religionists. Then, in the first part of the sixth century the bishops of Rome had dealings with the Arian Ostrogothic kings, but the latter were anxious to handle the city of Rome tactfully. The reconquest by Justinian later sounded the death knell for Roman Arianism, and above all that of Ravenna.

– THE BISHOP OF ROME AND HIS ENTOURAGE –

Between the fourth century and the sixth the Nicene bishop of Rome became the head of western Christendom. Indeed, Roman tradition made the apostle Peter the proto-bishop of the city. Consequently, unlike their colleagues in most other cities, Roman bishops were the successors of an apostle. That legitimised the claims of Rome and its bishop to exercise primacy over other sees. These claims developed chiefly from the second half of the fourth century, at a time when the bishop of Rome was beginning to be called *papa* – father. Verse inscriptions found in Rome considered the apostolic chair as a sacred source and summit. The holder of Peter's throne was regarded as the guide of God's people, a shepherd who guaranteed the unity of his flock, endowed with goodness and dispensing his teaching. Pope Hormisdas (514–23), it was said, healed the body of the homeland;[2] Boniface II (530–2) was hailed as gathering together the scattered sheep; Pelagius was praised for preserving the dogma; and Gregory for protecting souls from the enemy. As may be seen, certain pontifical virtues bore a strong resemblance to those which had been attributed to emperors or other great imperial figures. Their power was even made known by the use of Rome's traditional political terminology; for instance, an inscription describes Sixtus III as *episcopus plebis Dei* (bishop of God's people). Similarly Leo called himself the 'vicar' of St Peter: since Diocletian's day, the vicariate had been the administrative dignity of the governors of dioceses, and the right-hand man of the prefect of the city also bore this title. As for the epitaph of Gregory the Great, it uses the title of the most enduring and prestigious of the Roman magistracies: he is designated 'God's consul'.[3] Having come from both Peter and Paul, Rome's apostolic tradition was bipolar; yet, in the course of late antiquity, this very tradition was subject to significant evolution. Although Paul's influence on the ideology of the Roman church was clearly perceptible until the Constantinian era, it subsequently diminished to the advantage of Peter's. Elevated to the status of proto-bishop, the latter was invoked to support the hegemonic ambitions of the Roman see, especially from the time of Damasus' papacy. Paul had urged loyalty to the Caesars, and now they no longer lived in Rome; by contrast, the model of Peter allowed the bishop's political aura to increase.

The bishop of Rome was elected, and in this election the college of priests and deacons played a fundamental role, while the people either accepted or rejected their choice. Sometimes the opinion of neighbouring bishops, such as that of Ostia, was sought. Once elected, the new bishop was consecrated, on a Sunday, in the Lateran basilica. He enjoyed great power, but in theory made his decisions only after the deliberations of his counsellors, assembled in a synod. In addition, he had himself represented on councils, or on embassies, by legates who, with a few rare exceptions, were priests of the Roman church, like Claudianus and Vito at the Council of Arles in 314, or Vito and Vincentius at the Council of Nicaea in 325.

From research carried out by Charles Pietri, it appears that the bishop of Rome in the fourth century had an annual income of some 30,000 *solidi* and possessed about half a tonne of gold in the form of liturgical vessels.[4] Although he could freely enjoy the sums collected from the faithful, the income from Church properties was allocated to the churches to which they belonged. During the fourth century, the increase in church possessions and in episcopal decisions brought about the need for an episcopal administration. It seems that this pontifical chancellery was created by Liberius. By the late sixth century, the pope had become the administrator of all areas of Roman life.

As early as the mid-fourth century, even before Christianity became the only religion upheld by the state, the bishop of Rome enjoyed an eminent position at the heart of Roman society. Jerome records a famous jest by Praetextatus, one of the leading figures of the nobility who had stayed pagan: 'Make me bishop of Rome, and I will turn Christian right away!' This jibe is none the less significant, indicating that the episcopal seat was worthy of the rank of an *illustris*, even if its revenues were much lower. The conjunction of nobility and episcopate did not come about, however, until the fifth century, but, by the middle of the fourth, the episcopal dignity had already attained such brilliance that Ammianus declared he was not surprised by the animosity that could grip competitors at election times. In his view, 'The contestant who wins is sure to become rich through the gifts of aristocratic ladies, to ride in comfortable carriages, to dress splendidly, and to serve feasts on a scale fit to rival the tables of kings.'[5] Ammianus reproaches the bishops of Rome for this luxury, for he thinks that they should take their inspiration from the modest example of colleagues in other cities.[6] But in the period when he was writing his *History*, at the very end of the fourth century, the church of Rome was already dominated by a clergy of patrician origins and supported by the lay heads of the great Christian families.

– ELECTORAL DISPUTES –

The election of Damasus (366)

The succession to Pope Liberius gave rise to a violent conflict which set the supporters of the deacon Ursinus at loggerheads with those of the arch-deacon Damasus until 371. In 366, following Liberius' death, the followers of Damasus attacked the basilica of Sicininus in which their adversaries had blockaded themselves. Among them were circus factions and gravediggers, summoned by Damasus to fight for him. Climbing up onto the roof, they removed tiles which they hurled down inside onto the Ursinians. Ammianus Marcellinus says that this dramatic episode ended in 137 deaths; an anti-Damasan text from the *Collectio Avellana* makes that 160.[6] Exasperated by this urban rioting, the prefect Viventius preferred to withdraw to his country house. Damasus took advantage of this to set the prefecture's police against his adversaries, whom he had banished from Rome. But Ursinus' partisans did not disarm, and re-organised themselves, occupying a church.

The conflict of 418–19

Twenty-four documents from the *Collectio Avellana* give us information on the serious conflict aroused by the succession to Pope Zosimus, who died on 26 December 418.[7] Three days later, the prefect of the city, Symmachus, a nephew of the great Symmachus – sent a report to the emperor Honorius. In this he announced that, once the death was known, he addressed the people and corporations of Rome, as well as the *vicomagistri* of the districts, urging them to make efforts to keep the city calm; but a disagreement erupted immediately. On one side, the archdeacon Eulalius was conducted by part of the people and clergy to the Lateran, where they spent two days, apparently in accordance with regulations, before proceeding with the election of Eulalius. However, at the same time, another section of the people and some priests had assembled in the church of Theodora, to elect the priest Boniface. Anticipating disruption and violence, Symmachus brought the two claimants together and asked them to follow the customary procedures scrupulously, but Boniface's supporters took him to the *titulus Marcelli*, on the Campus Martius, there elected him bishop and took him in procession to St Peter's basilica. Symmachus ended his report by asking the emperor's advice.

The latter replied from Ravenna on 6 January 419, acknowledging in his letter the validity of Eulalius' election, and pardoning Boniface's supporters provided that Boniface was exiled from Rome. As soon as they learned of these measures, they addressed a request to the emperor. According to their account, Eulalius in fact besieged the Lateran with deacons, priests and a crowd of troublemakers. By contrast, in their eyes Boniface was a man filled with outstanding qualities, formally elected by seventy priests and nine bishops. Honorius was persuaded by this message; he annulled his previous decision and, to obtain the fullest information, summoned the two adversaries to Ravenna on 8 February. Furthermore, he ordered a council to be held in Spoleto on 13 June. In the meantime, it was understood that Eulalius and Boniface must refrain from living in Rome, and that Easter was to be celebrated in the city on 30 March by the bishop of Spoleto, Achillaeus. However, this last letter did not reach the prefect of the city until the evening of 18 March, whereas the disturbances had broken out at midday. In a letter of 23 March addressed to the future emperor Constantius III, who was by now the most powerful individual at Honorius' court, the prefect reported that, unbeknown to him, Eulalius had entered Rome during the day of 18 March, escorted by an armed mob. Symmachus tried to calm them down by making a speech, but was unceremoniously driven back, together with the *vicarius*, as far as the Forum of Peace. At that point some slaves, similarly armed, attacked the Eulalians. When he heard this item of news, Constantius sided against Eulalius, whom he ordered to leave Rome, but he did not obey, and gathered his supporters at the Lateran on Easter Eve. The prefect's men had to evict them by force, and Boniface was officially recognised by the emperor as Zosimus' successor.

This turbulent episode shows that papal successions were not always achieved in a climate of serenity. It bears witness to the strategic importance of one place, the Lateran, the city's first great Christian basilica and residence of the bishop, but also to the importance of one day, Easter, during which papal authority manifested itself through the celebration of baptism. In contrast, respect for the rules did not exclude resorting to force. Despite his goodwill, the prefect of the city seemed to be overtaken by events and, apart from some attempts to pacify the situation on his own initiative, sought rather to inform the court at Ravenna, asking for advice. The election of the pope had become an affair of great importance in Rome, involving the opinions of both laymen and clerics. Anxious to maintain public order, and wanting to ensure that such events did not recur, Honorius issued a new edict in 422. Henceforward, if two successors came to be elected, each by his partisans, both would be driven from the city.

The succession to Anastasius (498)

A sign of the times, in 498 a member of the Symmachan family was elected to Peter's see. This election provoked challenges causing a nine-year schism in Rome. There was an anti-pope, Laurentius, whose supporters intended to bring Symmachus to trial, accusing him of various misdeeds, but the latter's partisans concocted forgeries to prevent them. It was from one of those apocryphal writings, the *Constitutum Silvestri*, that there developed the legend of Pope Sylvester healing the emperor Constantine of leprosy and subsequently baptising him. Moreover, this papal conflict reflected deep-seated political rivalries. Laurentius had the backing of the emperor Anastasius in Constantinople, while Symmachus was supported by Theoderic, the Gothic king at Ravenna. The latter succeeded in driving Laurentius out of Rome in 506.[8]

– CONFLICTS WITH EMPERORS –

In late antiquity there were a few cases of disputes between emperors and bishops of Rome which, though rare, deserve a mention. They were also similar, in that the emperor was determined to have a decision approved that the bishop of Rome refused to recognise. In 356, for instance, Liberius refused to condemn Athanasius, the champion of the Nicene arguments in the east, although the Arian emperor, Constantius II, had asked him to do so. In the face of this refusal, the emperor ordered the prefect Leontius to have him arrested. In 526, king Theoderic sent Pope John I to Constantinople to plead the cause of the Arians, but John was a convinced Nicene and the mission failed. Theoderic held him responsible and had him put in prison, where he died. In 543–4, Justinian wanted Pope Vigilius to recognise his condemnation of Monophysite texts. Judging the emperor's demand too Nestorian, Vigilius refused, and, in January 547, he was carried off by order of the emperor, taken to Constantinople and illegally confined. Until 554 he endured exhausting and repeated pressure to draw up a text in keeping with the emperor's wishes. He composed several, but retracted on various occasions without doing what was expected of him. He died in 555, during his return journey to Rome.

– THE CLERGY –

The number of men dedicated to the church in fourth-century Rome was not large. Among some 800,000 inhabitants of the city, of whom some tens of thousands were Christian, there were at most a few hundred people who had enjoyed fiscal immunity since the time of Constantine. They were to be found either in the immediate entourage of the bishop of Rome, or allocated to religious services in the titular churches. Each of these had at least two priests, a number which rose to three in 419. As there were twenty-five *tituli* in Rome at that time, the number of priests appointed to them fluctuated between fifty and seventy-five. They were assisted in their ministry by clerics belonging to minor orders. Acolytes brought from the Lateran to their titular church a piece of bread, the *fermentum* consecrated by the bishop, which the priests then used for consecration. Lectors, whose title appears in inscriptions in 338, conducted liturgical celebrations.[9] The bishop appointed them by handing over the Holy Book to them. At the same rank were the exorcists, whose task was to drive out demons prior to a baptism. In all, then, about ten clerics assisted the priests, which means that each of the twenty-five *tituli* had about a dozen clerics, giving a total personnel of 300 people, not counting the deacons, sub-deacons and priests forming the papal curia, among whom the archdeacon played an eminent role. It was from the city's priests and the curia that popes chose their legates to represent them, for example, at councils. Ages varied greatly: epitaphs show lectors aged from nineteen to sixty-three, and deacons from thirty to eighty.[10]

There were seven deacons and seven subdeacons, whose duty, in each of the seven districts, was to administer ecclesiastical property and collect money from the faithful in order to display the proceeds on the Lateran's seven altars so that they could be offered on Sundays to widows and the poor. Priests, by contrast, were ordained by bishops by the laying on of hands. They were the only ones allowed to celebrate the eucharist. In the Church of Rome, therefore, there were two career paths, one leading to a diaconate, the other to the priesthood; this was an original feature, different from that found in the eastern churches.

Pope Leo the Great paid the closest attention to the recruitment of the clergy, which in his time was carried out more strictly and according to a precise career structure. The minor orders of acolyte and lector were indispensable to gain access to a subdiaconate, diaconate and priesthood. This strictness resulted in the new emergence of a cultured ecclesiastical élite. Moreover, while the Roman population dwindled in number during the fifth and sixth centuries, the rising number of church foundations meant that the ecclesiastical structure regularly increased in size. In the early fifth century, there were some hundred priests for 800,000 inhabitants; one hundred years later, there were three times as many for a population that had declined to fewer than 300,000 inhabitants. The proportion of ecclesiastics thus increased significantly, conferring on clerics a mounting influence over the Roman population.

It is noteworthy that the clergy, including bishops, were allowed to be married, and many were. Damasus was the son of a bishop, and Anastasius of a priest; Leo the Great was married; Gregory the Great, at the heart of the Anicius family, was the great-grandson of Pope Felix III. Celibacy was subsequently imposed only by the triumph of a monastic tendency in clerical discipline.

– ASCETIC CIRCLES –

Athanasius, bishop of Alexandria, who stayed in Rome in the middle of the fourth century, played an all-important role in the birth and development of asceticism in the city. Indeed, he taught the Romans about the lives of St Anthony and St Pachomius, the great founders of eastern monasticism. These accounts exerted such fascination on Christian noblewomen that a number of them opted for a simple and secluded life. While secretary to Pope Damasus, Jerome frequented and taught a group of ascetic women who met in an aristocratic house on the Aventine. Paula, Marcella, Eustochium and Blesilla became his friends, and he continued to correspond with them even after he left Rome and settled in Bethlehem in 385. They wore modest clothing, fasted, prayed, studied the Scriptures and practised charity. Some did so in rather radical fashion, like the young Blesilla, who died from excessive fasting, meaning that such behaviour attracted the disapproval of noble families. Fabiola, for her part, founded a *nosokomion* around 380, which was the first hospice for the sick in Rome.[11]

Born in the eastern empire at the same time as male monasticism, female monasticism arrived in Rome much later. In the fourth century, only Asella created an embryo of community life on the Aventine. Women chose virginity, and received the veil, which consecrated it, from the hands of the bishop. They publicly renounced earthly marriage in favour of a mystical marriage with God, choosing a life of abstinence, based on chastity and frugality. In Roman society, virginity had connotations not merely of childhood but also of the legal status of celibacy and the virtue of a deliberately chosen sexual abstinence.

In the mid-third century there were 1500 widows of the Church in Rome. They formed a special category, but one which was not an entirely clerical order. Jerome and inscriptions praise non-remarriage as much as the choice of chastity. Quite a few of these women were very young, and pledged their widowhood to their children and God. Like the poor, they benefited from the Church's practical assistance, and like the dedicated virgins, formed a sort of lay apostleship.

Originating in Egypt and Syria in the late third century, monasticism had developed in the east during the fourth century. The first monastic foundations in the west took place in the second half of that century and in the beginning of the fifth, notably in Gaul, but urban monasticism was more timid. Certainly, the life of women practising asceticism in the home or in their country residences bore some resemblance to the monastic way of life, but was different because it was not communal.

The first mention of a monastic foundation in Rome is datable to the pontificate of Sixtus III (432–40). Indeed, the creation of a monastery *in catacumbas*, that is, near S Sebastiano, the church with a burial ground that lay farthest from the city, is attributed to him. Under his successor, Leo, other foundations followed, for example, the monastery of SS John and Paul. Hilarus was the first pope to found a monastery within the city walls, on the site known as *ad Luna*. This seems also to have been the first to be conceived of independently of a basilica, and possessed its own oratory. Monastic communities installed in the vicinity of the suburban *martyria*, for example St Peter, S Paolo fuori le Mura and S Lorenzo fuori le Mura, soon saw residential areas grow up around them. At that time the number of monks in the city of Rome increased remarkably, to the point where they sometimes came into conflict with the clergy on the occasion of papal elections. Gregory the Great, who had been a monk, maintained a sympathetic attitude towards the monastic life, but for reasons of ecclesiastical discipline opposed its clericalisation, prohibiting baptism in monastery chapels. During his pontificate, the advance of the Lombards precipitated an influx of refugees to Rome, 3000 of whom were women from convents.

THE PATRIMONY AND REVENUES OF THE ROMAN CHURCH

Constantine ordered the restoration to the Roman church of the possessions that had been confiscated from it during the persecutions of 303–11. To this property were added donations from the imperial family and wealthy citizens. Furthermore, Constantine authorised the church to receive gifts. During the fourth century, and even more in the following centuries, that enabled the Roman church to amass a patrimony in coin, precious metals, furnishings, buildings and land, with the additional bonus of tax exemption. Take, for example, the Constantinian basilica of the Lateran: the emperor had presented it with its balustrades, seven golden altars and patens, an altar and a precious chalice and, for lighting, candelabras and large *metretae* to hold oil. He gave it land in Sicily and Campania, which guaranteed it an annual income of 4390 *solidi*. As for the baptistery, that received estates on the Appian Way, in the Sabine region and Africa, obtaining for it an income of 10,234 *solidi*. He guaranteed the other basilicas an income varying from 700 *solidi* (Sta Agata) to 7700 *solidi* (church of the Labicana). Compared with the imperial donations, those of the bishops of Rome were modest: 255 *solidi* for the *titulus* of Sylvester, and 145 for that of Mark.[12]

In the second half of the fourth century, the heritage of the Roman church could be assessed at one tonne of gold and six of silver in the form of sacred vessels, lamps, censers and liturgical gold and silverware. At a time when one tonne of gold equalled 119,400 *solidi* the annual income from the church of Rome's properties was about 26,000 *solidi*. Compared with the quantities of gold handled by the Roman aristocracy – where the estimated annual income of the less wealthy *clarissimi* was between 80 and 90,000 *solidi* – these sums appear modest. These riches came principally from income from landed properties granted to the church, around half of which were scattered through Italy, and the rest overseas. It has been estimated that the land revenues presuppose property of between 4000 and 5000 hectares. In addition, from their properties situated in the east, the Roman churches received papyrus, flax, pepper, saffron and cloves, much of which was most probably sold. This regular income was increased by gifts, donations and the proceeds of collections. In the sixth century, however, the Roman church's landed wealth came to grief as Spanish, African and Gallic possessions were lost. Nevertheless it remained the foremost landowner in Italy, with estates in Etruria, Romagna, Liguria, southern Italy, Sicily and Sardinia. These were run by the papal administration which, moreover, supplemented or replaced failing civil institutions. By the end of the sixth century, it was looking after the *annona* and even the payment of troops stationed in the city.

A taste for wealth among certain clerics is discernible from the sources. In a law of July 370, Valentinian I accuses clergy of appropriating the inheritances of widows and orphans, and prohibits them from receiving legacies. The period of Damasus witnessed the blossoming of luxurious tastes in a Roman church where clerics increasingly came from wealthy circles. Those who were critical, like the priest Macarius, ran the risk of being beaten up. Damasus himself was accused of being the 'earpick of great ladies'.[13] Jerome, whose position as the former secretary of Damasus did not restrain him from blunt criticism, made no secret in his letters some time later of his exasperation with clergy who were worldly socialites, with curled hair and concerned with the elegance of their clothing.[14]

− PRACTISING CHARITY −

The gradual conversion to Christianity of the aristocratic strata of Roman society during the fourth and early fifth century led rich Romans to practise the evangelical duty of charity. This manifested itself chiefly by almsgiving and visiting the sick. Thus, in the early fifth century, we see Melania and her husband doing the rounds of the sick, taking in and feeding passing strangers, helping the poor, visiting convicts in prisons and mines, and paying off what was owed by those who had been imprisoned for debt.

Some did this in an ostentatious and hypocritical way, such as the Roman matron whose actions Jerome described in a letter to Eustochium, but whom he is wary of naming. During his stay in Rome, Jerome reports, he had witnessed a scene that had outraged him: this woman had presented herself at St Peter's basilica escorted by eunuchs, and had given a coin to each poor person. An old woman covered in rags, who had already received one, rejoined the queue in the hope of getting a second. The noble matron hit her in the face so hard as to make her blood run. Is that, asks Jerome, how one should show charity?[15]

− LITURGY AND WORSHIP −

True entry into the community of the faith presupposed the observance of sacraments, the first being baptism. Not all Christians were baptised, however: the crowning point on the road of faith, this sacrament had to be earned, and required a way of life in pursuit of saintliness. It was therefore not given to small children unless they appeared in danger of dying, though Roman epitaphs show that, in a context of high infant mortality, this was quite frequent. The most widespread case was that of the baptism of adults, notably on their death bed, *in extremis*. Baptism was a major act of faith, and candidates went through a period of preparation of just under three years. They were the subject of inquiries, followed a course of doctrinal education that was verified by grading tests, and were exorcised. They underwent three examinations during Lent. These candidates were called catechumens and prior to baptism could attend the first part of Church services, the liturgy of the Word.

In Rome, baptisms took place for the most part on Easter Eve, chiefly in the Lateran, which was lit by over 100 lamps, lanterns and gold and silver candelabras. The catechumens had to pass an evening in prayer, publicly recite a profession of faith and renounce the devil; following which, they received the sacrament by immersion in the baptistery's font. After unction from the priests, they received anointment with oil from the hands of the bishop, who traced the sign of the cross on their forehead. They were then admitted to the Mass, where they were offered a chalice of wine, milk and honey. The newly baptised, called neophytes in the fourth and fifth centuries, would be clothed in white during Easter week. Funerary inscriptions sometimes mention the status of the deceased: 'Catechumen', like Bonifatius, who died at over sixty in 397: 'Neophyte', like Junius Bassus, who died on 25 August 359, at the age of forty-two, while he was prefect of the city.[16] The baptised were known as 'the faithful', and their baptism was mentioned by verbs – *accipere, percipere, consequi* – indicating that they had received the grace of God and accepted the faith. Let us take the example of young Severus: born on Easter Day 457, he had been given the usual name *Pascasius*, derived from *Pascha*, the Latin term for Easter. His epitaph shows that he had received baptism on the eve of his sixth birthday, before dying and being buried a week later on 28 April 463.

> Pascasius by name, [and] born one of the Severi on the day before the Nones of April, the day of Jupiter, in the consulship of the *clarissimi* Flavius Constantinus and Rufus. He lived six years, received [baptism] on the eleventh day before the Kalends of May and, wearing the white of Easter week, was laid in the tomb on the fourth day before the Kalends of May, in the consulship of the *clarissimus* Flavius Basilius.[17]

The baptised continued their training and had to follow a rigorous way of life, strictly in keeping with the Gospel. Those who strayed from this line were sentenced to expiate their sins for several years, or even their entire life, after publicly doing penance. The expiation, consisting of fasting, prayer and almsgiving, could end by the sacrament of penance, which could be given only once in a lifetime. The penitents were then admitted to the reconciliation, which took place in Rome on the Thursday preceding Easter.

In late antique Rome, the Greek word *synaxis*, meaning 'meeting', was still used to designate the liturgical office. Up to the Constantinian period, the *synaxis* assembled small communities in the *tituli*. The building of churches and basilicas on a large scale enabled the Roman church to impart new grandeur and solemnity to its liturgy. Thus processions developed, in imitation of pagan ceremonies, of which there were three during the *synaxis*:

at the introit, the offertory and the consecration. Unlike in eastern churches, the Roman altar was placed before the chancel and the priest officiated facing the faithful. The first part of the service was called the Proper, in which texts, extracts, epistles and gospels were read. Choosing them had been the subject of intensive selection and allocations: passages from the Scriptures were chosen for every day of the year. Such ritualism was well and truly Roman. Reserved for the baptised faithful, the eucharistic part was next opened by the Preface, which dismissed the catechumens. The priests consecrated the bread and wine with a fragment of bread, the *fermentum*, brought by acolytes from the episcopal church, and symbolising the church's unity. The term *fermentum* meant the yeast which caused bread to rise. It must be interpreted here in the figurative sense, as the yeast of the consecration and mystery of the Last Supper, transforming bread and wine into the body and blood of Christ.

In the Roman *synaxis*, Greek had at first been the liturgical language, but was superseded by Latin during the fourth century, not only because it was the vernacular but doubtless also because the theological use of Latin was expanding during that period. It has been said that liturgical Latin, a learned, stylised priestly language, placed 'Roman gravity in the service of the expression of the sacred'.[18] For this reason, the word *missa* (whence the English word *Mass*) belatedly supplanted that of *synaxis*. It was uttered at the end of the office to dismiss the faithful. Semantically, the *synaxis* assembled the Roman Christians, henceforward, the 'Mass' sent them out into the world.

The part played by music in the expression of Christian piety must be emphasised. At first, music had provoked a reaction of rejection on the part of cultured Christians, as it had the connotation of secular rejoicings and pagan rites; but the chanting in synagogues and the Old Testament tradition of psalmistry probably influenced the birth in Rome of Christian chanting, free of such associations. In the reign of Constantine, Bishop Sylvester I founded a *schola cantorum*, intended to train the church's cantors. In the fourth century, hymns and psalms were sung. Jerome, who revised the psalter at Damasus' request, wrote that the young Blesilla sang psalms in Hebrew, as well as *the alleluia, modulata voce*.[19] This expression argues the case for a melodic chant. In the development of liturgical chant, much is ascribed to Gregory the Great, probably more than is his due: the roots of so-called 'Gregorian' chant went much further back than the date of its presumed creation in his pontificate. Gregory had the antiphonary perfected and rebelled against the excessive aestheticism to which chanting gave rise. Indeed, he complained in one of his letters that more deacons were recruited for their fine voices than for the extent of their knowledge.[20] But Jerome puts it well: as Nicenes – believers in the Triune God – it was only natural for the Romans to sing in unison. This unison, accompanying processions, expressing prayers, was a testimony to the unity of the Christian people.

Finally, it is noteworthy that, in the architecture of the great basilicas, the processions, the language, the liturgical rituals and vestements, 'Christian ceremonial drew largely on courtly sources.'[21] Christian liturgy was influenced not by pagan rituals, but by imperial protocol. Just consider the way in which bishops and saints are dressed in the sixth-century Roman mosaics – they bear a strong resemblance to senators.

IV

Saeculum: *Worldly concerns*

CHAPTER 9

Life and death:
Material civilisation and mental attitudes

− Food and famine −

As early as the second century BC, keeping Rome supplied with food had been a thorny problem. Its population was large, and neither Latium nor the neighbouring regions of Italy could by themselves provide for its enormous daily needs. The building of aqueducts between 312 BC and AD 225 had endowed the city with a considerable flow of water, but it was quite another matter for wheat, oil, meat and wine. The chief food consumer in the Roman world, the city thus received, during the 'open sea' months between April and October, supply convoys organised by the state to offset the inadequacy of private commerce in satisfying the city's requirements. The goods were stored in the *horrea* (warehouses) situated by the Tiber in the south and west of the city.

The founding of Constantinople, to which Egyptian grain was sent, gradually deprived Rome of one of its most important sources of supply. From the reign of Constantine onwards, the city became increasingly reliant on grain from Africa. Its transport was still the responsibility of the public service of the *annona*, which supervised its route from source to distribution point.

In the Romans' diet, it is estimated that three-quarters of the calories were provided by bread. The remainder came from meat and the produce of Latium and Italy, such as honey, eggs, milk products, vegetables and poultry. Supplies of wheat were therefore of capital importance.

− Bread distribution −

Romans could buy their bread from private bakeries. The poorest had to be content with that provided by the *annona*, which was at first sold at a reduced price, then from 369 distributed free.[1] For the better off, it formed a complement. In fact, the *annona*'s aim was not only social − to feed the poorest – but also civic – to feed Roman citizens. Those eligible to receive it were, of course, first and foremost those without means of subsistence, but they were not the only ones. In contrast, certain Romans were excluded from free distributions: for instance, among others, employees in public offices, senators and their slaves. During the fourth century, those eligible to receive the *annona* distributions formed a large *clausus* (strict quota) of 200,000 citizens.[2] Those who died or emigrated were replaced, within the limits of this figure, by drawing lots.

Romans did not get their *annona* ration directly from the bakers: indeed, according to a law of 365, it was even illegal to go and get it from a public bakery.[3] The eligible had to go to certain distribution points known as *gradus*. There were 117 in Constantinople, but it is not known how many Rome possessed. As its name indicates, the *gradus* was a tiered platform, where bakers daily carried out distributions, under the supervision of magistrates and scribes. In fact, each eligible person was inscribed on the list of a *gradus*. In theory, this list was engraved on a bronze table and affixed to the *gradus*. It bore the names of the eligible – the *incisi* – and the quantity of bread to which they were entitled, which varied depending on the size of the family. It is probable that each *incisus* had a *tessera*, or token, qualifying him to receive his bread, but that has not been verified. The public nature of the distribution – the *erogatio* – was highly important: it had to be made in the sight and knowledge of all, not only because the annona was a public service but also in order to avoid fraud.

Until 369, those who were eligible could buy at low cost twenty 1.35 kilogram loaves. When in that year Valentinian I instituted free distributions, rations fell to six 980 gramme loaves, but of better quality. As the number of *incisi* was 200,000 until 410, the *annona* may be estimated at two quintals of wheat per person per year, or a total of 160,000 tonnes of wheat, of which half was distributed gratis. Of course, the department of the *annona* was supposed to check the quality of the flour and bread by inspecting the bakeries,[4] but that mostly depended on the grain, and storage conditions were precarious. The bakeries produced three qualities of bread: white bread, which was of a superior kind, second-quality bread and, lastly, mediocre bread – *panis sordidus*. In 396, Symmachus harshly criticised Rome's bread: of execrable quality, it made people ill, and Symmachus thought eating it was worse than fasting.[5]

– Meat distribution –

The *annona* pork represented about 1000 tonnes per year. In 419, it was divided into 4000 daily rations, the *opsonia*, each of 5 pounds, or 1.6 kilograms. Texts of laws indicate that the distribution was carried out under the responsibility of an *erogator opsoniorum*, whose existence was still attested in the sixth century.[6] It did not take place throughout the entire year, but only during five months. The 120,000 eligible thus collected five monthly rations of 5 pounds. If the distribution was staggered, which seems likely, it means that 1600 recipients were served every day for 150 days. So a Roman family could have 25 lbs or 8 kilograms of pork each year, offered by the *annona* service. The needy were satisfied, while those with the financial means could buy pork, mutton or beef at the market price.

− OIL AND WINE DISTRIBUTION −

The olive oil consumed by Rome's inhabitants came from Italy, but also Tripolitania, Spain and Africa, which provided an annual *canon*. If we are to believe the *Historia Augusta*, Septimius Severus started free daily distributions, and Aurelian established the custom, like that of distributing meat. The laws of the *Theodosian Code* show that they were still going in the fourth and fifth centuries.[7] Until the end of the fourth century there were daily distributions, carried out in 2300 shops, the *mensae oleariae*. We do not know whether this oil, intended for both lighting and cooking, was sold or given out free.

Up to the Ostrogothic period, wine was sold at a low price by the state treasury under the porticoes of the temple of Sol. So that Romans could benefit from wine at 25 per cent of its price on the free market, a sum of money, the *canon vinarius*, was levied in central and southern Italy and, starting in 354, in northern Italy. This money, used to buy wine, was put into a fund, the *arca vinaria*. The wine arrived at Rome by boat in amphorae, and, as soon as they had been unloaded, the amphorae were opened and tasters tested the quality. If it was suitable, the wine was put in casks and stored or sold. Storing it allowed reserves to be built up in case of a shortage, for Romans became very bad-tempered when there was a lack of wine.

− SHORTAGES AND RIOTS −

Political and military vicissitudes sometimes cut the city off from its African granary, as happened, for instance, in 308–10, 383–4, 398–9 and 410–11.[8] It therefore had to diversify its sources of provisions and resort to Sardinian, Spanish and Gallic grain supplies. The *annona* was even more seriously upset by the Vandals' conquest of Africa between 429 and 439. Rome then had to fall back on the Italian peninsula and Gaul to meet its needs, which even if they were certainly diminished by comparison with earlier centuries nevertheless remained very large.

Keeping Rome supplied with cereals depended largely on the African *annona*, so the city felt the pinch very keenly when there were African problems. In 310, the usurpation of Domitius Alexander halted the grain convoys to Rome, and thus provoked a riot in the city. Maxentius put it down, but at the cost of 6000 lives, according to Zosimus.[9] In 328, the prefect of the *annona*, Naeratius Cerialis, imposed a contribution of 138,000 *modii* of grain on Campania, to make up for insufficient African deliveries.[10] In 356, there was a riot near the Septizodium, because of a shortage of wine. Despite the entreaties of his entourage, the prefect Leontius went there in his carriage. Part of his escort deserted him when they encountered the vociferous mob shouting gibes at the prefect. Keeping a cool head, the latter pinpointed one of the ringleaders, Peter Valvomeres, had him arrested, strung up and whipped, while the demonstrators chose to beat a retreat. The ringleader was later exiled to Picenum.[11] In 359–60, contrary winds caused a delay in the *annona* convoys coming from Africa. The disgruntled mob gave the prefect Tertullus a rough time and, to calm them down, he showed them his young children who were also suffering from these shortages. To ward off bad luck, he had a sacrifice performed in the temple of Castor and Pollux at Ostia.[12]

In 375, the former prefect Symmachus the Elder was driven from Rome when there was a dearth of wine and the mob set fire to his Trastevere *domus*. Why? He was no longer prefect, but he was a landowner, and a malicious rumour had been spread in the town that he had declared, 'Rather than sell my wine at the price they are offering me' – in other words, the public price below the market price – 'I would sooner keep it to slake lime.' He was recalled after a petition and decision of the Senate the following year.[13] In 384, during his urban prefecture, his son had to confront one of the major crises of the *annona* in the fourth century. The African harvest of 382 had been catastrophic, and the following year the empire had suffered a great drought. Symmachus expelled the *peregrini* from Rome, as Orfitus had done thirty years previously. He appealed to the emperor and managed to obtain a convoy of Egyptian wheat. In 388, because of a new shortfall in the harvests, the quantity of wheat imported to Rome proved inadequate, and the following year, contrary winds again prevented the transport of the *annona*, compelling the emperor to send Macedonian grain to Rome.[14]

The same problem arose in 397–8, at the time of Gildo's rebellion in Africa. Claudian says Rome was exhausted by a long scarcity of wheat and oil which, together with an epidemic and grave flooding, transformed it into a ghost town. Symmachus went so far as to despatch a letter to Stilicho asking for imperial aid.[15]

The years 408–10 were particularly gloomy. Alaric's first blockade of the city caused an initial famine, which cost the prefect Pompeianus his life in February 409 when he was murdered in the Forum during a riot.[16] In 409–11, rebellion against Alaric's puppet emperor, Attalus, by Heraclian, the governor of Africa, merely aggravated a situation already rendered precarious by the Goths' sieges of the city. As the African ports were blockaded, Rome no longer received either wheat or oil. The prices rose all the more dramatically because merchants hoarded and speculated. It was during this famine that the infamous cries rang out in the circus, addressed to the prefect of the city: 'Fix the price of human flesh!' (*pretium imponi carni humanae!*)[17].

– THE *ANNONA* IN THE FIFTH AND SIXTH CENTURIES –

Until the sack of 410, the Roman population had numbered roughly 800,000 inhabitants; and up to that period the *incisi* had stayed at around 200,000. According to recent findings, this figure fell to under 100,000 after the sack of the city, to rise again to 120,000 in 419, before experiencing a regular drop: 80,000 in 452, around 15,000 in 530. This fall was matched by the loss of provinces that had been indispensable to the *annona*, such as Africa, conquered by the Vandals between 429 and 439. In the sixth century, Rome no longer needed a contribution from overseas provinces, but its 60,000 or so inhabitants still made it the largest city in the west, and an important consumer centre; so the *annona* did not disappear. At the time of his visit to Rome in 500, King Theoderic added an endowment of 2000 rations of wheat, which was modest in comparison with the figures of earlier centuries, but must have formed a far from negligible contribution.[18] The Ostrogothic kings feared Roman rebellions, and the praetorian prefects, such as Cassiodorus, saw to it that the prefect of the *annona* scrupulously carried out his duties of inspection and control. At that time wheat came from Sicily, while meat, as before, came from southern Italy, and wine from the north of the peninsula.

From the late fifth century, the bishop of Rome played a growing part in keeping Rome provisioned. Indeed, the *Liber Pontificalis* mentions that Gelasius I saved the city from famine during his pontificate (492–6). Rome experienced many difficulties during the war between the Goths and the Romans of the east, as prices rocketed in the many sieges to which it fell victim. It was doubtless at this point that the church's granaries began to play a decisive role. At the end of the conquest, Justinian's *Pragmatic Sanction* maintained the system of the *annona*, but Procopius is the last source to mention the public granaries.[19] The church had thus taken the *annona* under its wing. In this regard, the situation under the pontificate of Gregory the Great (590–604) is unequivocal. Gregory managed the church's granaries, which he filled with products levied by the *defensores* from the ecclesiastical estates situated in Italy, Sicily, Sardinia, Africa and Gaul. The wheat was sent to Rome at the end of the summer under the responsibility of the *rector patrimonii* of the Roman church, requisitioning the services of merchants. The wheat fund – *arca frumentaria* – formerly under the aegis of the Senate, was henceforward the responsibility of the pope. The latter, like the emperor of Constantinople, who continued to endow the Roman *annona*, could allocate supplementary sums to obtaining provisions: for example, Gregory paid 3600 *solidi* to buy a wheat supplement.[20] It seems that his successor Sabinianus (604–6) put an end to the free *annona*. When Rome was hit by shortages under his pontificate, he sold the wheat from the church's granaries instead of giving it out free. It was an unpopular move, and in 606, Sabinianus' funeral cortège had to make a long detour to carry his remains to St Peter's basilica in order to avoid angry demonstrations by the Roman people.

If we consider the figures available to us and the assessments that can be inferred from them, the state took charge of almost half the food requirements of poor Romans, or those on a low income. The very poorest depended entirely on the rations of the *annona*: around 200 kilograms of bread and 8 kilograms of pork annually, with free oil, and wine at the public price. The more comfortably off, perhaps, saw it as a welcome free or low-priced supplement. Lastly, the better-off *incisi* found it a source of goods which they could redistribute to their clients, their household staff and slaves. From this point of view, the *annona* certainly played a role in maintaining a large population in Rome.

– MEDICINE –

Until the reign of Valentinian I, there were only three public doctors in Rome. By 'public' we must understand doctors who were paid, not by their patients, but in public *annonae*, namely the doctors of the Xystus, the Vestals and Portus, and that there were others attached to trade corporations. It is true that in this respect Rome was less well endowed than the other cities in the empire. Indeed, in the middle of the second century, Antoninus Pius had issued a rescript authorising cities of Asia Minor to recruit several public doctors, on the decision of the local *ordo* of decurions. Their number was set at five or seven, depending on the city's population. In exceptional circumstances, the largest cities could recruit ten, but that would concern hardly more than three or four centres in the empire. By this measure Antoninus had extended a Hellenistic custom of having municipal doctors, the *archiatroi*, and this name was preserved for them in the text of the rescript, Latinised into *archiatri*.

On 30 January 368, in a letter addressed to Praetextatus, prefect of the city, Valentinian I decided to create fourteen posts for *archiatri* in Rome, or one for each of the city's districts.[21] The emperor's intention is made quite clear in the text: these *archiatri* had the mission of tending the poor without charge, and they were prohibited from swelling their income by making rich Romans pay for consultations. Their method of recruitment was clearly laid down in another edict, dated 10 March 370.[22] A hierarchichal order had to be strictly followed, and the fourteen were classed according to seniority. If a post became vacant through death, those who followed went up one step and the newly elected took the fourteenth place. An infringement of this practice created a scandal in 384, because Theodosius had wanted to introduce a certain Iohannes at the same rank as the doctor who had died.[23]

Rome's *archiatri* were certainly less well paid and less conspicuous than those attached to the imperial palace, but under the law they benefited from fiscal privileges, chiefly in exemptions from duties.

This institution had a remarkably long life, surviving the end of the western empire, and it appears that Theoderic kept it going during his reign (493–526). It then went out of fashion for about thirty years, but, when Justinian had reconquered Italy, he re-established the fourteen *archiatri* in Rome and their public *annonae* in his *Pragmatic-Sanction* of 554. It is in this period that the presence of certain deacons among the doctors is noticeable.

Alongside the public doctors were 'private' ones who accepted fees, even though the exercise of a liberal art was supposed not to be venal. Their consulting rooms were much frequented by Romans who could afford their services. According to Jerome, they were even 'the ultimate salon where one can have a chat'; he was grumbling, as he often did, about those at a loose end who spent their time gossiping in waiting rooms.[24]

– DRESS AND SOCIAL STATUS –

In Chapter VI of the 14th book of his *History*, Ammianus Marcellinus settles his scores with the population of Rome. As he pursues his long indictment, he lists their failings and vices, at every level of society. He starts by denouncing the pretensions of the rich and powerful who have themselves immortalised in statues. He next criticises their luxurious and ostentatious lifestyle: their carriages, which are higher than ordinary carriages, their long cloaks with trailing fringes and their tunics with multicoloured embroideries depicting animals, which they move sinuously with a gesture of their left hand. In the ceremonial garb of senators, the time of the traditional toga was long past. The immense semi-circular piece of white material, arranged in clever drapery with the help of slaves, had been replaced by the stitched tunic with sleeves, which constricted the body less. Bas-reliefs, mosaics and ivory diptychs show us that the toga had not completely vanished. Now more simple, it was worn over the tunic, like a long, rectangular shawl wound round the chest and back to end in a final fold over the forearm. It remained the distinctive sign of the senatorial nobility.[25]

Criticisms similar to those of Ammianus can be found in his contemporary, Jerome, who in his letters enjoys decrying the sartorial snobbishness of Roman men and women. Young people had their hair carefully combed, and wore linen. From Jerome we learn more about feminine toilette, mentioned six times in his letters. His stay in Rome, when he had been in the company of women of the Roman aristocracy – to the extent that his enemies' tongues started wagging – had allowed him to be a privileged observer of female elegance. Thus through him we know that Roman ladies outlined their eyes in black with antimony, and painted their faces with carmine and white lead. They sometimes tinted their hair red, had it waved or arranged in braids, holding them in place with a diadem. In the second half of the the fourth century it was also considered very smart to bring the hair forward over the forehead and the ears, the latter being pierced to take jewellery. Thanks to Jerome's criticisms, whose detailed descriptions were intended to convey violent disapproval of excessive attention paid to the body, we know too how Roman women liked to dress. They wore crimson or white garments, with narrow, close-fitting sleeves. The fashion was for a seamless tunic, leaving the shoulders bare, which women covered with a mantilla. Their breasts were confined by strips of cloth and supported by a gathered sash. On their feet, Roman women wore gilded clogs or leather bootees that creaked when they walked. All this interest in appearance, of course, is cited by Jerome as the height of affectation, a worldly snare which he reproves with the utmost acrimony. These beauties formed only a limited contingent, but they were part of the society from which his wealthy ascetic female friends originated.[26]

– SEXUALITY –

In the second part of the twentieth century, Roman sexuality has been the subject of studies as original as they are remarkable. However different they may be, those of Michel Foucault, Aline Rousselle and Peter Brown all present us with the incontrovertible conclusion that, starting in the fourth century, Roman society experienced a powerful trend of 'renouncing the flesh', 'controlling the body' and even 'sensory deprivation'. The question is whether this was the result of Christianity alone. After all, Greek philosophical tendencies and those of the Romanised 'oriental' cults advocated this self-control over the body, the former so as not to yield to the passionate excesses of the flesh, supposedly leading to dissoluteness, and the latter to avoid a state of pollution. As early as the second century, a doctor such as Soranus of Ephesus was advocating sport as a way of diverting the young from love, while the emperor Marcus Aurelius practised abstinence. Besides, we should remember, as Paul Veyne has emphasised, that a certain amount of reserve in sexuality went well with the concept of *gravitas* and *dignitas* of the Roman senatorial circles, so it was not a novelty when the Christians, in all their diversity, advocated such a reserve fairly rigorously.[27] Moreover, Christians directed as much disapproval to sexuality as they did to gluttony. The more flexible among them condemned only excess, recommending moderation; the more radical, influenced by monastic asceticism, condemned even satiety as an excess, and advocated a struggle with the body, which could be subdued only by privation.

If we are to believe the district records, Christian Rome in the fourth and early fifth century had forty-six *lupanaria*, run by *lenones*. No text mentions a ban on these brothels, whereas those in Carthage were closed by Arian Vandals, so Salvian of Marseilles tells us. Among the characteristics of the city, therefore, Prudentius evokes its scented brothels with their foul rooms, designated as such not because they were dirty, but because of the erotic pictures decorating the walls. There was no attempt, however, on the part of Christians in Rome to close them down, only indignation. The reason is perhaps because the Church's main preoccupation was with the conduct of Christians, who were in constant danger of falling into sin, without any claim to regulate that of non-Christians. What was a sin for a Christian was part of the normal order of things for a pagan, so pastoral activity concentrated on conversion. One has only to recall a popular saying recorded by Augustine: 'Let him do it, he's not baptised yet'. It was mainly by becoming a catechumen that one entered the moral framework of the Church.

– ROMAN MARRIAGE, CHRISTIAN MARRIAGE –

Pinianus and Melania provide a good example of the matrimonial customs of Christian Roman nobles. It was the parents who arranged the marriage of their children, and Melania was married, at the age of fourteen, to her cousin Pinianus, who was seventeen. This age was not unusual. Epigraphy reveals the very early ages at which marriage took place, and the life of the young Hilaritas, as evidenced by her inscribed epitaph, is fairly typical. Affianced at the age of eleven, she was married seven years later; her conjugal life lasted seven years and she died at the age of twenty-five. She was buried on 16 August 390 in the cemetery of Commotilla.[28]

Devoted to asceticism, Melania wanted to remain chaste in her marriage, but Pinianus, imbued with the values of their social circle, wanted to have children to ensure the continuance of his family line. The couple worked out a compromise: they would choose continence after the birth of a child. A little girl was born of their union, and her virginity consecrated. As patrilineal continuity was thus not assured, Pinianus insisted on a second child although Melania wished to remain chaste. When she again became pregnant, her second confinement was difficult. Weakened and very upset, Melania, who was still not yet twenty, made her husband swear that they would remain chaste from then on. Scarcely had she recovered her health when their daughter died.

Summed up in this way, the early married life of Pinianus and Melania teaches us a great deal. From the demographic viewpoint, we can pick out close-kin marriage, the early age of marriage, and the depletion caused by infant mortality. From the anthropological viewpoint, we may remark the masculine desire to perpetuate lineage and, in Melania, the importance of the value of chastity, which was due to religious teachings. Moreover, we have to acknowledge that a Roman wife, with the extra endowment of a decisive temperament, was not absolutely under her husband's thumb. The young couple also remained under the authority of their parents, whose permission they sought to lead an ascetic life. This was refused, however, and the parents' motive throws light on the mental attitudes of the nobility. Melania's father was less afraid of seeing her health decline than of being the target of reproaches from pagan senators. He died when Melania was about twenty, and his death released her from obedience to him. She and her husband left Rome for a villa in the neighbourhood of the city, to lead what Gerontios calls 'her angelic life'.

In the view of the Scriptures, marriage was not to be discredited by Christians – quite the reverse. It was even the guarantee of chastity, whose prime definition was sexuality within marriage, and in many inscriptions we find young couples described as *virgines*. A number of clerics and bishops were married, yet were in no way considered slaves of the flesh. On the contrary, marriage could seem a bastion against temptation. By contrast, the remarriage of widowers and widows was ill regarded, and even condemned. To dissuade one of his female correspondents, Jerome showed great severity, at the same time waxing eloquent about the many disadvantages of marriage, including squalling brats. The discrediting of matrimonial union, with its connotation of fleshly union, must be imputed to monastic radicalism, which increasingly influenced Christianity from the late fourth century. As regards adultery, Christianity was in harmony with Roman legislation, which condemned it. In the time of Maxentius,[29] a prefect of the city was sentenced to exile on a charge of adultery. In the 340s, the emperor Constans made it a capital crime, on a par with homosexuality and abduction.

– ROMAN ATTITUDES TO DEATH –

– CEMETERIES AND TOMBS –

Romans practised inhumation and buried their dead outside the *pomerium*, though they were not obliged by law to do so in communal cemeteries. Everyone could build a tomb where they liked, as long as it was outside the walls, so burials formed cemeteries around the periphery of the city, especially along the roads. They were not enclosed areas more or less hidden from sight, but impinged directly on the major thoroughfares. The traveller arriving at Rome therefore paid an obligatory visit to the society of the dead before passing through the city wall. He could admire the mausolea and tombs, run his eyes over the stelae or carved epitaphs which were often directly addressed to him. In this way cemeteries and their inscriptions formed a connection between the dead and the living.

Roman legislation made burial a *res religiosa* or religious matter, violation of which was a crime. A law of 28 March 349, for instance, ordered the prefect of the city, with the help of pontiffs, to keep an eye on the tombs and cemeteries under Rome's authority.[30] Epitaphs even contained threats regarding possible violators; in late antiquity, these threats became violent imprecations, even curses, wishing death and a tombless grave on any who might dare to make the attempt. Nevertheless, despite the respect for the dead evinced by the Romans, some of the cemeteries were overturned when major works were being carried out, notably on the Aurelianic defence wall and St Peter's basilica. From the late second century and early third century, Christians began to have their own cemeteries.

Many Romans sought to acquire or build a tomb during their lifetime. Well aware of their own mortality, they therefore paid out, some for a *loculus* (small casket or receptacle), some a sarcophagus, some a *cubiculum* or an *arcosolium* (funerary chamber), according to their financial means. It was doubtless a sign of pride, for the epitaphs do not forget to mention that the tomb was paid for *de suis propriis*, that is, at one's own expense. The deceased thus continued to live in *his* house, the inscription bearing witness to his right to ownership, which had been properly acquired from the *fossores*, whose duty it was to maintain and administer the cemeteries. As their activity included some of the aid given to the poor, in the fourth century they were exempted from the *chrysargyron*, the tax falling every four years on tradespeople.

The family tomb was a Roman tradition which continued in late antiquity, but from the early fourth century the cult of saints became so popular that more and more Christians wanted to be buried near to them. A feeling of belonging to another family, of the communion of Christians and saints, was thus grafted onto the ordinary spirit of family.

The day of death was rarely mentioned on the epitaphs. One or two days, in exceptional cases more, separated deaths from burial. A pagan custom was to hold a funerary banquet, which the living came to celebrate at the tombs of the dead. To keep the latter from torment, they were brought food and drink which were introduced into the tomb by way of a tiny barred window. This custom was known as the *refrigerium*, 'refreshment', for it was supposed to refresh the dead. Christians in Rome practised this too, mainly in the second half of the fourth century. They went in a group to the tombs of their nearest and dearest or of revered martyrs; there they ate and drank, praying to God to grant happiness and blessing to the deceased. *Graffiti* known as 'proskynemes' bear witness to these *refrigerium* meals, such as at the *triclinium* of the cemetery *ad catacumbas*.[31] This custom came to an abrupt end in the late fourth and early fifth century when bishops attacked its excesses and pagan aspects.

− THE CATACOMBS −

Several received ideas about the catacombs used to be, and still are, prevalent: the first would have it that they were places for clandestine worship of a scarcely tolerated, not to say persecuted, Christianity at Rome in the early empire. Although this false notion has been attacked many times, it is still alive, and I have to dispel it once again. In fact, the Roman catacombs, which have been the subject of numerous studies, some of them very recent,[32] were not places of worship but cemeteries. Their generic name 'catacombs' is derived from the generalisation of the place-name *ad catacumbas*, which designated a Christian necropolis on the surface of the ground, situated on the Via Appia. Another erroneous theory consists in thinking that the use of the catacombs corresponded only with the 'primitive', pre-Constantinian phase of Roman Christianity. Far from it: archaeology and epigraphy provide formal evidence that the catacombs underwent their most important development during the second half of the third century and chiefly the fourth, and that burials took place there until the early sixth century. In the catacombs, the dead were wrapped in a shroud and placed in horizontal rows of recesses in the walls known as the *loculi*. These were stopped up with a thin marble or limestone partition, or with tiles sealed with terracotta. On these partitions the funerary inscriptions were carved, though a good many *loculi* had no epigraphy. Lastly, the catacombs were not the only Christian cemeteries. There were others in the open air, known as *subdiales*, and during the fifth century these became the majority. A little over sixty early Christian cemeteries have been listed around Rome, and four Jewish cemeteries.

THE *MEMORIAE* OF
THE MARTYRS AND BURIAL *AD SANCTOS*

Starting in the fifth century, Christians greatly altered their funerary customs and consequently the topography of burial, becoming increasingly keen in Rome as elsewhere to be buried near the tombs of saints and martyrs. Indeed they believed that a holy corpse diffused virtues which might be instilled into their own remains, so plots situated in the *martyria* and their vicinity were greatly coveted. Relics, the object of veneration from the second half of the fourth century, were kept in churches, so a real revolution took place during the fifth century: the dead began to be interred in churches situated within the walls.

It was Pope Damasus (366–84) who gave the decisive impetus to establishing a cult of martyrs in Rome. In some fifteen tombs situated outside the walls on the periphery of the city, he had poems – *carmina* – placed in their honour. He had them carved by the finest Roman calligrapher of his time, Filocalus, the very man who had created the famous codex known as the *Calendar of 354*. This act was accompanied by various rearrangements which embellished and 'monumentalised' the tombs, resulting in attracting the piety of ever-increasing numbers of pilgrims between the late fourth and late sixth century. The tombs of St Peter and St Paul were the most honoured in Rome, of which they were now the patrons.

– THE EXPERIENCE OF DEATH –

While literary texts are certainly the major sources for a study of Romans' feelings regarding death, there can be no doubt that epitaphs are the most concrete and direct source. Rome's epigraphic corpus is immense: more than 65,000 inscriptions, 25,000 of them Christian, have been found and listed. In the nineteenth century, the latter were collected in a monumental anthology by Gian Battista De Rossi. This collection, called the *Inscriptiones Christianae urbis Romae*, or the *ICUR*, was continued after his death, and now amounts to seven volumes. Of these inscriptions, eight out of ten are funerary, and provide a rich source of material to study Roman perceptions of death.

Nevertheless, in the case of many inscriptions, it is impossible to say whether they are pagan or Christian. In fact, the cultural fundamentals were the same, and many Christian epigraphs make use of the traditional imagery of pagan literature. In the epigraphic corpus of the third century, Christian inscriptions were still in the minority. In contrast, their number increased throughout the fourth century, whereas pagan inscriptions grew fewer. They were intended to perpetuate the *bona memoria* (good memory) of the deceased, at the same time inviting the living to pray for them, thereby both testifying to the past and looking to the future.

Study of the words in the funerary inscriptions enables one to obtain a reasonably complete idea of the way in which Romans regarded death. In the first place, there is the regret of the living for the death of persons who were dear to them. Grief is aroused by the separation, mostly of spouses, but also of children and parents. Their sorrow is accentuated by listing the qualities of the deceased, such as the innocence of children, or the kindness and uprightness of adults. The epitaph for one child, Boethius, who died in 577, reveals the heartbreak felt by his mother Argenta: 'Because of your death, your mother wanted to die: she would have been happy (she says) if she could have joined you.' In the event, she did so less than a month later.[33] Death was therefore looked upon first as a halt, a departure, even an abduction in the case of children or sudden death. It was undergone as an element of fate or God's will, which took away light. Thus Christians and pagans alike addressed a last farewell to the dead, a paradoxical *Vale!*, sometimes accompanied by a consolatory phrase 'No-one is immortal!' or 'Take courage!'

But once the moment of grief had passed, Christians were distinguished from pagans by hope. For the latter, death was a plunge into an eternal sleep which, for people influenced by Greek philosophies, might be a return to the stars, to the ether, or to the sky. In pagan ways of thinking, life was a loan, a debt to the Parcae (the Fates), to *fatum*, to *fortuna*, settled by a death regarded as a return. This concept of ephemeral life handed back was not alien to Christians nourished on Scripture. In Christian epitaphs, too, especially the *carmina* after the middle of the fourth century, one finds Orphic, Platonic or Stoic influences in a dualist conception of the soul and body. Death freed the soul from corporal ties and chains; the soul could attain the divine world, whereas the body joined the earth. In this instance, death could be perceived as rest and liberation, an idea shared by pagans, Jews and Christians.

For Christians, however, death also meant a new birth: the day of death was regarded as a *dies natalis*. For them, baptism guaranteed entry into the Kingdom of Heaven and death a rebirth in Christ who washed away sins. Thus the verb *vivere* – 'to live' – is almost ubiquitous in Christian epitaphs. With immortality of the soul, we touch on one of the fundamental points of Christian eschatology. As is indicated in a *carmen* attributed to Pope Celestine, 'Earth now covers what is earthly, while the soul which is unaware of death, lives and consciously rejoices in the presence of Christ.'[34] Death was only that of the body, resting in the slumber of peace; but the soul was received into the light of Christ.

In the study he has devoted to the Christian epitaphs of Rome, Jos Janssens has noticed different trends between laity and clergy. Lay inscriptions tended to have more classical themes, closer to pagan perceptions. In contrast, those of the clergy revealed far more Christian beliefs, in particular the immortality of the soul waiting for resurrection and eternal life. In fact, according to the Christian faith, the soul was destined to return to the body at Judgement Day. So says the epitaph of Gregory the Great: 'The earth shall give up the body when God restores it to life.'[35] While awaiting the Second Coming, a sojourn of bliss with God and His saints rewarded the soul of anyone who had done good on earth. The soul lived in God, *in Christo*, in celestial light and peace. Here, perhaps, we have one of the fundamental differences from pagan ideas about death. For pagans, life meant light, and beyond the tomb lay a realm of shadows; for Christians, it was almost the opposite, as death brought light in the next world.

CHAPTER 10

Transforming the calendar

The evolution of the Roman calendar is a major feature of the city's history in late antiquity, and demonstrates that there was no sharp break but, on the contrary, a slow modification. Its chief characteristic is the gradual superimposition of Christian time on pagan time. Until Dionysius Exiguus worked out a specifically Christian computation in the sixth century, the calendar had been a hybrid affair, reflecting the overlapping of pagan and Christian traditions. There is one outstanding document in evidence of this – the beautifully calligraphed codex called the *Calendar of 354*, executed by Filocalus for an *illustris* of the city named Valentinus – and in it we find not only the festivals and games of the old republican tradition, with imperial anniversaries, but also the Christian festivals, including those of the martyrs.

– MARKING TIME –

Several centuries after the birth of Christ, the Romans had still not perfected a computation of the Christian era, so the points of reference used to date events were traditional, and their large number enabled datings to be pinpointed more sharply. The oldest, of course, was the foundation of Rome, and up to the sixth century chronicles were still using this point of departure.

Since the republic, Roman consuls had been eponymous magistrates, which means that their two names had been used to date the year in which they had held office; this system of dating was used as a major reference point until the end of the ordinary consulate in 541. It must be noted that in the fifth and sixth centuries there were some years when there was one consul only, and even some with no consul at all. For example, the year 477, which had none, was known as 'the year after the consulate of Basilicus and Armatus'. The same thing happened in 531, 532 and 536. After 541, inscriptions and chronicles resumed the practice of years without consuls, establishing the use of dating by postconsulate starting from the last, Flavius Anicius Faustus Albinus Basilius Iunior.

The indiction was a year for taking an inventory of land in order to establish the basis for the land tax, the *iugatio*, imposed by Diocletian. The interval between two indictions was initially fixed at five years, but in 312 was extended to fifteen. These periods were used for counting up years, and the word indiction tended to take on another meaning – that of the period in between.

The Romans used the century – *saeculum* – as a unit of time. It formed an interval of 110 years between the games that were known, for this reason, as *saeculares* – secular. The last secular games had been held at the beginning of the third century, so, according to the calculation of the years, it was incumbent on Constantine and Licinius to hold the games at the time of their third consulate, in 313, but they did not do so. Zosimus reproached them for it, and blamed Rome's later misfortunes on this failure to observe tradition.[1]

– THE DURABILITY OF THE TRADITIONAL CALENDAR –

The Romans followed the Julian calendar, which Caesar had had established during his dictatorship by the Egyptian astronomer and computator, Sosigenes. It was a solar calendar, dividing the year into twelve months and adjusting it every four years by doubling up the sixth day – *sextilis* – of the kalends of March, namely, 23 February. In this way the divergence from the astronomical calendar was reduced to a minimum.

The term 'Roman calendar' must not mislead us. It was not a calendar that would have been followed throughout the empire; on the contrary, there was a multiplicity of calendars, often peculiar to individual cities, such as that observed at Alexandria. By 'Roman calendar' we must understand the one that was in use in the city of Rome.

– THE MONTHS AND THEIR DIVISIONS –

The twelve months bore the name of deities or traditional festivals (Janus, Februus, Mars, Aprilia, Maia, Juno), of emperors (Julius, Augustus), and their place in time (seventh, eighth, ninth, tenth). They are represented by allegories in Filocalus' illustrated *Calendar of 354*.

The year began on 1 January, the date when the consuls took up office, and the months contained 28, 30 or 31 days. Each day had a corresponding letter, from A to H, thus defining the cycles of eight days, the intervals between markets, the *nundinae*. Each day was numbered by counting backwards from the kalends (the first day of the month), the nones (which fell between the fourth and seventh day of the month) and the ides (roughly in the middle of the month). However, tradition was not devoid of innovation, and it is fairly certain that, as early as the first century, days were beginning to be given the names of planets. The way time was reckoned in Rome was not only traditional, but also traditionalist. An examination of the chronological points of reference demonstrates this: although new reference points were invented and established, the old ones were by no means abandoned. A movable calendar table that was discovered in an annexe of Trajan's baths, but is lost today, had been incorporated into a church during the late period. It was evidence of a desire for a variety of ways of enumerating the days. Indeed, notches in it allowed movable parts to be inserted showing the day of the lunar month, the zodiacal sign and the planet giving its name to the day. The designation of any given day could therefore be made following three criteria: lunar, astrological and planetary.

Through epigraphy, another innovation can be dated to the fifth century – fixing the day by its numerical order. It was found on a fragment of an inscription discovered in the cemetery of Domitilla: DIES XX MENS – that is to say, the twentieth day of the month. This fragment means that, in Rome, people had begun to move away from the traditional enumeration of the days of the month. Instead of working in reverse by numbering so many days before the kalends, nones or ides, they were calculating the days from the first to the last of the month.

– THE HOURS OF THE DAY –

Hours were numbered in the same way as in the times of the republic and early empire. An hour was the twelfth part of the day, so its value varied continually, and it equalled our sixty minutes only twice a year, at the equinoxes. At the winter solstice, an hour was shorter, about 45 minutes, but, at the summer solstice, it was longer, about 75 minutes. In late antiquity, Christians' perception of a day differed from that of the Roman tradition. For Romans, as for us today, a day extended from midnight to midnight, or from the twelfth hour to the twelfth hour. In contrast, for Roman Christians a day finished when the sun set, at which point another day began.

The passing of the hours could be shown materially by sundials and *clepsydrae* (water clocks). On the campus Martius there was a *gnomon*, a giant sundial laid out in the first century AD on the ground on an area of 110 x 60 metres, and with an obelisk as its pointer. In the fifth century, the construction of the church of S Lorenzo in Lucina encroached on the pavement of the *gnomon*, which had been useless for a long time. Even so, the technological know-how was not lost: in 507 Boethius, who was then

Magister officiorum, was ordered by Theoderic to devise a sundial and a *clepsydra* for the king of the Burgundians.

– CHRISTIAN TIME –

Contrary to an idea spread by folklore enthusiasts, the Roman episcopate did not seek to Christianise pagan festivals. Instead, it helped to establish a Christian year which tended to compete with and marginalise them. In the eyes of educated Christians time belonged to God, its Creator and Master. The bishops of Rome, like those in the provinces of the Roman empire, undertook to make the march of time fall in line with the periods and festivals of the Christian liturgical calendar. During the fourth and fifth centuries a calendar of saints was thus established, and in 336 a calendar of the year's festivals was fixed.

The *Calendar of 354* includes in its *Depositio martyrum* a list of thirty-five martyrs, mostly Roman, whose twenty-two anniversary dates are recorded, together with their place of burial. It contains also the anniversary date of the burial of twelve bishops of Rome from Dionysius, who died in 269, to Julius, deceased in 352, nine of whom were buried *in Callisti*, the cemetery of Callixtus.

With meticulously carved metrical inscriptions, Pope Damasus honoured some fifteen additional martyrs, whose tombs, marked by oratories, formed a sort of diadem around the city. The Roman calendar continued to be compiled during the fifth and sixth centuries, and additions were made to the anniversary tables in the *Calendar of 354*. The catalogue of saints feast days known as the *Martyrologium Hieronymianum* took its inspiration from it, and in return inspired later additions. Thus in the time of Gregory the Great the Roman Church had available a comprehensive list, in which nearly all the martyrs were named for each day, and Masses were celebrated in their honour.

– THE WEEK –

Rome is certainly one of the places where the earliest references to the 'week' can be seen. The possibility of pagan or Jewish influences has been the subject of conflicting arguments. Jewish influence is undeniable; indeed, from long tradition the Jews uniquely lived their lives in periods of seven-day weeks. This had derived from the seven days of the Creation, the first ever hebdomad, and ended in the Sabbath, a day of obligatory rest and fasting. This particularly Jewish custom was already well known in Rome at the time of Augustus. The hebdomadal rhythm of the Sabbath may even be said to have had an influence that spread widely beyond the synagogue alone, not only over Christians but also over Romans as a whole. In the second century, Christians

Table 10.1 **Combination of pagan and Christian elements in the Calendar of 354**

	Mens Augusti		Month of August	
1	N. D. Pertinacis C.		Birthday of Emperor Pertinax (193)	
2		D. Stephani		Burial of Stephen
3				
4	Victoria Senati. Circenses		Victory of the Senate. Circuses	
5	Natalis Salutis. Circenses		Birthday of Salus. Circuses	
6		D. Xysti		Burial of Sixtus
7	N. D. Constantii C.		Birthday of Constantius II	
8	Ludi Votivi		Votive Games	
9		D. Secundi, Carpofori, Victorini et Severian		Burial of Secundus, Carpoforus, Victorinus and Severianus
10		D. Laurenti		Burial of Laurence
11				
12	Lychnapsia		Festival of lamps (Cult of Isis)	
13	Natalis Dianes		Birthday of Diana	
14		D. Ypoliti		Burial of Hippolytus
15				
16				
17	Tiberinalia		Festivals of the Tiber	
18				
19	N. D. Probi C.		Birthday of Emperor Probus (276–82)	
20				
21				
22		D. Timotei		Burial of Timothy
23	(Ludi) Vulcanalici. Circenses		Games of Vulcan. Circuses	
24				
25				
26				
27				
28	Natalis Solis et lunae. Circenses		Birthday of the sun and moon. Circuses	
29		D. Hermetis		Burial of Hermes
30				
31				

whose origins lay in Judaism still observed the Sabbath. In his *Apologia*, Justin tolerated this practice, but asked that newly-converted Gentiles should not be subjected to it. It was quite a different matter in the fourth and fifth centuries, when observing the Sabbath was likened to a heresy. Nevertheless, fasting continued to be encouraged on the Sabbath day, as on the Friday which preceded it. Unlike the eastern provinces, Italy and Rome had therefore eliminated Sabbatical celebration from Christianity.

	Mens Septembris		Month of September
1			
2			
3			
4			
5	Mammes vindemia		Grape harvest festival (Cult of Liber)
6		D. Acinti	Burial of Acintus
7			
8			
9	N. D. Aureliani C.		Birthday of Emperor Aurelian (270–5)
10		D. Gorgoni	Burial of Gorgonus
11	Natalis Asclepii		Birthday of Asclepius
		D. Proti, Iacinti	Burial of Protus and Hyacinthus
12	Ludi romani		Roman Games
13			
14		D. Cypriani	Burial of Cyprian
15			
16			
17			
18	N. Traiani		Birthday of Emperor Trajan (98–117)
19	N. Pii Antonini C.		Birthday of Emperor Antoninus Pius (138–61)
20			
21			
22		D. Basillae	Burial of Basilla
23	N. Divi Augusti C.		Birthday of the Divine Augustus
24			
25			
26		D. Eusebii	Burial of Eusebius
27	Profectio Divi C.		Departure of the Divine Caesar
28	(Ludi votivi)		Votive games
29	Ludi fatales		Games of the Fates
30			

In Roman: Roman festivals   *In Italics: Christian festivals*

Between the third century and the fifth, Christian bishops tried to draw a distinction between Christianity and paganism or Judaism in their organisation of time. This was achieved by departing not only from the practice of keeping the Sabbath but also from astrological concepts, which were very much in fashion between the second and fourth centuries. But they did not depart from the number seven, which matched the original hebdomad and the seven archangels, and also the seven stars and planets. It would appear that the custom of naming the days of the week originated in Egypt in the early third century.

The eight-day nundinal cycles, still mentioned in the *Calendar of 354* but in actual fact falling into disuse, had been replaced by hebdomadal cycles of seven days and this transformation had begun during the early empire. In the week itself, the days first received a number known as a *feria* replacing the old letters. Thus, after Sunday, which was regarded as the first day of the week – the day of creation – Monday became the second *feria*, and so on until Saturday the seventh. This usage is retained in Portuguese from Monday to Friday, which are known as the second to sixth days. The choice of the word *feria* to designate each day of the week and year thus corresponded with a Judaeo-Christian conception of time: since time belonged to God, every day could be looked on as a feast day or holy day.

During the empire, however, the habit had prevailed of attributing a planetary quality to the days. They were in fact given names inspired by those of the planets – the Moon, Mars, Mercury, Jupiter or Jove, Venus (the new name for Lucifer), Saturn and the Sun – and these names are retained in French, Italian and Spanish, for example. The fairly rare references in Christian inscriptions and texts to the planetary names of the days should not be regarded as a concern with astrological matters or even as a pagan survival. Educated Christians from the third to the fifth century were very anxious to refute popular astrology. In their view the stars had no effect at all, direct or indirect, on the elements or mankind, but planets and stars had been arranged by God to help men calculate time. Of course, the planets had the names of pagan deities, but Christians had distanced themselves from such things, so planetary nomenclature could be used without any suspicion of idolatry. However, the days of the week are rarely mentioned in inscriptions. Their use mainly reflected an emotional echo when a death, for instance, had occurred on a particular holy day. This was the case of a child, Aurelius Melitius, whose epitaph shows that he died *die Saturni Pascha:*[2] the Paschal Saturn's day was Holy Saturday, the eve of Easter Day, a special moment in the Christian year, because baptisms were held then.

In one of his treatises, Boethius places above all forms of music the *musica mundana*, in other words the inaudible harmony of the heavens, the earth and the planets. Influenced by Plato and Pythagoras, he established an equivalence between the seven celestial bodies (the Moon, the Sun and five other planets) and the scale of notes. He maintained that the seven days of the week were ordered in accordance with this scale, each of the days being separated by an interval of a fourth or fifth.

– SUNDAY –

It is widely held that Sunday, *dies dominicus* – the Lord's day – was instituted by the emperor Constantine, but that is not so. The first mention of the

Lord's day in a Latin text can be found in Justin's *Apologia*, which dates from the mid-second century. It corresponded with the *dies solis*, day of the sun. Christians had chosen this day for their assemblies because it was the day when the world was created, the day when Christ was resurrected and the day of Pentecost. True, the popularity or Manichaeism and the cult of Mithras, as well as the institution of the cult of the Unconquered Sun – *Sol Invictus* – by Aurelian, between 270 and 275, had helped to favour the day of the sun – *dies solis* – as the focus of the week. Indeed, even in the mid-fifth century, Pope Leo the Great was still censuring Christians for turning to greet the rising sun while they were standing on the forecourt of St Peter's.

Sunday for Christians was less strict than the Sabbath was for Jews. Texts that mention it make it a day of communal joyfulness rather than one given over to rest, and it is significant that they use terms such as *laetitia*, which denote Rome's secular rejoicings. Now, however, such celebration focused on the creation of the world and the Easter mystery of the Resurrection. This communal joy was intended to make a distinction between Christian people and those who were non-Christian. Constantine's well-known law relating to Sundays is dated 3 March 321, and is addressed to the *vicarius* of the city, Helpidius. It asked judges, the trades *corpora* and the populace in general not to work on the *dies solis*. Farmers in Rome's countryside were exempt from this obligation because of the imperative need for work in the fields. The object of the law was to avoid the occurrence of activities liable to be unworthy of a day devoted to God.[3] On 3 July following, Constantine authorised exceptions to be made for the freeing of slaves and the emancipation of children.[4] According to Constantine's proscriptions, then, Sundays were therefore not really 'days off': the only activities to be suspended were those deemed incompatible with the dignity of the day, such as trials or circus games. Forced labour was also banned, so as to enable the labourers and slaves to attend church in the morning and rest in the afternoon.

After Constantine the *dies solis* became the *dies dominicus*: indeed, a law of 3 November 386 mentions the *dies solis* as being customarily called *dies dominicus* in religious rituals.[5] Liturgical use thus imposed its term for this day on the profane world, and that is one of the striking signs of the way in which time became Christianised, and also of the pre-eminence of liturgical time in the Christian concept of the year.

– CHRISTIAN FESTIVALS –

At some date before 336 the Roman Church issued a *feriale*, a calendar of the year's festivals and feast days. Of course, it contained the most important highlights of Christianity, such as Easter, Pentecost and the

Nativity, but also the feast days of saints. The *Calendar of 354* made use of this catalogue and expanded it to include a list of the anniversary days of the burials of bishops, and one of the burials of martyrs. Later on, Damasus added some fifteen names of martyrs, establishing their tombs. As churches were built, they were allotted to one festival or another, and thus in Rome there developed a liturgical topology known as 'stational', whereby a certain festival would be celebrated at a certain place. Among many examples, we have the celebration of Christmas at St Peter's, and of Easter at the Lateran.

It is in the *Calendar of 354* that, for the first time, the Nativity is attested as a festival on the date of 25 December, but it was already included in the 336 *feriale*. The first celebration of the Nativity at St Peter's that we know about took place during the pontificate of Liberius, when Ambrose of Milan's sister received the veil of consecrated virginity.

Veneration of SS Peter and Paul occupied an eminent place in the Roman Church's calendar. On 22 February was the festival of *natalis Petri de cathedra*, celebrating Peter's teaching in the city, and Rome's two proto-martyrs were jointly celebrated on 29 June.

– ANNIVERSARIES OF THE MARTYRS –

The day kept for celebrating the martyrs was their burial date. The *Calendar of 354* includes a list of the *depositio martyrum*, which accompanies that of the bishops, the *depositio episcoporum*. Remarkably, the celebrations of martyrs' feasts followed a rhythm which managed to fit in the essential activities of rural life with those of religious life; thus none occurred between February and April, the period for ploughing and sowing. Similarly, the Easter period was completely free of them. The *Calendar of 354* locates the saints' tombs and invites the faithful to pilgrimage and prayer. Devotions to the saints were performed chiefly in the summer, so of the twenty-five anniversaries of the martyrs recorded in this document thirteen fell between July and September.

– COMPETITION WITH THE PAGAN CALENDAR? –

The day of *natalis Petri* was also that of the old festival of Caristia, when Romans traditionally paid homage to their dead, but this is no more than coincidence. The institution of a Christian calendar which played an increasingly lively part in the rhythms of life at Rome resulted in its competing with and, in the course of time, engulfing the old calendar. Here we touch on a major point in the metamorphosis of Rome between the fourth and sixth century, in that urban space was not the only area encroached upon by Christianity. We have already seen how a large number of Christian edifices was built both inside and outside the walls, and that together with these developed processions, pilgrimages and stational religious services. But occupying time, too, was an important matter: 'the conquest of time' was a basic requirement if a truly Christian Rome was to be achieved.[6]

When studying the chronology of the process by which Rome succumbed to Christianity, we may quite rightly note that space was conquered before time. Whereas Constantine gave the first impetus in both areas, his successors, up to Theodosius, were chiefly concerned with closing the temples and scrupulously helping with the construction of Christian basilicas. It would appear (although this is a hypothesis that needs to be checked by research which still remains to be done) that the conquest of time was a concern that emerged from a more belated awareness. Fifth-century popes, in particular from Leo to Gelasius, realised that the calendar preserved the rhythms of the old pagan festivals, such as the Lupercalia, and they wanted to be rid of them.

If the pagan and Christian elements of the *Calendar of 354* are super-imposed, it is noticeable that some pagan and Christian festivals fell on the same day: for example, on 15 January the commemoration of the burial of Marcellinus took place on the day of the Carmentalia, while on 22 February Christians celebrated the *natalis Petri de cathedra*, and pagans the Caristia. In March the burial of Luke was celebrated at the same time as the *navigium Isidis*, and that of the martyrs Perpetua and Felicitas during the *Lunonalia*. In all, there were fourteen times during the year when the feasts of paganism and Christianity coincided.

– Celebrating Easter –

Easter Day was the culmination of the Lenten fast. During that time, which was devoted to prayer, catechumens who were candidates for baptism underwent examination. On Holy Thursday, penitents, like Jerome's friend Fabiola, were reconsecrated, and then on Easter Eve the faithful would assemble in the Lateran basilica. During the all night vigil, those catechumens who were to be initiated into the Church would receive the sacraments of baptism and communion. The initiation was followed on Easter Sunday, the supreme day of rejoicing, with great celebrations.

Easter, then, was the major festival of the Christian year, the occasion not only for the celebration of the Paschal mystery and the Resurrection, but also for baptisms in the Rome of late antiquity. Yet when it came to fixing the actual date for Easter, chaos reigned among Christian communities. Its origins lay in the Jewish Passover, which was fixed on the fourteenth day of the month of Nisan, the first month in the lunar year; but since the Christians followed the Julian, and therefore solar calendar, discrepancies soon arose. It became the custom in Rome to celebrate Easter on the first Sunday after the full moon following the spring equinox which, in Rome, was 25 March. In Alexandria, the centre of astronomy and computation, however, Easter was celebrated at the full moon following 21 March. These divergences had created a gap between the churches, as Easter could be celebrated a month apart in Rome and Egypt. Besides, the movability of the festival could cause it to oscillate between 22 March and 25 April, so the dates of Easter had to be calculated in order to establish a paschal cycle. The *Calendar of 354* includes one such cycle. It begins in 312, at which date bishop Miltiades reorganised the Roman Church in the wake of the persecutions carried out under the Tetrachy, and in its original form it continued up to 358. Then, at a later stage, additions were made to the cycle, extending its calculations down to 410.

– THE CALCULATIONS OF DIONYSIUS EXIGUUS –

In 525, the pontifical chancellery entrusted a monk, Dionysius, who was well known for his computing abilities and his knowledge of Greek and Latin, with the task of putting forward a date for Easter that might win universal acceptance. He advocated the adoption of the Alexandrian calculation, but that had been based on the reign of Diocletian, which began on 29 August 284. Although in Christian eyes Diocletian had been a persecuting emperor, the Alexandrians had retained this system of computation for convenience. Since Dionysius probably had some scruples about getting the Roman Church to adopt it, he worked out a new computation based on the birth of Christ. He thus established an equivalence between the first year of the Christian era and the 754th year of Rome. However, he omitted the scriptural reference according to which Herod the Great had died during Rome's 750th year, Jesus having been born a few years earlier. His calculation, set up in 526, was therefore already out by some years, but could be used as a point of reference. Its application, basically intended to establish Easter Day, took a long time to gain acceptance and was not put into effect before the seventh century.[7]

CHAPTER 11

Festivals and entertainments

– TRADITIONAL FESTIVALS –

If, then, late antiquity was the period when Rome became Christian, it did so by way of a gradual metamorphosis, to which, as we have just seen, the calendar of its festivals bears remarkable witness. The rites and festivals of Roman religion, which Christians were beginning to call 'pagan', were still very much alive during the fourth century. Although the laws aimed by Gratian and Theodosius at pagan worship certainly caused them serious upset, such festivals continued to be celebrated throughout the fifth century, revealing a notable loyalty to these ancient cults. Here again, contrary to a widespread misconception, Christian festivals did not replace pagan ones, but were interspersed among them, adding their dates to those of the old festivals. The calendar of fourth- and fifth-century Roman festivals was therefore a combination, and it was only in the late fifth century that Christian festivals tended to gain a monopoly.

The *Calendar of 354* clearly shows the juxtaposition of the ancient festivals with those of Christianity. It is a traditional calendar, including pagan festivals that date back to the republican era, and adding some new elements. Imperial anniversaries were the signal for about a week of votive games – *ludi votivi*. Nine imperial victories were also celebrated, all preceded by five days of *ludi* and one of *circenses*.[1] Imperial celebrations alone thus represented a little over sixty days of games in the calendar. If one adds the games, *ludi et circenses*, that for some thirty days accompanied twenty-odd festivals in honour of various deities, one arrives at a total of ninety-days-worth of games. To this must be added those given by magistrates, quaestors, praetors and suffect and ordinary consuls. In other words, Romans in the mid-fourth century had between 100 and 120 days of the year when they could go to the amphitheatre or the circus, an average of one day out of three. From this we may infer that the games were little short of an addiction!

– THE CIRCUS AND THE GAMES –

First under the republic, and then under the empire, the Romans had spread a taste for circus games all around the Mediterranean. This popularity, or even fervour, did not flag in late antiquity – quite the reverse. Even modest-sized towns possessed an amphitheatre, and the larger ones boasted a hippodrome as well. The new fourth-century capitals, such as Trier and Constantinople, had one, based on the archetypal model of Rome's Circus Maximus.

Games were presented by magistrates taking up office or by benefactors. An entertainment greatly appreciated by the populace, games were nevertheless a political lever for the Roman élite. In Rome the holding of games followed the traditional yearly calendar, that is, of religious festivals, for some of these were accompanied by games; for example, the festival of Cybele, with the Megalesian games, or of Apollo, with the Apollonian games. One of the most important dates in the Roman calendar was 21 April, the *Dies natalis Urbis*, the anniversary of the founding of the city, which was regularly commemorated. On that day the suffect consuls presented the games. Others, such as the praetorian or consular games, were given by magistrates entering office, for instance. In addition to the regular games were those given in exceptional circumstances, such as the Secular Games, held only once a century.

December and January were the peak times for games in Rome. On 8 and 20 December, candidates for the quaestorship presented theirs. In the same month, the fiscal *arca* offered them, in place of quaestors without the financial means to do so: from 4 to 6, then on 19, 21 and 23 of the month. Until the early fifth century, they consisted of gladiatorial combats.

The praetorian games took place from 1 to 7 January. The praetors presented wild animal shows in the amphitheatre and chariot races in the Circus Maximus. On 3 January, in the middle of these games, the *vota publica* to the emperor were proclaimed. Games were also held in Constantinople, but those in Rome hugely surpassed them in the amount of expense involved and the scale of the spectacles. Roman aristocrats accumulated the sums necessary for their sons' praetorship for many years before the day came. Symmachus' letters show that he was preparing several years ahead for the praetorship of his son, Memmius. He wrote to the Spanish horse-breeders who had been recommended to him, in order to buy good runners; he complained about delays, and corresponded with dealers in wild animals. When his son eventually became praetor in 400–1, Symmachus paid out 2000 gold *librae* for his games. Such vast expenditure was not unique: Petronius Maximus spent 4000, around 412, and Probus 1200 in 423–5. This obligation to raise enormous sums for praetorian games gave rise during the fourth century to the custom of appointing future praetors several years in advance, so that, during the intervening period, fathers could save up their money, contact and chivy animal suppliers, and engage charioteers. Family honour would depend on such preparations when the time came for the games. Successful games were the ones that caused astonishment, leaving a lasting impression in people's minds, perpetuating the name of a family as the dispenser of unequalled munificence.

Until the fifth century, as in the early empire, the games comprised four great kinds of spectacle: gladiatorial combats, hunts, chariot races and theatrical shows. Claudian recalls those given by Mallius Theodorus in 399 for his consulate when there were horse races, gymnastics and wrestling in the circus. According to Polemius Silvius, the races were held twice, which meant five days of games. The wild beast hunts called *venationes* were held in the amphitheatre. Lastly, the theatre was the venue for a wide variety of shows: mimes and pantomimes, comedies, tragedies, acrobatics and mock sea battles, all accompanied by the music of flutes and hydraulic organs, to say nothing of pyrotechnics.

Gladiatorial combats still enjoyed great popular enthusiasm in the fourth century, and were moreover the least costly show to put on for those presenting the spectacles. Contrary to a widely held belief, Constantine did not ban them, but only limited them. When Valentinian I then banned them for Christians this shows that they continued to take place throughout the fourth century. *Venationes* were staged amid scenery in the arena. They were very expensive, as the organisers had to import wild animals from Africa or Asia, and not all arrived in Rome in the best condition, so it was preferred to put them on show rather than massacre them as in the past.

During the fourth century horse races gradually replaced gladiatorial combats in Roman popularity, and the building of a hippodrome adjoining the imperial palace in Constantinople is in part an indication of this. During the sixth century the circus definitively supplanted the amphitheatre, and chariot racing tended increasingly to symbolise the games. The ivory diptychs that ordinary consuls presented as gifts to commemorate their entry into office thus depicted them in the act of throwing the *mappa* onto the track to commence the races. Charioteers were great favourites among the Roman populace, who would compare their respective qualities in interminable arguments. The extent of this popularity can be gauged from how, when the prefect Leontius had the charioteer Philomorus arrested in 356, he immediately set off a riot. He sent his police officers against the demonstrators, some of whom were arrested, others tortured and exiled to an island.

Starting in the mid-fourth century, the spectators split into factions which supported different charioteers; at first there were two, the Greens and the Blues, then four, with the Reds and the Whites. The four factions are represented on the famous polychrome marble *opus sectile* which adorned a *domus* belonging to Junius Bassus, and which is preserved today in the Palazzo Vecchio in Florence. In Constantinople, these factions sometimes clashed violently, but in Rome there is no written trace of such violence. This was probably due to the absence of the emperors, whereas in Constantinople the factions corresponded to political leanings. In fact, the circus was the only place where the emperor showed himself before a populace assembled in vast numbers, and where the latter could manifest their affection or anger. The imperial box – called the *pulvinar* in the Circus Maximus in Rome, and the *kathisma* in Constantinople's hippodrome – was directly connected to the Palace. At once protected and separated from ordinary mortals, the emperors thus displayed their superhuman presence to the people, in ceremonial fashion.[2]

During the first half of the fifth century, the last gladiatorial combats were to be seen. When Honorius gave the games in the Circus Maximus to celebrate his sixth consulship, early in 404, they comprised *venationes* and military parades. Describing them, Claudian indeed reports that only horse races were given in the circus. He is glad that the martial demonstrations by the troops were only enactments and that the combats produced no victims, so he approves Honorius' decision to abandon the bloody spectacle of gladiatorial fights: henceforward, only the blood of wild animals would redden the sand of the arena.[3] Perhaps the emperor had been sensitive to the entreaty addressed to him by Prudentius at the end of his diatribe against Symmachus, around 402–3. He deplored the cruel pleasure derived from these gory fights by the Vestal Virgins, for whom the best places were reserved. He depicts them rising from their seats as the decisive blows were struck, and gesturing with their thumbs in order to see the losers finished off. 'May Golden Rome no longer witness this kind of crime', he entreats: 'this is the prayer I address to you, O most august ruler of the Empire of Ausonia; command the abolition of these horrible sacrifices, as you have commanded that of all the others'.[4] But the crowds remained very fond of such combats. Theodoret of Cyrrhus recounts that in 404, at the games given for Honorius' sixth consulate, a monk named Telemachus had been stoned by spectators, who were provoked to fury when he tried to place himself between the gladiators. Yet Claudian was congratulating himself that there were no gladiatorial fights at these same games. We may suppose, perhaps, that the combats were suppressed when the games had already started.

Valentinian III (425–55) re-established gladiatorship, but only for a very short time, as he abolished it again in 438. As for the military parade of 404, it comprised the presentation of troop exercises and manoeuvres rather like a modern military tattoo. A *magister* cracked a whip to give orders to the soldiers: they gripped their shields and brandished them over their heads, at the same time striking them with their swords, thus combining, in Claudian's words, the deep resonance of bronze with the sharp clatter of steel. After bowing before the emperor, the soldiers next performed mass manoeuvres at the double, following an intricate geometrical pattern. First they made lines resembling a labyrinth, and then formed precise circles.

In 494 the consul Asterius introduced wild animal fights and theatrical presentations between the chariot races. This innovation shocked the Romans, because it overturned a well-established custom according to which each day provided appropriate spectacles, and the rule was not to mix them.

– OPPOSITION TO THE CIRCUS –

Opposition to circus games was a recurring subject for the Fathers of the Church, but was not the province of Christian writers alone. A pagan such as Ammianus Marcellinus did not, of course, criticise the games *per se*, but for the state of devouring passion into which they threw the Romans, especially the most humble plebs. In the late fourth century, he deplored the fact that people spent so much time in the taverns tirelessly comparing the respective merits of charioteers.

When Augustine criticised the games, he was continuing a tradition begun by Tertullian two centuries earlier. In his *Confessions* he gives one of the finest passages in condemnation of the circus when he describes in vivid detail the misadventure of one of his friends, Alypius. The latter had preceded him to Rome, to study law, thus following a route taken by many talented young Africans. He had resolved to give up attending the circus, and the law could only strengthen him in this resolution. But once when he was leaving a banquet, some fellow-students dragged him off, despite his protests, to see a gladiatorial show. Having yielded in the face of such insistence, there he was sitting in the tiers of the Flavian amphitheatre, but still putting up a token resistance by closing his eyes. Then there was a great shout as a gladiator went down, and unable to hold out any longer, overcome by curiosity, Alypius opened his eyes, whereupon the last vestiges of his resistance vanished into thin air. He was fired with passionate enthusiasm and shouted and yelled with all the rest of the crowd.[5]

Salvian, the mid-fifth-century Marseillais priest originally from Trier, was also inimical to the games. He laments the misfortunes of Trier, sacked four times within the space of a few years, and complains bitterly about the attitude of its élites, who, amid so much ruin, continued to clamour for games. In his view, it is a sign of moral blindness, even madness, for such misfortunes should encourage a change in the way of life, a conversion to an ascetic Christianity. But beyond the criticism, one can glimpse a basic tenet of imperial civilisation: circus games were so central a part of the Roman art of urban living that the wish to continue to hold them, no matter what dramatic events occurred, manifested a desire for continuity, for maintaining an identity.

As we have seen, the Christian calendar in Rome, from the middle of the fourth century, included the celebration of martyrs in the sanctuaries of the city's suburban diadem. Some of those anniversary days of the *depositio* of the martyrs fell while the games were being held, such as in August, during the *Ludi apollinares*. The cult of the martyrs therefore had the effect of diverting from the circus and amphitheatre those faithful who were not yet baptised.

– IMPERIAL *ADVENTUS* –

The visit of a Roman emperor to a city was the occasion for the ceremony of *adventus*, in which he made a solemn entrance into the city amid crowds of its inhabitants. Such processions were accompanied by general rejoicing, the distribution of lavish gifts by the emperor, and, in many cases, the minting of special medals that showed the emperor on horseback or in a chariot entering the city[6]

Rome had not been the emperors' ordinary place of residence since early in the fourth century, but received visits from them now and then. We know about a certain number of them from texts and the reverse side of coins. These *adventus* were distinguished from those made by the emperors to other cities, for Rome enjoyed a special place in the empire. 'Mother of kings and leaders', in Claudian's words,[7] it had incomparable prestige and an exceptional wealth of monuments that might intimidate some emperors. Everywhere else, the emperor dominated the cities he visited; in Rome it was a different matter, and by its sheer scale the city seemed to dominate its august visitor.

Constantine came to Rome three times. His first entry into the city occurred at the end of 312, when he was around forty years old and had just defeated Maxentius and his army at the Milvian Bridge. He stayed in the city in December 312 and January 313, but did not settle there. During his brief sojourn, he was anxious to establish good relations with the Senate, which conferred the title *Maximus* upon him. Moreover, he pronounced the disbanding of an old and famous corps of troops, the praetorian cohorts, who had in fact supported Maxentius. Constantine paid a second, equally brief, visit in 315 for the celebration of his *decennalia*, during which his triumphal arch, near the Colosseum, was inaugurated. His last visit took place in July 326, for the solemn celebration of his *vicennalia*. This had been discreetly celebrated in Nicomedia the year before because of the holding of the ecumenical council in Nicaea. The site of Constantinople had been consecrated in 324, and the city that was to be the new imperial place of residence was under construction. It was probably for this reason that Constantine, accompanied by the Caesars, his sons, together with his family and court, came to Rome, and the *vicennalia* gave him the opportunity of celebrating his triumph over Licinius. During one of these three visits, according to Zosimus, who reproaches him for it, Constantine left the triumphal procession before it ascended to the Capitol, thus distancing himself from pagan religious rites.

The *adventus* that we know best was that of Constantius II, who visited the city for the first time in 357, which Ammianus Marcellinus describes in detail in his XVIth book. The imperial procession was greeted on the outskirts of the city by senators, accompanied by the wax *imagines* of their dead ancestors. Constantius' first source of astonishment was the cosmopolitanism of the Roman populace in general. Preceded by a double file of standard-bearers, he entered the city seated alone in a gold chariot adorned with gemstones. Around him dragon standards woven of purple thread billowed in the breeze from the tips of poles. Among his escort, with their dazzling cuirasses, Ammianus makes special mention of the *clibanarii*, horsemen entirely covered in coats of mail, who could have been mistaken for statues. Cheered on by the crowds, the procession went to the Rostra, near the Senate house in the Forum. Throughout the journey the emperor maintained a rigid pose:

> Indeed, he inclined his tiny stature when going through the high gates and, as if he had his neck caught in an iron collar, he kept his eyes fixed straight ahead of him, turning his head neither right nor left; like a statue, he was never seen to move with the jolting of his chariot, not spit, nor mop or rub his face or nose, nor even move his hand.[8]

From this description we can judge what sort of image of their office fourth-century emperors wished to put across: lofty and distant, more reserved than haughty. After making a speech to the Senate, and then another to the people, he went to the Palace, where he stayed from 28 April to 29 May.

– THEODOSIUS AND HONORIUS –

Following his victory over the usurper Eugenius in 394, Theodosius went to Italy, accompanied by his young son Honorius, whom he appointed consul for 396, and on this occasion the poet Claudian delivered a panegyric. In this he describes the warlike pomp of the procession in which the emperor and his son had the starring role, going through the city standing in the same chariot, amid the cheering crowds of young maidens, mothers, old men and children. The procession that made its way to the Palace blazed with colour and sound. Claudian conjures up the rippling plumes, the forest of unsheathed two-edged swords, bows, javelins, pikes and, of course, standards. Puffed out by the wind, snake-like banners hissed, snapped and rustled with redoubled force.[9]

Honorius next came back to Rome to inaugurate his fourth consulship, of 398, and then his sixth, of 404. Claudian composed two other panegyrics for these occasions, and that for 403–4 gives a good description of the procession and festivities. The crowds of Romans were massed between the Milvian Bridge and the Palatine, flowing through the streets and cramming into the houses right up to the attics. Honorius made an innovation by refusing to let the members of the Senate precede his chariot, and insisting that they walk on a level with him, in the same ranks as his nearest and dearest. With his trusted general Stilicho at his side, the emperor wore a consular toga glittering with emeralds, and a diadem on his head. The crowd could hear the dragon banners whistling and admire the *clibanarii* who, like their horses, were completely covered with steel plates. Above the procession bobbed helmet tops, adorned with plumes. Scarlet silk sashes fluttered from the soldiers' shoulders, falling in folds on their golden breastplates. Honorius paid a visit to the city's magistrates, who had assembled in the temple of Victory, and to the senators, before going to his residence on the Palatine.

The tradition of the *adventus* was not lost in the fifth century. The sources indicate that it was perpetuated in the west by the 'barbarian' kings well after 476. Hence it was in the manner of the emperors that Theoderic made his entry into Rome in 500, for his one and only visit to this, the mother of cities. Like them, he distributed money and gave the people games, adding bread to his gifts. In other words, the Ostrogothic king lavished *panem et circenses* – bread and circuses – on the Romans, thus showing that he had adopted the imperial model.[10]

CHAPTER 12

Education and culture

– STUDIES AND LIBRARIES –

In late antiquity Rome was indisputably one of the great centres of study in the empire; today such centres would be called 'university towns', but that is a term too laden with medievalism to be used in respect of education in antiquity. Let us say, rather, that Rome was one of the capitals of the liberal arts, as they were taught to the most deserving young men graduating from the grammarians' lessons. In the mid-fifth century, Sidonius Apollinaris still regarded it as the seat of law and the *gymnasium litterarum*.[1] Others were: Athens, for philosophy; Alexandria, chiefly for medicine; Beirut, for law; Constantinople, Milan and, in the fourth century, Trier, for rhetoric.

As well as the private libraries of rich intellectuals, like those of Quintus Aurelius Memmius Symmachus in the late fifth century, or of Boethius, gleaming with gold and ivory, in the early sixth century, Rome was endowed with public libraries. Two of them, one Greek and the other Latin, were in the Forum of Trajan, one of the focal points for teaching, together with the Forum of Augustus. Statues of great rhetors and poets continued to be erected in their vicinity well into late antiquity, such as those of Marius Victorinus in 353, and Claudian, Merobaldus and Sidonius himself, in 456.[2]

The fourth century was the time when the scroll, the *volumen*, was gradually making way for the *codex*, a book of bound pages. This new practice, which was the forerunner of books as we know them today, offered an incomparable ease of reading by comparison with the *volumen*, which necessitated continual unrolling and re-rolling, with help from another person. Henceforward, one could just turn the pages. We may imagine what a boon this was in the work of someone like Jerome, who was a voracious reader, indefatigable translator and ceaseless writer. He had to handle and consult innumerable books in the course of his work, so in this way his new

Latin translation of the Hebrew Bible, ordered by Pope Damasus, was certainly made easier.

In a society where public reading was also a performance, where Latin was pronounced with long and short vowels, reading was traditionally done aloud. When in autumn 384 he left Rome for Milan as the city's new professor of hetoric, Augustine encountered the city's bishop Ambrose, who became hoarse very easily. To his great surprise, he saw Ambrose reading in silence, only moving his eyes.[3] This was most unusual and also, perhaps, the genesis of a more individual and internalised way of reading that foreshadowed a decline in the art of rhetoric.

– STUDENT LIFE –

Many young men came to Rome to follow more advanced studies, arriving from all over the western provinces, especially, so it seems, from Africa, known throughout the empire as a veritable breeding-ground for lawyers, and Gaul, famed as a land of educated men. During the fourth century, a period when the Latin language was in the ascendant, Roman schools also received students from the east.

Through legal texts and various pieces of evidence that have come down to us, we have a fairly good idea of how student life was lived in Rome. For example, in 370, a letter addressed to the prefect of the city by Valentinian I, Valens and Gratian strictly regulated the period to be spent in Rome by students coming from other places.[4]

The first obligation of young men coming to Rome to study was to have themselves registered. To do this, they had to go to the offices of the *magister census* and produce their letters of recommendation: the authorisation of the governor of their province of origin, a certificate showing the city from which they had come, their identity, the name of their parents and their academic references. They then had to declare the course they intended to follow in the city. They were still not allowed to settle in, however, until the *censuales* had filled in a police file giving the student's address in Rome, so that he could be monitored at any time.

A law of 370 stipulated that students deemed to be 'serious' could stay in Rome until the age of twenty. Once that birthday had passed, they had to leave on their own initiative, failing which the services of the urban prefecture would expel them and conduct them back to their home town. This was a very strict aspect of the law, and, in order to ensure that it was observed to the letter, the census office had to draw up a monthly report containing an exact list of students who had arrived and those who were due to depart. Only students who were duly inscribed in a Roman professional corporation could defer this obligation and remain in Rome.

A student's stay in Rome could, however, be brusquely interrupted because of his behaviour. Indeed, if the *censuales* noticed that a student was guilty of public misbehaviour in gatherings, taking part in the activities of unruly groups, or spending too much time at shows or parties, they could inflict a double penalty on him: a public whipping followed by immediate dispatch home by the first available ship. In contrast, brilliant students had the opportunity to see an equally brilliant career opening up before them. Indeed, each year the prefect of the city had to send the imperial offices a report on the best individuals, so that the possibility of their recruitment into the imperial bureaucracy could be assessed.

As may be seen, these measures were simultaneously guided by demographic, public order and academic concerns. First, there was a concern to control the influx of arrivals, who could then take up residence but be kept under surveillance. Next, a concern for public order and the reputation of the liberal arts, which could not be tarnished by excesses in behaviour. For students, therefore, Rome must be no more than a temporary residence and place for study. But in most cases Roman laws were made not to anticipate problems but to try to remedy them, and we know from several sources that students could disturb public order in large towns. Augustine complains about the attitude of his students in Carthage, where he taught between 374 and 383. Their noisy students' rag processions gatecrashed classes to which they did not belong: Augustine calls them *eversores* (destructive hooligans), and his was no isolated experience; Libanius describes student boisterousness at Athens in similar terms. Augustine cites this as the reason for his departure to Rome, as rumour had it that students there were more peaceable and disciplined, which may be seen as a possible result of the law of 370. He thought he would find more serene working conditions, which he did, in fact, but only to discover other problems. There were no hooligans in Rome but, more disillusioning, students who deserted their courses when the moment came to pay their teacher his fee. This failure to pay up made Augustine very bitter, and in 384, after a mere year's stay in Rome, he left to take up a chair of rhetoric in Milan.[5]

– CHRISTIANITY AND THE CLASSICAL TRADITION –

Roman education was marked by strong traditionalism,[6] and the academic *cursus* of someone like Augustine was the same as that of a young man in the early empire. He went from the first lessons of the *magister* to those of the grammarian and, finally, of the rhetors. The characteristics of education were classicism and variety: classicism because it favoured the memorising of great classical texts, such as those of Cicero and Virgil; variety because students came into contact with all the liberal arts. Augustine, and Boethius to an even greater extent, were learned men capable of writing on many subjects, able to hold forth equally well on arithmetic and music, astronomy and grammar. But if there was one art that prevailed over the rest, it was rhetoric, which enabled a coherent and persuasive discourse to be constructed, making use of the speaker's knowledge of literature and history. Ancient rhetoric was a science concerned not only with the composition of texts but also with the art of oratory, in which the pitch of the voice, pronunciation of words, prosody and accompanying gestures played a fundamental role. During his brief stay in Rome, Augustine encountered the scorn of pronunciation purists: in his *Confessions* he recounts that his African accent did not allow for the aspiration of the initial *h* in certain words, and he was mocked for that reason.[7] The art of rhetoric also proved outstandingly useful to Christian pastoral work as the preaching of homilies and sermons adopted its rules in order to be more persuasive.

Good students of rhetoric were sought after by the emperors' headhunters, who were anxious to recruit them into the *militia* of the imperial offices. To do very well in rhetorical studies and to get oneself noticed was the promise of a brilliant administrative career, so knowledge of the art of discourse was closely linked to power in the Roman empire, and no less so in Ostrogothic Italy in the sixth century. In late antique society, rhetors were eminent personages, who were listened to, respected and sometimes feared.

A famous law of Julian, promulgated in 362, revealed a possible contradiction between the teaching of rhetoric and Christian faith. An extreme example of pagan reaction against an increasingly powerful Christianity in the second half of the fourth century, Julian wanted to deprive Christian rhetors of the chance of teaching in state professorial chairs. In his opinion, teaching literature that was imbued with mythology and elements of pagan religions was incompatible with Christianity. This short-lived law came as a grievous surprise to Christian rhetors, who had taken on the Homeric, Platonic, Aristotelian, Ciceronian and Virgilian heritage without raising an eyebrow, and it implicitly presented them with the opportunity of forming a Christian culture that would break away from the classical. Yet a biblical, exegetical and patristic culture could not be built up by excluding traditional culture – quite the reverse in fact. In the fourth and fifth centuries, the Greek and Latin heritage, like rhetoric, was put to the service of Christian apologetics. But many well-read men, such as Ambrose, showed that they were not taken in by the rhetoric of pagan hardliners. In both his and Symmachus' opinion, the language of erudite literati charmed and dazzled like gold, but was merely a coating on an ordinary metal.

The conversion of great rhetors to Christianity had an incalculable effect on Roman society and the advance of the Christian faith, as those who became bishops, like Augustine and Sidonius Apollinaris, used their oratorial skills in preaching. In his *Confessions*, Augustine relates the account Simplicianus had given him of the conversion of the best-known Latin rhetor in the fourth century, Marius Victorinus.[8] This immensely cultured man had taught many senators and translated some of Plato's works into Latin, and so great was his fame that a statue of him had been erected in Trajan's Forum, the usual site for writers' statues. Being a pagan, he had celebrated rites in honour of the Roman gods, but his intellectual curiosity had drawn him to read the Bible and books by Christian authors, which led him to become a Christian himself in his old age. Fearing the animosity of his pagan friends, he would not attend church, despite Simplicianus' encouragement, but the latter's persistence made him take the big step of becoming a catechumen, which would lead to baptism. When the great day came, to save his embarrassment, the priests offered him the choice of making his profession of faith in private, but in the event he did so before the assembled faithful, according to Roman custom. Everyone knew him, and his profession of faith was greeted by chanted acclamations of his name. This episode clearly shows how in the fourth century Rome was divided between a widespread Christianity and a lively paganism. Marius Victorinus had hesitated for a long time before making public his Christianity precisely because he was apprehensive of the reaction of the pagan nobility, many of whom he had taught. Thus the great joy evinced by Christians when he publicly underwent baptism was one of victory: Marius Victorinus was well and truly the sort of convert who was likely to strengthen the Roman Church by his example, and Christians certainly felt that his baptism was an invitation to other cultured pagans to do likewise.

In the sixth century some voices were raised in an attempt to dissociate Christian discourse from its grammarian and rhetorical roots, but they were not unanimous. On the contrary, and in spite of certain bishops' suspicions about classical studies, the Church made sure in many instances that they were maintained. In the sixth century the bishops of Rome, and others besides, became aware that a lack of learning among the clergy could only be deleterious to the Church, so they undertook to ensure education in Rome, where the old academic structures of the Empire had wavered. It was with this intention that, in 535, Pope Agapetus created a sort of centre for religious studies, endowed with a library.

– LITERARY OCCUPATIONS AND PUBLISHING –

The Roman aristocracy formed a milieu of well-read men who, besides their political and administrative activities, indulged in the pleasures of reading and writing. Many of the *illustres* who held the office of urban prefect left letters and poetical, philological and historical writings, only some of which, unfortunately, have come down to us. Nobles owned often sumptuous private libraries which they enriched with purchases from Roman book-shops, or by having copies made of books borrowed from friends. Less wealthy readers and students could make use of the public libraries.

Guglielmo Cavallo's researches into books and reading in late antiquity have enabled the chief characteristics to be established.[9] In the late fourth or early fifth centuries, Macrobius wrote the *Saturnalia* in the form of a philosophical dialogue between Roman men of letters of his time. The people he depicts belonged to the fourth-century pagan senatorial back-ground, the circle of the Symmachi and Nicomachi. All the indications we possess suggest that up to the dawn of the fifth century there had been something of a pagan revival, and literary classicism was its preferred means of expression. These nobles read, commentated, corrected and re-edited the works of the great Latin authors. Virgil, Juvenal, Lucan, Statius, Livy, Plautus and Terence were the objects of their pious veneration. We know that in 395, Sallust, one of Symmachus' close friends, held a debate on the works of Apuleius, in the Forum of Augustus, chaired by the rhetor Endelechius. In 401, Flavius Gennadius Felix Torquatus did the same for Martial's works. Symmachus and Nicomachus Flavianus themselves edited and oversaw production of an edition of the first ten books of Livy's history, turning it into 'a sort of Bible of pagan Roman civilisation', to quote Cavallo. This intense activity was at that time part of a desire to see the political restoration of state paganism. Whereas in Constantinople the imperial family supported a more specifically Christian editorial activity, Rome's pagan senators did so with the aim of maintaining tradition.

How then should we interpret the pique of Ammianus Marcellinus, criticising the poor taste of senators when it came to reading matter? It could be anti-Roman prejudice, but could also be a remark applying only to some less-cultured senators. But that must be measured against Ammianus' general tone, which is one of nostalgia tinged with feelings of decline – a feeling that was by no means new, but rather a commonplace of Roman historiography.

Although the conversion of the élite to Christianity brought about changes in the editing of books, it did not put an end to the practice. In the late fifth century, Turcius Rufus Apronianus Asterius paid for a new edition of Virgil, and in the sixth century, with the help of the rhetor Felix, Agorius Basilius Mavortius published Horace's *Epodes* and some works by Prudentius. It was probably the same Felix, the last great representative of the Roman school of rhetoric, who revised the works of Martianus Capella early in the sixth century. The literary activity of the Roman élite, therefore, was not confined to dictating their own works: rather these cultured men liked to anthologise those of their forebears. Among the Petronii family, for instance, during the fourth century, Probus dedicated to Theodosius a collection of the poems of his grandfather, Probianus, his father Probinus, and his own, written on a manuscript of Cornelius Nepos.[10] But, as we have seen, literary interest went farther than mere family glory, as aristocrats surrounded themselves with rhetors to amend and correct classical works, which they produced in new high-quality editions on costly parchment. Similarly, from the fourth to the sixth centuries there was an intense activity in translating from Greek to Latin. In the fourth century Marius Victorinus translated works by Plato and Aristotle: in the sixth, Flavius Josephus and Cassius Dio, as well as great treatises on grammar and medicine, were published in translations made from the impressive Italian heritage of Greek manuscripts.

Another major aspect of the literary history of this period was the change brought about by Christian influence on the use of the *codex* in place of the *volumen*. Several kinds of books existed in the fourth century of which the cheapest were the little *codices* made up of pages of papyrus. Although less numerous than in the east, their modest price made them a sort of second-class book. They provided the basic raw material for a popular Christian literature, in the form of small, easily portable books. Beginning in the fourth century, Christians started to use parchment in books with sewn pages, first of all for copies of the Bible; indeed, for Jerome, the term *membrana*, referring to the animal skin from which parchment was made, is synonymous with the Holy Scriptures. In their concern for legibility, Christian copyists created the Latin uncial, a calligraphy that brought a cursive roundness to Roman capitals. They were also the creators of a new page layout: on the almost square pages of the *codices*, the text was arranged in two narrow columns. In Rome – the seat of Law – secular publications adopted this method, with a very wide margin in legal texts to allow readers to add their own glosses and annotations.

Words played a fundamental role in Christian pastoral work. The circulation of sermons, taken down in abbreviated notes by scribes, exegetical texts, theological treatises and lives of saints, joined that of biblical texts and caused something of an explosion in the Roman book-selling business. Traditional copying studios, which could be described as secular, could no longer cope with the task, but rather than growing in number they declined. Instead, the Church ensured the publication of Christian texts by means of its own copying offices, the *scriptoria*, and those secular studios that survived in Rome in the fifth and sixth centuries, such as that of Gaudiosus, specialised in de luxe editions. Booksellers extended their production to Christian literature and became artistic craftsmen servicing a clientele of rich bibliophiles. Soon after 400, the *Life of St Martin*, written by the Gallic monk Sulpicius Severus, reached Rome, and immediately became a huge success, helped by Roman booksellers. While this best-seller might conceivably have led them to 'industrialise' copying, in the event it turned out to be a momentary phenomenon. In fact, the preferred way of acquiring books in fifth and sixth-century Rome was to have a copy made privately. Friends and admirers lent one another books, thus maintaining in an institutional Church the personal relationship that had ensured the spread of Christianity. Copies were made on papyrus or parchment, the latter's higher cost resulting in the use of the palimpsest, whereby old or redundant texts were erased from the page to make way for new texts.

While the publishing of Latin classics benefited from this heightened quality, the solemnisation of the liturgy and a desire to glorify sacred writings led to the development of ceremonial editions of Christian works. In Rome, as early as the Theodosian period, gospel books were calligraphed in silver or gold lettering on crimson-dyed parchment. True works of art, these precious manuscripts enabled one to visualise the treasure formed by the Divine Word. Jerome railed in vain against this luxury on the part of the Roman Church: in his view it was indecent, when the poor continued to die at its gates. But the practice continued throughout late antiquity, culminating in the sixth century, in the Ostrogothic period, thanks to the support of King Theoderic, and men such as Cassiodorus and, later, Pope Gregory the Great. Far from being a period of decline, the sixth century was the era of the first blossoming of books in the west, the outcome of veneration for the Latin classics and the sacredness of Christian texts.

CHAPTER 13

The influence of Christian Rome

– ARBITRATION AND MISSION –

The power of dissident theologies – Arianism, then Nestorianism and Monophysitism – in the eastern part of the Roman empire established the bishop of Rome as a moral and political authority to whom the eastern Nicene Christians could appeal, mostly during the fifth century. Thus Pope Julius I absolved Athanasius, the Nicene bishop of Alexandria, when he came to Rome, while Damasus was entreated to intervene in the quarrel between Basil of Caesarea and his Arian rivals, declaring himself in 377 clearly in favour of Basil's Trinitarian theology. Even the bishop of Constantinople, John Chrysostom, harassed by his adversaries, asked Pope Innocent to intercede on his behalf with the emperor Arcadius.

In 418–22 first Boniface, then Celestine, condemned Pelagianism. This doctrine, spread by the monk Pelagius, stressed free will and the possibility of salvation through good works, to the point of forgetting about original sin. In 449 it was Leo's turn to intervene, this time in the Nestorian affair. Nestorius had denied that the Virgin Mary could be called *Theotokos* – mother of God – and saw in Christ a dual nature that was dominated by his human side. Leo composed a document condemning Nestorian thinking, the *Tomus ad Flavianum*, which he sent to the east and which was used as a reference at the Council of Chalcedon in 451 to condemn the Nestorians. Religious disputes led the emperor Zeno, in 482, to attempt a compromise between Nestorians, Nicenes and Monophysites, by means of an edict, the *Henotikon*, and, even though Pope Felix III condemned it in 484, the dispute persisted until 519.

All these examples show that the bishop of Rome did not stand back from the theological controversies of the east, and intended to give the apostolic see an authority that extended beyond the bounds of Rome and Italy. From the time of Damasus and his successor, Siricius, the bishops of

Rome enjoyed a disciplinary authority and jurisdictional power throughout the west. For instance, in 417–18 Zosimus, and in 461–8 Hilarus, intervened in Gaul to arbitrate between the bishops of Vienne and Arles in their struggles for supremacy. Innocent, Leo and Gelasius increased the number of such regulations, taking Rome from a position of arbitration to one of command. In this area, too, the influence of Rome's word was not confined to the west, a fact eloquently demonstrated by the translation of Gregory the Great's treatise on *Pastoral Care* into Greek in 604.

Nevertheless, it would be wrong to ignore the difficulties experienced by the bishops of Rome in imposing their role of arbitration and command. As early as 313, at the council assembled in Rome against the Donatists, Pope Miltiades had not managed to resolve the problem, which forced Constantine to convene another council in Arles, the following year. Throughout the fourth century, the Roman pontificate was exposed to the ambitions of other episcopal sees, not least that of Milan, when it was occupied in the Theodosian era by the striking personality of Ambrose. Certainly, Pope Innocent played a far from negligible political role at the time of the Gothic sieges of Rome, in 409–10, since he took part in two embassies that went to Ravenna to plead the city's cause to Honorius. Even so, the position of the bishops of Rome remained delicate. This is well demonstrated by the fate undergone by Pope Vigilius in the sixth century, because of his stance in the dispute over the emperor Justinian's condemnation of the writings known as the 'Three Chapters'. Justinian kept him in captivity in Sicily, and then Constantinople, in order to force his condemnation of the texts at issue.

Prosper of Aquitaine recounts in his *Chronicle* that in 428, Pope Celestine sent bishop Germanus of Auxerre to Britain to combat the Pelagian ideas that were developing there. This was at the instigation of the deacon Palladius who, two years later, was sent by Celestine to the Irish 'who believed in Christ', to be their bishop. The Roman papacy therefore sent reliable men to the western regions that were threatened by heresy. It also helped to strengthen existing Catholic communities by providing them with senior clergy.[1] In 597 Gregory the Great sent missionaries to Britain under the leadership of the monk Augustine who, in a very short space of time, managed to convert the king of Kent, Ethelbert, and founded an episcopal see at Canterbury.

After the baptism of Clovis, and the adoption by the Franks of Nicene doctrine in the late fifth century, and in 587 after the conversion from Arianism of Reccared, the Visigothic king of Spain, these missions had the effect of extending Roman influence over the west. They are a true reflection of the main concerns of the fifth- and sixth-century popes. Ireland, then known as Hibernia, had never been under Roman rule.

As for Britain, it had witnessed Roman administration and troops finally withdrawn around 410. Christianity had certainly managed to penetrate these regions, but it had been influenced by the Pelagianist heresy; hence the bishop of Auxerre, Germanus, had gone to Britain twice in the mid-fifth century to combat it. Gregory wanted to consolidate and give a firm base to a vulnerable Christianity by means of ecclesaistical institutions: strong links between the British Isles and Rome were central to this movement.

– MARTYRS AND PILGRIMS –

We have seen that, during his pontificate, Damasus had broadened the cult of martyrs by increasing the prestige of their tombs, which were situated on the outskirts of the city. In the middle of the fourth century, however, Roman churches did not yet bear the names of saints, but those of the donors who had enabled their construction to take place. However, once Sixtus III dedicated his basilica on the Esquiline to the Virgin Mary, there arose a veritable riot of name-giving, and during the fifth and sixth centuries the custom of dedicating churches to saints became general. In some cases the donor's name became beatified: for instance, the *titulus-Sabinae* turned into the church of Sta Sabina; that of Chrysogonus in Trastevere, became S Chrysogono. Others changed their name: the *titulus* of Bizans became the church of SS Giovanni e Paolo, while Nicomedes' was placed under the patronage of SS Peter and Marcellinus. In the majority of cases Roman martyr saints were honoured, with Peter, Paul, Laurence and Sebastian being in the forefront, but the importing of relics allowed St Stephen to be revered as well. By the sixth century all the *tituli* bore the name of a saint, which was the result of a desecularisation of the church buildings themselves and the fruit of the success of the cult of saints. Books of legends, compiled by Roman clerics, tended to portray these churches as the places where the saints had lived, been imprisoned or martyred. This staging of a fictional past is the sign of a deliberate ecclesiastical policy, at the heart of which pilgrimages would henceforward play an eminent part. By attracting a growing number of pilgrims Rome affirmed both its position as the capital of Christianity and its role in bringing unity to Christendom. Already in the first half of the fifth century that had already been the concern of Sixtus III. On the architrave of the splendid new Lateran baptistry he had inscribed:

> *Unus Fons, Unus Spiritus, Una Fides*
> One fount, one spirit, one faith[2]

One might add *unum caput* – one head – a position to which Rome fully aspired.

To fulfil this role, the Roman Church did not rely only on Roman saints. The first pillar of its supremacy was to possess the tombs of Peter, Paul and Laurence; but it also celebrated the burial of African saints, such as Perpetua and Felicitas, and the bishop Cyprian. In 415, the relics of the protomartyr Stephen were discovered at Jerusalem, and Rome received some of them, for which the circular church of S Stefano Rotondo was built. Then, around 500, Pope Symmachus dedicated a church to the important Gallic saint, Martin of Tours. This policy reveals a desire to connect Rome with the worship of Christianity's major saints: from St Stephen, the first known martyr, of Jerusalem, to a bishop saint who had founded monastic establishments in the Touraine and acquired immense fame thanks to his biography, written by Sulpicius Severus in the early fifth century. The Roman Church thus embraced both Jerusalem and Tours, brought east and west together and firmly welded hagiography to the Gospel. It claimed to represent the whole of Christianity, by a double action of absorption and spreading influence. By the end of the sixth century, hundreds of martyrs, real or fictitious, were honoured in Rome.[3] Relics, and faith in the miracles they could accomplish, attracted an ever-growing number of pilgrims. Although Roman law had banned trafficking in them as early as the Theodosian period, bones were much sought after: in the time of Gregory the Great, for instance, some monks were caught in the act of digging up the ground in a pagan cemetery not far from the basilica of S Paolo fuori le Mura, searching for bones for resale as relics.

Throughout the fifth and sixth centuries, alterations were carried out which helped to give more space to church buildings, and endow them with hostel facilities, like the *xenodochia*, which enabled the practice of pilgrimages to expand. Indeed, during the fifth and sixth centuries, an impoverished city could derive many economic benefits from pilgrimages. Among the treasures of Monza Cathedral are some phials in which a pilgrim from the time of Gregory the Great had collected a little of the oil that burned in the lamps of the Roman *martyria*. On each of these phials is a label on which the pilgrim had written where he had obtained the oil. He had brought them back from a pilgrimage to Rome to present them to the Lombard queen, Theodelinda.

– A NEW ROME –

Between the pontificates of Damasus and Gregory, or from 366 to 604, the image of Rome as *sedes Petri*, the unique apostolic see in the Christian world, gradually compelled recognition. As Charles Pietri has clearly shown, the Christian community in Rome, which, in the fourth century, represented only the city's Church, became the representative of the whole of Christianity and a model for Christian expansion destined to go beyond the limits of the former Roman empire. *Roma christiana* was imbued with the structures and mental attitudes of *Roma augusta*; in other words, although Rome had become Christian, Christianity had also become strongly Roman. The sacks of 410 and 455 had made Roman Christians inclined to dissociate their destiny from that of ancient Rome, whose gods had experienced their twilight. This is one of the teachings of Augustine's *City of God*. Pope Leo the Great similarly professed this dissociation, and in the Forum, SS Cosma e Damiano replaced the shades of the pagan Dioscuri, whose temple stood nearby. But Peter and Paul formed the fundamental pair, exalted by Leo the Great, and became the patron saints of Rome. In one of his sermons he even compared them with Romulus and Remus: the two saints had shed their blood in order that a Christian Rome should arise. But in demonstrating the break and the new state of things, was not Leo resuming the pagan theme of the founding heroes? Ecclesiastical terminology, too, reveals a Roman institutional heritage, the pope being often given the title *vicarius Christi*. The term had previously designated an imperial official who was immediately subordinate to the highest administrators, the prefects. To consider the pope as *vicarius* was to look on Christ as a divine prefect. Following the same line of thought, the apostle Peter was regarded as the *patronus* of the city; in other words, like a great Roman notable, he was the protector and benefactor of a civic community. Lastly, to establish its supremacy in Christendom, Rome claimed that the fact that it was an apostolic see, the only community founded by an apostle, conferred *auctoritas* upon it. This ancient privilege of the Roman Senate, later embodied by Augustus (whose very name was derived from the word *auctoritas*), indicated the capability of giving the best opinion. To the Church of Rome, this meant passing on the teachings of Peter, of which it was the custodian.

What is called 'Christian Rome' was thus steeped in the traditions and political terminology of ancient Rome. One should not look, therefore, for a cultural break; rather, the process was more a matter of the assimilation of Christian and Roman ideologies. The years 608–9, at which the narrative of this book closes, contained two highly symbolic events. In 608 an imperial monument was erected on the Forum that was to be the last of its kind: the column, still visible today, dedicated in honour of the emperor Phocas. That marked the perpetuation of an ancient tradition, which showed how eminent a place Rome still maintained in the eyes of the emperors in

Constantinople. The very next year, 609, under Pope Boniface IV, Agrippa's Pantheon, which had been rebuilt already by the emperor Hadrian, was transformed into a church. This was a precedent that opened up a new path for the integration of classical and Christian Rome. Here again we can only record the fact that the Roman Church was slipping into the garments of ancient Rome. In other words, Rome remained Rome, and anything new was tightly embroidered onto the old fabric.

– A NEW JERUSALEM –

Even before the capture of Jerusalem by the Arabs in the seventh century, the growing influx of pilgrims was Rome's closest resemblance to that city, and owed much to the exaltation of the sanctity of Peter and Paul, as well as to precious relics. This influence was such that the empress Constantina, wife of the ill-fated emperor Maurice, asked Gregory the Great to send relics of the two saints to Constantinople, but he refused indignantly, for he considered it an intolerable sacrilege to touch a hair of the saints' bodies. In the fifth and sixth centuries, enthusiasm for St Peter drew a growing flood of pilgrims. Up to the pontificate of Gregory the Great, a tiny window opened into the interior of the tomb through which pilgrims could put their head and throw a handkerchief on the tomb, which was supposed to absorb the saint's virtues. Gregory had to adapt the site to the large number of visitors, constructing an annular crypt under a raised platform, making it much easier for pilgrims to circulate around the apostle's shrine.

Conclusion

Rome is unique, not only in western but in universal history: first because it was a city that conquered and administered a vast empire; secondly because that empire had an exceptionally long life; and lastly, because, identified with its empire by its very name, it set itself up as the Eternal City.

Beginning in the early fifth century, the empire suffered territorial losses on such a scale that the Romans came to doubt the eternity of their *imperium*. With no emperor, and a population in decline, the city nevertheless continued to be generally regarded as the capital of the world, queen of the universe, mother of leaders and the metropolis of trophies. The beguiling power of the name survived even if, in Gregory the Great's words, the old eagle had lost its plumage; and therein lies the miracle of Rome. It must be said that Rome was also *sedes Petri*, a designation which affirmed its supremacy during late antiquity in Italy and an unevenly Christianised west. There was thus a continuity between imperial and pontifical Rome. Although the expression 'end of the Roman Empire' can make sense, the 'fall of Rome' has no historical reality. Rome did not fall, but was transformed by keeping its special characteristic of mythical and historical capital. In the fourth century, many writers had the feeling that Rome was enjoying a venerable old age, but educated Christians spread the idea that Christianity might give it renewed youth. By doing so they were resuming the theme of renewal and regeneration that was recurrent in the empire's history. Shortly after 400, Prudentius was a witness to this transition and upholder of this *renovatio*: 'Now I am rightly called venerable and the capital of the world; today the helmet and red plume that I shake are covered with olive leaves, my proud sword-belt is hidden under a green garland and, beneath my military show, I adore God without stain of bloodshed.'[1] Yet the events of the fifth century were repeated spurs to reconsider Rome's history in other terms than those of venerable and peaceable vigour.

In one of his epigrams, Pope Damasus invoked the Dioscuri – Castor and

Pollux – but held St Peter and St Paul to be the *nova sidera* – new stars.[2] In the mid-fifth century, Pope Leo the Great compared the two saints to Romulus and Remus, thus vesting the myth of the founding twins in Christian garb. Gregory the Great is also symbolic of this metamorphosis: scion of the Anician family, he was prefect of the city; elected pope, he became, in the terms of his epitaph, 'God's consul'.

During the fourth century, and even more so after the Arab conquests, Rome's image underwent a change entirely due to its conversion. Once derided as another Babylon, and punished for that very reason, it now became a new Jerusalem on which flocks of pilgrims converged. The pilgrim itineraries that were drawn up to make their journeys easier provided emphatic proof that all roads still led to Rome.

Notes

Introduction: The City
between antiquity and the Middle Ages

1. Aelius Aristides, *Oration*, 14 (*To Rome*) § 93.
2. For an emphatic statement of the utility of urbanisation, see P. Garnsey and R. Saller, *The Roman Empire: Economy, Society and Culture* (London, 1987), pp. 26–40. A good summary of the characteristics of Roman cities may be found in W. Liebeschuetz, 'The end of the ancient city', in J. Rich (ed.), *The City in Late Antiquity* (London, 1992), pp. 1–49, esp. 1–15.
3. Liebeschuetz, 'End of the ancient city', p. 1.
4. Gregory of Tours, *On the Seven Sleepers of Ephesus*, 7.
5. Pausanias, *Description of Greece*, X.4.1.
6. Ammianus Marcellinus, 15.11.12.
7. *ILS*, 6091 = MAMA, vii.305. Cf. F. Millar, *The Emperor in the Roman World (31 BC–AD 337)* (London, 1977), pp. 394–410, for a discussion of this and similar appeals.
8. Fredegar, *Chronicle*, ed. J. M. Wallace-Hadrill (London, 1960), 4.71.
9. J. K. Hyde, 'Medieval descriptions of cities', *Bulletin of the John Rylands Library*, 48 (1965–6), pp. 308–40 (reprinted in id., *Literacy and Its Uses: Studies on Late Medieval Italy* [Manchester, 1993], pp. 1–32).
10. For a selection of such studies, see the Guide to Further Reading.
11. B. Ward-Perkins, 'Re-using the architectural legacy of the past, *entre idéologie et pragmatisme*', in G. P. Brogiolo and B. Ward-Perkins (eds), *The Idea and Ideal of the Town between Late Antiquity and the Early Middle Ages* (Leiden, 1999), pp. 242–3.
12. B. Ward-Perkins, *From Classical Antiquity to the Middle Ages: Urban Public Building in Northern and Central Italy AD 300–850* (Oxford, 1984), pp. 179–86.
13. For Verona's religious topography in the fourth century, see M. Humphries, *Communities of the Blessed: Social Environment and Religious Change in Northern Italy, AD 200–400* (Oxford, 1999), p. 210.
14. For the Gallic episcopate and its role in urban life, see especially J. Harries,

'Christianity and the city in late Roman Gaul', in Rich, *City in Late Antiquity*, pp. 77–98.

15. Paul the Deacon, *History of the Lombards*, 2.10 (Paulinus) and 12 (Felix).

16. For these events, see M. Humphries, 'Italy AD 425–605', in A. Cameron, B. Ward-Perkins and M. Whitby (eds), *The Cambridge Ancient History*, 14, *Late Antiquity: Empire and Successors, AD 425–600* (Cambridge, 2000) pp. 500–1.

17. Good discussion of the coronation and of Charlemagne's assumption of the title *patricius Romanorum* in J. Herrin, *The Formation of Christendom* (Oxford, 1987), pp. 454–62.

– 1. Looking at the city –

1. There is another model, comparable with Gismondi's, the work of the French architect Paul Bigot (1870–1942), and exhibited in the Maison de la Recherche en Sciences Humaines of Caen University (France) which owns it. Presentation and virtual visit is available on the Internet (http://www.unicaen.fr/rome).

2. A. Chastagnol, *Les Fastes de la Préfecture de Rome au Bas-Empire* (Paris, 1962), No. 107; *CIL*, VI, 1188–90.

3. Claudian, *Panegyric on the Consulship of Stilicho*, III. 130ff.

4. On this point, see Louis Duchesne, *Scripta minora* (Rome, 1973), pp. 36–43, 109, and his edition of the *Liber Pontificalis* (I, p. 364, n. 7), as well as the update by Henri-Irénée Marrou, 'L'origine orientale des diaconies romaines', *Mélanges d'Archéologie et d'Histoire*, 47 (1940), pp. 95–142, reprinted in *Patristique et humanisme* (Paris, 1976), pp. 81–117. Cf. P. Llewellyn, *Rome in the Dark Ages* (London, 1971), pp. 136–7.

5. Claudian, *On the Sixth Consulship of Honorius*, 521.

6. Claudian, *The War against Gildo*, 17–43.

7. Procopius, *BG*, IV, 22.

8. J. Le Gall, *Le Tibre, fleuve de Rome dans l'Antiquité* (Paris, 1953), p. 319.

9. F. Guidobaldi, 'Roma: Il tessuto abitativo, le *domus* e i tituli', *Storia di Roma*, 3, *L'età tardoantica*, II, pp. 69–83 (72).

10. Procopius, *BG*, II, 27.

11. Procopius, *BG*, II, 4–5.

12. Procopius, *BG*, I, 26.

13. F. Coarelli, *Roma*, Guide archeologiche Mondadori, 2nd edn, 1994 (Trad. française, Hachette, 1995), p. 41.

14. J. Durliat, *De la ville antique à la ville byzantine: Le problème des subsistances* (Rome, Coll. de l'École française, 136, 1990), Ch. 1, II, B (pp. 37–184 are about Rome).

15. Durliat, *De la ville antique*, table on p. 117.

16. Juvenal, *Satires*, III, 1, 58ff.

17. A. Degrassi, 'L'indicazione dell'età nelle iscrizioni sepolcrali latine', in *Akten des 4tes internazionalen Kongresses für griechische und lateinische Epigraphik* (Vienna, 1964), pp. 89–90.

18. L. Homo, *Rome impériale et l'urbanisme dans l'Antiquité*, L'évolution de l'humanité (Paris, 1951, revised 1971), pp. 496ff.

– 2. Transforming the city's image –

1. Ammianus Marcellinus, 16.10.
2. Claudian, *On the Sixth Consulship of Honorius*, 35ff.
3. H. Jordan, *Topographie der Stadt Rom im Altertum* (Berlin, 1871).
4. Allusion to *Inventaire*, a poem by Jacques Prévert.
5. Claudian, *On the Sixth Consulship of Honorius*, 407ff.
6. Jerome, *Letters*, 107, 1, to Laeta (AD 400).
7. *CIL*, VI, 1750.
8. A. Chastagnol, *La fin du monde antique* (Paris, 1976), pp. 133–4.
9. Coarelli, *Roma*, p. 180.
10. Chastagnol, *Les Fastes*, No. 59.
11. Chastagnol, *Les Fastes*, No. 38.
12. Chastagnol, *Les Fastes*, No. 40.
13. Chastagnol, *Les Fastes*, No. 43.
14. Ammianus Marcellinus, 17.4.
15. Ammianus Marcellinus, 18.4.
16. Here I use the term hallowed by use. In his book, *Roman Circuses* (London, 1986), pp. 175–6, John Humphrey sought to show that their central ridge had been called *euripus*. We know that in Rome this word was applied to the water-filled trench surrounding the circus (Suetonius, *Julius Caesar*, 39).
17. *Theodosian Code*, VI, 35, 13.
18. *ICUR*, II, p. 150, No. 19 = *ILCV*, 92.
19. On this subject, see L. M. White, *Building God's House in the Roman World* (Baltimore, 1990), and R. Krautheimer, *Three Christian Capitals* (Berkeley, 1983).
20. J. Guyon, 'Roma: Emerge la città cristiana', *Storia di Roma*, 3, *L'età tardoantica*, II, pp. 53–68 (67).

3. The phoenix city: War and invasion in the fifth and sixth centuries

1. G. Dagron, *Naissance d'une capitale: Constantinople et ses institutions de 340 à 441* (Paris, 1974).
2. Ammianus Marcellinus, 14. 6.
3. Claudian, *Panegyric on the Consulship of Stilicho*, III.99 and 175.
4. Zosimus, *New History*, IV, 45.
5. Zosimus, *New History*, V, 39.
6. Zosimus, *New History*, V, 29.
7. Zosimus, *New History*, V, 39.

8. Zosimus, *New History*, V, 41.
9. Zosimus, *New History*, V, 45.
10. Orosius, *History against the Pagans*, VII, 39–40.
11. Jerome, *Letters*, 127, to Principia; Rutilius Namatianus, *On His Return*, I, 1. 47ff.
12. *CIL*, VI, 1718 and *CIL*, VI, 1703 = *ILS*, 5715.
13. Rutilius Namatianus, *On His Return*, I, ll. 201–2.
14. Procopius, *BG*, III, 5, 1–6.

– 4. Urban administration –

1. Chastagnol, *Les Fastes*.
2. Chastagnol, *Les Fastes*, Nos 11 (Aelius Helvius Dionysius, prefect in 301–2), 38 (Anicius Paulinus Iunior, prefect in 334–5) and 50 (Ulpius Limenius, prefect in 349).
3. Sidonius Apollinaris, *Letters*, I, 10.
4. Chastagnol, *Les Fastes*, No. 59.
5. Ammianus Marcellinus, 27.3.
6. On this affair, Symmachus, *Relationes*, XXV and XXVI.
7. Symmachus, *Letters*, IV, 70, and V, 76.
8. It must be noted, however, that Romans of Rome formed the majority of the 200 Christian senators listed by Diehl in the *ILCV*.
9. Sidonius Apollinaris, *Letters*, I, 9 (467).
10. Gerontios, *Life of St Melania*, 44.
11. Ammianus Marcellinus, 14. 6.
12. Ammiunus Marcellinus, 28.1.
13. Symmachus, *Letters*, I, XIII. On this point, see P. Bruggisser, 'Gloria novi saeculi. Symmachus et le siècle de Gratien', *Museum Helveticum*, 44 (1987), pp. 134–49.
14. Chastagnol, *La fin du monde antique*, pp. 109–14.
15. Chastagnol, *La fin du monde antique*, pp. 125–6.
16. Boethius, *Consolation of Philosophy*, I, 8–9.
17. Gregory the Great, *Homilies*, II, 6, 22.
18. R. Bagnall, A. Cameron, S. Schwarz and K. Worp, *Consuls of the Later Roman Empire*, Philological Monographs of the American Philological Association, 36 (Atlanta, 1987), p. 7ff.
19. Claudius Mamertinus, *Speech of Thanks to the Emperor Julian*, II.
20. Cassiodorus, *Variae*, VI, 1.
21. R. Delbrueck, *Die Consulardiptychen und verwandte Denkmäler* (Berlin, 1929).

– 5. The nobility, 'elite of the human race' –

1. *Theodosian Code*, VI, 7, 1 and 9, 1 (5 July 372).
2. Zosimus, *New History*, VI, 7; cf. Ammianus Marcellinus, 16.8.3.

3. *CIL*, VI, 1753 = *ILS*, 1267.

4. M. T. W. Arnheim, *The Senatorial Aristocracy in the Later Roman Empire* (Oxford, 1972), p. 142.

5. Sidonius Apollinaris, *Letters*, I. 9 (467).

6. Taken from Jean-Pierre Callu in his edition of the letters of Symmachus (Books I–II), Paris, Les Belles Lettres, 1972. See also J. Matthews, *Western Aristocracies and Imperial Court* AD 364–425 (Oxford, 1975), pp. 1–31.

7. Ammianus Marcellinus, 14.6.

8. Gerontios, *Life of St Melania*, 15.

9. Gerontios, *Life of St Melania*, 18.

10. Novella 8, 1–2; A. Chastagnol, *La fin du monde antique*, pp. 116–18.

11. Gerontios, *Life of St Melania*, 14.

12. Claudian, *Panegyric on the Consulship of Mallius Theodorus*, 175ff.

13. Cassiodorus, *Variae*, VIII, 31. On this point, C. Lepelley, 'Un éloge de la cité classique dans les *Variae* de Cassiodore', *Haut Moyen-Âge, culture, éducation et société; Mélanges P. Riché*, Éd. européennes Érasme (1990), pp. 33–47.

14. Ammianus Marcellinus, 14.6.

15. Ammianus Marcellinus, 27.3.

16. Ammianus Marcellinus, 28.4.

17. Chastagnol, *Les Fastes*, Nos 66 and 90.

18. Gerontios, *Life of St Melania*, 23 and 26. For Blesilla, see Jerome, *Letters*, 39, 1.

19. Macrobius, *Saturnalia*, I, 2, 30.

20. Symmachus, *Relationes*, 3, 10. An idea refuted by Prudentius in his *Against Symmachus*, II.

21. On the *contorniates*, A. and E. Alfoldi, *Die Kontorniat-Medaillons*, 2 Text (Berlin–New York, 1990).

22. Jerome, *Letters*, 107, 2; Prudentius, *Against Symmachus*, I, 561ff.; Chastagnol, *Les Fastes*, No. 79.

23. Prudentius, *Against Symmachus*, I, 566–8, and II, 440–1.

24 Gerontios, *Life of St Melania*, 53.

25. *Liber Pontificalis*, 42. Chastagnol, *La fin du monde antique*, pp. 97–8.

– 6. TRADESMEN AND PLEBS –

1. On the shipmasters and other offices connected with the *annona*, see: J.-M. Carrié, 'Les distributions alimentaires dans les cités de l'Empire romain tardif', *MEFRA*, 87 (1975), pp. 995–1101; Durliat, *De la ville antique*; H. Jaidi, *L'Afrique et le blé de Rome aux IVe et Ve siècle*, Université de Tunis, Publications de la faculté des Sciences humaines et sociales, 34 (1990); B. Sirks, *Food for Rome: The Legal Structure of the Transportation and Processing of Supplies for the Imperial Distribution in Rome and Constantinople* (Amsterdam, 1991); and E. Tengström, *Bread of the People: Studies of the Corn Supply of Rome during the Late Empire*, Acta Instituti Romani Sueciae, 12 (1974).

2. *Theodosian Code*, XIV, 15, 2 (366).

3. *Theodosian Code*, XIII, 5, 33 (409).
4. *Theodosian Code*, XIV, 21, 1 (364).
5. *CIL*, VI, 1759 = *ILS*, 1272.
6. *Theodosian Code*, XIV, 4, 9 (417) and 15, 1.
7. Tengström, *Bread of the People*, pp. 65–72.
8. *Theodosian Code*, XI, 14, 1 (365).
9. *Theodosian Code*, XIV, 3, 4.
10. *Theodosian Code*, IX, 40, 3.
11. *Theodosian Code*, XIV, 3, 12 (370) and 3, 17 (380). For inheritance and obligations: XIV, 3, 5–6 (364).
12. Sirks, *Food for Rome*, Ch. 13, 'Importation and distribution of meat', pp. 361–87. Law of Valentinian I: *Theodosian Code*, XIV, 4, 4.
13. *Theodosian Code*, XIV, 4, 2 (367).
14. *CIL*, VI, 1682 = *ILS*, 1220.
15. Novella 5 (440); Chastagnol, *La fin du monde antique*, pp. 114–15.
16. Ammianus Marcellinus, 14.6, 19. The reader is recommended to read the whole of 14.6, a bravura piece of pamphleteering.
17. *Theodosian Code*, XIV, 10, 4.
18. Ammianus Marcellinus, 14.6.
19. *Theodosian Code*, I, 29, 1–3. It may be that *defensores plebis* were instituted only in Illyricum, on an experimental basis.
20. *Theodosian Code*, IX, 40, 2 (316); IX, 12, 1 (319); IV, 7, 1, (321).

− 7. Ancestral cults −

1. *Theodosian Code*, XVI, 10, 10.
2. *CIL*, VI, 102 = *ILS*, 4003.
3. Zosimus, *New History*, IV, 36.
4. F. Cumont, *Les religions orientales dans le paganisme romain* (Paris, 1963), p. 190.
5. *CIL*, VI, 1779 = *ILS*, 1259. Also *CIL*, VI, 1778,
6. *CIL*, VI, 512 = *ILS*, 4154.
7. Cumont, *Les religions orientales*, p. 188.
8. M. Vermaseren, *Mithra, ce dieu mystérieux* (Paris–Brussels, 1960), p. 143.
9. Zosimus, *New History*, IV, 59; see notes 212 and 213 of F. Paschoud, vol. II, 2, pp. 468–73.
10. Zosimus, *New History*, IV, 3.
11. On this affair, Symmachus, *Relationes*, 6; Ambrose, *Letters*, 27 and 28. These texts are translated, with comprehensive commentary, in B. Croke and J. Harries, *Religious Conflict in Fourth Century Rome* (Sydney, 1982), pp. 28–51.
12. Zosimus, *New History*, V, 38.
13. Zosimus, *New History*, V, 41.
14. *Theodosian Code*, XVI, 5, 42.
15. Gelasius, *Letter to Andromachus*, 31.

16. An analysis of these trials can be found in J. Matthews, *The Roman Empire of Ammianus* (London, 1989), 209–18.
17. Ammianus Marcellinus, 26.3.

– 8. THE EXPANSION OF CHRISTIANITY –

1. Tertullian, *Apologeticus*, 37, 4.
2. *ICUR*, NS II, 4150.
3. *ICUR*, NS II, 4156, 1. 15.
4. C. Pietri, *Roma Christiana: Recherches sur l'Église de Rome, son organisation, sa politique, son idéologie, de Miltiade à Sixte III (311–440)*, 2 vols (Rome, BEFAR, 224, 1976), p. 84.
5. Ammianus Marcellinus, 27.3.14.
6. Ammianus Marcellinus, 27.3.
7. Ammianus Marcellinus, 27.3, and *Collectio avellana*, 1, CSEL, 35.
8. *Collection avellana*, 14–37; extracts in Chastagnol, *La fin du monde antique*, pp. 102–7.
9. On the political implications of this schism, itself derived from the Acacian schism, refer to P. Llewellyn's 'The Roman Church during the Laurentian Schism: Priests and Senators', *Church History*, 45 (1976), pp. 417–27.
10. *ICUR*, NS III, 8719.
11. J. Janssens, *Vita e morte del cristiano negli epitaffi di Roma anteriori al saec. VII*, Roma, Analecta gregoriana, 223 (1981), II, Ch. 3.
12. Jerome, *Letters*, 39, 1 and 6 (Blesilla) and 77, 6 (Fabiola).
13. Pietri, *Roma christiana*, vol. I, pp. 3–96. Summarised in Pietri, 'La Roma cristiana', *Storia di Roma*, 3, *L'età tardoantica* (Einaudi, 1993), I, pp. 697–721 (697ff.).
14. *Collectio avellana*, 1, 9.
15. Jerome, *Letters*, 22, 28, 52.
16. Jerome, *Letters*, 22, 32.
17. *ICUR*, NS I, 2812 (Bonifatius). *ICUR*, NS II, 4164 (Junius Bassus).
18. *ICUR*, NS VI, 15, 895.
19. H. I. Marrou, *Nouvelle histoire de l'Église*, vol. I (Paris, 1963), p. 487.
20. Jerome, *Letters*, 38 and 39, 1.
21. Gregory the Great, *Registrum*, V, 57.
22. C. Heitz, 'Les monuments de Rome à l'époque de Grégoire le Grand', in *Grégoire le Grand*, Actes du colloque de Chantilly, 15–19 sept. 1982 (CNRS, 1986), pp. 31–8 (p. 32).

9. LIFE AND DEATH: MATERIAL CIVILISATION AND MENTAL ATTITUDES

1. *Theodosian Code*, XIV, 17, 5.
2. Durliat, *De la ville antique*.

3. *Theodosian Code*, XIV, 17, 3.

4. Cassiodorus, *Variae*, VI, 18, 1.

5. Symmachus, *Letters*, VI, 14, 2.

6. Cassiodorus, *Variae*, XII, 11. *Theodosian Code*, XIV, 4, 10, 5.

7. *Historia Augusta*, Severus, 18, 3; Aurelian, 48, 1.

8. H. R. Kohns, *Versorgungskrisen und Hungerrrevolten im Spätantiken Rom* (Bonn, 1961).

9. Zosimus, *New History*, II, 13.

10. Symmachus, *Relationes*, 40, 4.

11. Ammianus Marcellinus, 15.7.

12. Ammianus Marcellinus, 18.10.

13. Ammianus Marcellinus, 17.3.

14. Symmachus, *Letters*, II, 6 and 7; *Relationes*, 35. For 388: *Letters*, II, 52 and 55, III, 82.

15. Symmachus, *Letters*, IV, 5 and 54.

16. Chastagnol, *Les Fastes*, No. 115.

17. Zosimus, *New History*, VI, 11.

18. Anonymus Valesianus (ed. and trans in J. C. Rolfe, *Ammianus Marcellinus*, Loeb Classical Library (London, 1939, vol. iii), 67; Paul the Deacon, *Historia Romana*, ed. A. Crivellucci (Rome, 1914), 15, 18.

19. *Pragmatic Sanction*, ed. R. Schöll and W. Kroll (Berlin, 1895), 22; Procopius, *BG*, V, 14, 17.

20. Gregory the Great, *Registrum*, I, 78. See also I, 42 and IX, 2.

21. *Theodosian Code*, XIII, 3, 8.

22. *Theodosian Code*, XIII, 3, 9.

23. Symmachus, *Letters*, X, 27.

24. Jerome, *Letters*, 50, 5.

25. Delbrueck, *Die Consulardiptychen*, p. 43ff.

26. Jerome, *Letters*, 117, 6; 54, 7; 79, 7; 22, 13; 107, 5; 108, 15; 117, 7.

27. P. Veyne, 'La famille et l'amour sous le Haut-Empire romain', *Annales ESC*, I, 1978, pp. 35–63.

28. *ICUR*, NS II, 6049. On this point see C. Carletti, 'Aspetti biometrici del matrimonio nelle iscrizioni cristiane di Roma', *Augustinianum*, 17 (1977), pp. 25–51.

29. This was Vettius Cossinius Rufinus: Chastagnol, *Les Fastes* , No. 26.

30. *Theodosian Code*, IX, 17, 2: the prefect was Limenus.

31. *ICUR*, NS V, 12 907–13096.

32. See J. Guyon, *Le cimetière aux deux lauriers: Recherches sur les catacombes romaines* (Rome, BEFAR, 264, 1987).

33. *ICUR*, NS II, 4187.

34. *ILCV*, 973, ll. 7–8.

35. *ICUR*, NS II, 4156, ll. 1–3.

– 10. Transforming the calendar –

1. Zosimus, *New History*, II, 7.
2. *ICUR*, NS VI, 15895.
3. *Justinian's Code*, III, 12, 2.
4. *Theodosian Code*, II, 8, 1.
5. *Theodosian Code*, VIII, 8, 3; II, 8, 18; XI, 7, 13.
6. C. Pietri, 'Le temps de la semaine à Rome et dans l'Italie chrétienne', in *Les temps chrétien de la fin de l'Antiquité au Moyen-Âge* (Paris, 1984), pp. 129–41.
7. The first historian to adopt Dionysius' computation was the Venerable Bede, in Britain, in the seventh century, in his *Ecclesiastical History*.

– 11. Festivals and entertainments –

1. The *ludi* chiefly meant gladiatorial combats. *Circenses* were races held in the circus.
2. On this point the standard work of reference is Alan Cameron's *Circus Factions*.
3. Claudian, *On the Sixth Consulship of Honorius*.
4. Prudentius, *Against Symmachus*, II, 1091ff.
5. Augustine, *Confessions*, VI, VIII, 13.
6. On this subject see Sabine MacCormack, *Art and Ceremony in Late Antiquity* (Berkeley and Los Angeles, 1981), pp. 15–89.
7. Claudian, *Panegyric on the Consulship of Stilicho*, 1. 175.
8. Ammianus Marcellinus, 16.10.9–10.
9. Claudian, *On the Third Consulship of Honorius*, 1. 126ff.
10. On the *adventus*, see J. Moorhead, *Theoderic in Italy* (Oxford, 1992), 60–5.

– 12. Education and culture –

1. Sidonius Apollinaris, *Letters*, I, 6, 2.
2. Augustine, *Confessions*, VIII, II, 4 (Marius Victorinus). *CIL*, VI, 1710 (Claudian). *CIL*, VI, 1724 and Sidonius Apollinaris, *Poems*, IX, 1. 301 (Merobaldus); VIII, 8 (Sidonius).
3. Augustine, *Confessions*, VI, III, 3.
4. *Theodosian Code*, XIV, 9, 1.
5. Augustine, *Confessions*, V, XII, 22.
6. H. I. Marrou, *Histoire de l'éducation dans l'Antiquité*, 2, *Le monde romain* (Paris, 1948).
7. Augustine, *Confessions*, I, XVIII, 29. Jerome scoffs at Roman women who, in his view, swallow half their words: *Letters*, 22, 29 and 107, 4.
8. Augustine, *Confessions*, VIII, II, 3.

9. G. Cavallo, *Libri, editori e pubblico nel mondo antico* (Rome & Bari, 1984), pp. 83–132, notes pp. 149–61.
10. Chastagnol, *Les Fastes*, No. 34, p. 83.

– 13. The influence of Christian Rome –

1. On this point, see Richard Fletcher, *The Conversion of Europe* (London, 1997).
2. *ILCV*, 1513.
3. On this point there are two classics: A. Dufourcq, *Études sur les Gesta martyrum romains* (Paris, 1900); H. Delehaye, *Études sur le légendier romain* (Brussels, 1936).

– Conclusion –

1. *Against Symmachus*, II, 662–5.
2. *Epigrammata damasiana*, ed. Ferrua, No. 20, ll. 3–7.

Chronology

272–9	Construction of the new circuit of walls by Aurelian and then Probus
283	Serious fire in the Forum
303	Vicennial celebrations of Diocletian and Maximian, decennial of Galerius and Constantius I; erection of columns in their honour in the Forum
306–12	Usurpation of Maxentius; restoration of the defensive walls.
310	Fire; food shortage
312	Constantine's victory over Maxentius at the Milvian Bridge; praetorian guard disbanded
315	Decennial celebrations of Constantine; his triumphal arch is inaugurated
319–29	Construction of St Peter's basilica
326	Constantine's vicennial celebrations
326–8	Helena has the Sessorian basilica built
350	Usurpation of Nepotian
354	The scribe Filocalus produces illustrated Calendar
357	Visit of Constantius II
366–84	Pontificate of Damasus; introduction of the cult of martyrs within the walls
367	Praetextatus, prefect of the city, has the portico of the temple of the *Dii Consentes* restored
369–71	Trials and executions in senatorial circles
379	Possible visit of Gratian
382–4	Subsistence problems in Rome; public disorder
383–4	Augustine teaches in Rome
384–5	Urban prefecture of Symmachus; death of Praetextatus and Damasus; food shortage
384–99	Pontificate of Siricius; building of S Paolo fuori le Mura
388	Food shortage.
398	Visit of Theodosius to Rome
398	War with Gildo in Africa; famine and floods in Rome

401–3 Restoration and extension of the defence walls
404 *Adventus* of Honorius for his sixth consulate
406–8 Visits by Honorius to Rome
408–10 Sieges of the city by Alaric's Goths
409–10 Attalus proclaimed Augustus, then deposed; famine in Rome
410 Sack of Rome
414 Rutilius Namatianus is prefect of the city
418 Pelagius and Celestius are expelled from Rome
418–19 Dispute between Eulalius and Boniface over the succession to Pope Zosimus
419 The new amount of *annona* rations is fixed
429 Earthquake
431 Rehabilitation of Nicomachus Flavianus
438 The Senate receives and acclaims the *Theodosian Code*
440–61 Pontificate of Leo the Great
440 Valentinian III protects Greek merchants in Rome
443 Earthquake
445–7 Valentinian III in Rome
450 Measures to support shipmasters
452 Embassy to Attila the Hun led by Pope Leo; *Novella* 36 of Valentinian III on the resources of the *suarii*
455 Petronius Maximus emperor; Vandals sack the city
458 Majorian pays his respects to the Senate; defensive measures to protect the city's public edifices
476 Anthemius and Sidonius Apollinaris in Rome
468 Sidonius Apollinaris prefect of the city
472 Rome captured by Ricimer
476 Deposition of the last western emperor, Romulus Augustulus
476–80 Disappearance of the suffect consulate
494 Pope Gelasius I condemns the Lupercalia
500 Theoderic visits Rome
507–11 Theoderic has the theatre of Marcellus restored
523 Last attestation of games in the Colosseum; last mention of the praetorship
526–30 Pontificate of Felix IV; first church on the Roman Forum (SS Cosma e Damiano)
527 Last ordinary consul for the west
530 Cassiodorus' measures for the *annona*
536 Belisarius seizes Rome
544–6 Siege and capture of Rome by Totila
547 Belisarius recaptures Rome
550 Totila recaptures Rome
552 Narses seizes Rome
554 Justinian's *Pragmatic Sanction*

568   Start of the Lombard invasion of Italy

573   Gregory (future pope) is prefect of the city

584   Last known attestation of a head of the Senate (*caput senatus*)

589   The Tiber rises: floods in Rome

590–604   Pontificate of Gregory the Great

590   Epidemic in Rome

592   Siege of Rome by the Lombard Agilulf

599   Last known urban prefect

603   The Senate receives and acclaims the portrait of Phocas

604–6   Pontificate of Sabinianus; famine; probable suppression of the free *annona*

608   Erection of Phocas' column in the Forum

609   The Pantheon is turned into a church: the first instance of a temple in Rome converted for liturgical use

Guide to further reading
Mark Humphries

The material available on late antique Rome, even in English, is of vast extent, and what follows is intended only as an introductory guide. Items marked with an asterisk (*) have especially useful bibliographies.

– PRIMARY SOURCES –

Important texts, including the narratives of Ammianus Marcellinus and Procopius, the letters of Sidonius Apollinaris, and the poetry of Ausonius, Claudian and Prudentius, may be found in the Loeb Classical Library. Ammianus is also available in an abbreviated but none the less excellent translation in Penguin Classics. Zosimus, *New History*, is available in a good English translation by R.T. Ridley (Canberra, 1984). For legal texts, see C. Pharr and others (trans), *The Theodosian Code and the Sirmondian Constitutions* (Princeton, 1952). Some understanding of the ceremonial aspects of urban life in late antiquity may be gleaned from imperial panegyrics, translated in C.E.V. Nixon and B.S. Rodgers, *In Praise of Later Roman Emperors* (Berkeley, 1994).

Several items of specific relevance to Rome and Italy are also available in English translation. *B. Croke and J. Harries, *Religious Conflict in Fourth-Century Rome* (Sydney, 1982), provides an extremely useful selection of sources – both literary and epigraphic – pertaining to religious matters. The relevant sections of the *Liber Pontificalis* and some related texts are translated in *R.P.Davis, *The Book of Pontiffs* (Liverpool, 1989); this volume also provides useful introductory material on ecclesiastical topography. Administrative topics are illuminated by R.H. Barrow, *Prefect and Emperor: The* Relationes *of Symmachus, AD 384* (Oxford, 1973), which translates the official correspondence of Symmachus from his term as urban prefect, and by *S.J.B. Barnish, *Cassiodorus: Variae* (Liverpool, 1992), which contains a selection of material for the Ostrogothic period.

– MODERN WORKS –

For the general history of the period discussed here, there is simply nothing to beat the thoroughness of A.H.M. Jones, *The Later Roman Empire: A Social, Economic and Administrative Survey, AD 284–602*, 3 vols (Oxford, 1964 paperback reprint in 2 vols. 1986). Shorter, more up-to-date and less arid treatments will be found in Averil Cameron's *The Later Roman Empire AD 284–430* (London, 1993) and *The Mediterranean World in Late Antiquity AD 395–600* (London, 1993). Much of the same period is covered in great detail by various authors in volumes 13 (Cambridge, 1998) and 14 (Cambridge, 2000) of the new edition of *The Cambridge Ancient History*. Social dynamics are given sophisticated treatment in P. Brown, *Power and Persuasion in Late Antiquity* (Madison, 1992). Among the most enthralling studies of late Roman society produced in recent decades, and containing much that is relevant to affairs at Rome, is J.F. Matthews, *Western Aristocracies and Imperial Court, AD 364–425* (Oxford, 1975). Architecture, art, and ceremonial are covered in R. Bianchi Bandinelli, *Rome, the Late Empire: Roman Art AD 200–400* (London, 1971), which boasts numerous excellent illustrations, H.P. L'Orange, *Art Forms and Civic Life in the Late Roman Empire* (Princeton, 1965), and S.G. MacCormack, *Art and Ceremony in Late Antiquity* (Berkeley, 1981). For the cult of saints, see P. Brown's seminal *the Cult of the Saints: Its Rise and Function in Latin Christianity* (Chicago, 1981), discussing *inter alia* some Roman material. Several authors have received detailed study: perhaps most relevant here is Alan Cameron's *Claudian: Poetry and Propaganda at the Court of Honorius* (Oxford, 1970).

For Italy in late antiquity, see: the general, but extremely illuminating and stimulating, survey by C.J. Wickham, *Early Medieval Italy: Central Power and Local Society 400–1000* (London, 1981); also M. Humphries, 'Italy, AD 425–605', in A. Cameron, B. Ward-Perkins, and M. Whitby (eds), *The Cambridge Ancient History 14 Late Antiquity: Empire and Successors, AD 425–600* (Cambridge, 2000) pp. 525–51. For more specific periods and topics, see: *P.Amory, *People and Identity in Ostrogothic Italy, 489–554* (Cambridge, 1997); T.S. Brown, *Gentlemen and Officers: Imperial Administration and Aristocratic Power in Byzantine Italy, AD 554–800* (London, 1984); N. Christie, *The Lombards: The Ancient Longobards* (Oxford, 1995); P. Heather, *The Goths* (Oxford, 1996); *J. Moorhead, *Theoderic in Italy* (Oxford, 1992); and J. Moorhead, *Justinian* (London, 1994).

The fate of Graeco-Roman cities in late antiquity has been the subject of intense scholarly investigation in recent decades. In English alone there have been three important collections of essays in the last ten years: J. Rich (ed.), *The City in Late Antiquity* (London, 1992); N. Christie and S.T.

Loseby (eds), *Towns in Transition: Urban Evolution in Late Antiquity and the Early Middle Ages* (Aldershot, 1996); and G.P. Brogiolo and B. Ward-Perkins (eds), *The Idea and Ideal of the Town between Late Antiquity and the Early Middle Ages* (Leiden, 1999). There exist some fine studies of individual cities in this period: C. Foss, *Ephesus after Antiquity: A Late Antique, Byzantine, and Turkish City* (Cambridge, 1979); C. Roueché, *Aphrodisias in Late Antiquity* (London, 1989); J.H.W.G. Liebeschuetz, *Antioch: City and Imperial Administration in the Later Roman Empire* (Oxford, 1972); S.T. Loseby, 'Marseille: A Late Antique Success Story', *Journal of Roman Studies* 82 (1992), pp. 161–85; and T.W. Potter, *Towns in Late Antiquity: Iol Caesarea and its context* (Sheffield, 1995). There is an excellent survey in B. Ward-Perkins, 'The Cities', in A. Cameron and P. Garnsey (eds), *The Cambridge Ancient History 13 The Late Empire AD 337–425* (Cambridge, 1998), pp. 371–411. There will soon be a synoptic study in English of the process in the Mediterranean world as a whole: J.H.W.G. Liebeschuetz, *The Decline and Fall of the Roman City* (Oxford, forthcoming). For western Europe, there is A. Verhulst, *The Rise of Cities in North-Western Europe* (Cambridge, 1999). For Italy, see especially B. Ward-Perkins, *From Classical Antiquity to Early Middle Ages: Urban Public Building in Northern and Central Italy AD 300–850* (Oxford, 1984); and on Northern Italy, M. Humphries, *Communities of the Blessed: Social Environment and Religious Change in Northern Italy, AD 200–400* (Oxford, 1999). Potter's *Towns in Late Antiquity* (cited above), although largely focused on the author's excavations at Cherchel (ancient Iol Caesarea) in Algeria, includes also a useful discussion of the important late antique and early medieval site at Mola di Monte Gelato in southern Etruria, providing useful comparative material for nearby Rome.

For the city of Rome itself, orientation is provided by a number of topographical guides and dictionaries. Among the most recent, A. Claridge, *Rome: An Oxford Archaeological Guide* (Oxford, 1998), is an excellent handbook. Also useful, and not only for the traveller, is the splendid and erudite Blue Guide: A. Macadam, *Rome and Environs* (6th ed.: London, 1998). More detail may be found in L. Richardson, Jr, *A New Topographical Dictionary of Ancient Rome* (Baltimore and London, 1992), and good photographs are available in E. Nash, *Pictorial Dictionary of Ancient Rome*, 2 vols (London, 1968); both Richardson and Nash, however, are weak on Christian buildings. For the administrative workings of Rome in the republic and early imperial period, see *O.F. Robinson, *Ancient Rome: City Planning and Administration* (London, 1992), including a very useful fold-out map of the ancient city. The architectural development of Rome in late antiquity (and beyond) is covered in R. Krautheimer, *Rome: Profile of a City 312–1308* (Princeton, 1980); for the fourth and fifth centuries, Rome's development is compared with that of Milan and Constantinople in R. Krautheimer, *Three Christian Capitals: Topography and Politics* (Berkeley, 1983). Krautheimer's works lay particular (though not exclusive) emphasis on churches. For other topographical concerns see, on the demise of paganism, J. Curran , 'Constantine and the ancient cults of Rome: the legal evidence'. *Greece and Rome* 43 (1996), pp. 68–80, and, for secular buildings, R. Coates-Stephens, 'Housing in early medieval Rome', *Papers of the British School at Rome* 64 (1996), pp. 239–59 and id., 'The walls and aqueducts of Rome in the early Middle Ages AD 500–1000', *Journal of Roman Studies* 88 (1998), pp. 166–78. A useful selection of papers (some of them in English), containing reports of recent archaeological work, is W.V. Harris (ed.), *The Transformation of Urbs Roma in Late Antiquity* (Portsmouth RI, 1999). For the fourth century, we eagerly await J. Curran, *Pagan City and Christian Capital: Rome in the Fourth Century* (Oxford, forthcoming).

In addition to architectural matters, modern research on Rome in late antiquity has tended to focus on the papacy. For general studies, see P. Llewellyn, *Rome in the Dark Ages* (London, 1971; reprinted with an afterword, 1993) and J. Richards, *The Popes and the Papacy in the Early Middle Ages* (London, 1979). Of the individual popes, Gregory the Great has been the subject of several studies in English, the best of which is R.A. Markus, *Gregory the Great and His World* (Cambridge, 1997). For a sophisticated assessment of the interrelationship of secular and ecclesiastical patronage, see K. Cooper, 'The martyr, the *matrona*, and the bishop: Networks of Allegiance in early sixth century Rome', *Journal of Roman Archaeology* (forthcoming). Dr Cooper's on-going study of the Roman martyr romances (*gesta martyrum*) is likely to yield exciting new insights into the city's social evolution in late antiquity. Such a project is indicative of the current vitality of research into late-antique Rome.

Mark Humphries

Index